Communications
in Computer and Information Science   1608

More information about this series at https://link.springer.com/bookseries/7899

Ana Fred · David Aveiro · Jan Dietz ·
Ana Salgado · Jorge Bernardino ·
Joaquim Filipe (Eds.)

Knowledge Discovery, Knowledge Engineering and Knowledge Management

12th International Joint Conference, IC3K 2020
Virtual Event, November 2–4, 2020
Revised Selected Papers

Springer

Editors
Ana Fred
Instituto de Telecomunicações
Lisbon, Portugal

University of Lisbon
Lisbon, Portugal

Jan Dietz
Delft University of Technology
Delft, The Netherlands

Jorge Bernardino
Polytechnic Institute of Coimbra – ISEC
Coimbra, Portugal

David Aveiro 🆔
University of Madeira
Funchal, Portugal

Madeira-ITI
Funchal, Portugal

Ana Salgado
Federal University of Pernambuco
Recife, Brazil

Joaquim Filipe
Polytechnic Institute of Setúbal
Setúbal, Portugal

INSTICC
Setúbal, Portugal

ISSN 1865-0929   ISSN 1865-0937 (electronic)
Communications in Computer and Information Science
ISBN 978-3-031-14601-5   ISBN 978-3-031-14602-2 (eBook)
https://doi.org/10.1007/978-3-031-14602-2

This Springer imprint is published by the registered company Springer Nature Switzerland AG
The registered company address is: Gewerbestrasse 11, 6330 Cham, Switzerland

Preface

The present book includes extended and revised versions of a set of selected papers from the 12th International Joint Conference on Knowledge Discovery, Knowledge Engineering and Knowledge Management (IC3K 2020), held via online streaming, during November 2–4, 2020.

IC3K 2020 received 133 paper submissions from authors in 44 countries, of which 6% were included in this book. The papers were selected by the event chairs and their selection is based on a number of criteria that include the classifications and comments provided by the Program Committee members, the session chairs' assessment, and also the program chairs' global view of all papers included in the technical program. The authors of selected papers were then invited to submit a revised and extended version of their papers having at least 30% innovative material.

The purpose of IC3K is to bring together researchers, engineers, and practitioners in the areas of knowledge discovery, knowledge engineering, and knowledge management. IC3K is composed of three co-located conferences, each specializing in at least one of the aforementioned main knowledge areas: the International Conference on Knowledge Discovery and Information Retrieval (KDIR), the International Conference on Knowledge Engineering and Ontology Development (KEOD), and the International Conference on Knowledge Management and Information Systems (KMIS).

The papers selected to be included in this book contribute to the understanding of relevant trends of current research on knowledge discovery, knowledge engineering, and knowledge management, including information extraction, data analysis, machine learning, natural language processing, semantic types, knowledge graphs, task knowledge, digital transformation, and enterprise social networking.

We would like to thank all the authors for their contributions and also the reviewers who helped ensure the quality of this publication.

November 2020

Ana Fred
David Aveiro
Jan Dietz
Ana Salgado
Jorge Bernardino
Joaquim Filipe

Organization

Conference Chair

Joaquim Filipe   Polytechnic Institute of Setubal/INSTICC, Portugal

Program Co-chairs

KDIR

Ana Fred   Instituto de Telecomunicações/University of Lisbon, Portugal

KEOD

David Aveiro   University of Madeira/Madeira-ITI, Portugal
Jan Dietz   Delft University of Technology, The Netherlands

KMIS

Ana Salgado   Federal University of Pernambuco, Brazil
Jorge Bernardino   Polytechnic Institute of Coimbra, Portugal

KDIR Program Committee

Muhammad Abulaish	South Asian University, India
Amir Ahmad	United Arab Emirates University, UAE
Mayer Aladjem	Ben-Gurion University of the Negev, Israel
Maria Aramburu Cabo	Universitat Jaume I, Spain
Eva Armengol	IIIA-CSIC, Spain
Vladimir Bartik	Brno University of Technology, Czech Republic
Gloria Bordogna	CNR-IREA, Italy
Amel Borgi	Université de Tunis El Manar, Tunisia
Pavel Brazdil	University of Porto, Portugal
Ivana Burgetová	Brno University of Technology, Czech Republic
Arnaud Castelltort	LIRMM, France
Chien-Chung Chan	University of Akron, USA
Keith Chan	Hong Kong Polytechnic University, Hong Kong
Chien Chen	National Taiwan University, Taiwan, China
Zhiyuan Chen	University of Maryland Baltimore County, USA

Patrick Ciarelli	Universidade Federal do Espírito Santo, Brazil
Paulo Cortez	University of Minho, Portugal
Luis M. de Campos	University of Granada, Spain
Emanuele Di Buccio	University of Padua, Italy
Thanh-Nghi Do	Can Tho University, Vietnam
Antoine Doucet	University of La Rochelle, France
J. Stephen Downie	University of Illinois Urbana-Champaign, USA
Markus Endres	University of Augsburg, Germany
Iaakov Exman	Azrieli College of Engineering Jerusalem, Israel
Thiago Ferreira Covões	Universidade Federal do ABC, Brazil
Panorea Gaitanou	Universidad de Alcala, Spain
Susan Gauch	University of Arkansas, USA
Nuno Gonçalves	Polytechnic Institute of Setúbal, Portugal
Jennifer Harding	Loughborough University, UK
Beatriz de la Iglesia	University of East Anglia, UK
Ahmedul Kabir	University of Dhaka, Bangladesh
Mouna Kamel	CNRS, France
Ron Kenett	KPA/Samuel Neaman Institute, Israel
Margita Kon-Popovska	Ss Cyril and Methodius University in Skopje, North Macedonia
Donald Kraft	Colorado Technical University, USA
Nuno Lau	Universidade de Aveiro, Portugal
Anne Laurent	LIRMM, University of Montpellier, France
Carson Leung	University of Manitoba, Canada
Rory Lewis	University of Colorado, USA
Jerry Chun-Wei Lin	Western Norway University of Applied Sciences, Norway
Michel Liquiere	University of Montpellier, France
Jun Liu	University of Ulster, UK
Ricardo Marcacini	University of São Paulo, Brazil
Sérgio Matos	University of Aveiro, Portugal
Edson Matsubara	Universidade Federal de Mato Grosso do Sul, Brazil
Dulani Meedeniya	University of Moratuwa, Sri Lanka
Engelbert Mephu Nguifo	LIMOS, Université Clermont Auvergne, France
Stefania Montani	University of Piemonte Orientale, Italy
Gianluca Moro	Università di Bologna, Italy
Yashar Moshfeghi	University of Strathclyde, UK
Mitsunori Ogihara	University of Miami, USA
Elias Oliveira	Universidade Federal do Espirito Santo, Brazil
Márcia Oliveira	Universidade Federal do Espírito Santo, Brazil
Fabrício Olivetti de França	Universidade Federal do ABC, Brazil

Sarala Padi	National Institute of Standards and Technology, USA
Colm Riordan	National University of Ireland, Galway, Ireland
Milos Savic	University of Novi Sad, Serbia
Simeon Simoff	Western Sydney University, Australia
Manuel Striani	University of Piemonte Orientale, Italy
Atsuhiro Takasu	National Institute of Informatics, Japan
Marco Temperini	Sapienza University of Rome, Italy
Ulrich Thiel	Fraunhofer-Gesellschaft, Germany
Predrag Tosic	Washington State University, USA
Alicia Troncoso Lora	Pablo de Olavide University of Seville, Spain
Domenico Ursino	Università Politecnica delle Marche, Italy
Xing Wei	Pinterest Inc., USA
Yan Zhang	California State University, San Bernardino, USA
Yi Zhang	University of Technology Sydney, Australia

KDIR Additional Reviewers

Mohammed Alqahtani	University of Arkansas, USA
Reem Alsaffar	University of Arkansas, USA
Jerry Bonnell	University of Miami, USA
Antonella Carbonaro	University of Bologna, Italy
Zheng Fang	Pinterest, USA
Pedro Faustini	Macquarie University, Australia
Andrew Mackey	University of Arkansas, USA
Michael Mbouopda	University of Clermont Auvergne, France
Omar Salman	University of Arkansas, USA

KEOD Program Committee

Alia Abdelmoty	Cardiff University, UK
Andreas Abecker	disy Informationssysteme GmbH, Germany
José Abreu Salas	Universidad de Alicante, Spain
Mamoun Abu Helou	Al-Istiqlal University, Palestine
Masanori Akiyoshi	Kanagawa University, Japan
Raian Ali	Hamad Bin Khalifa University, Qatar
Francisco Antunes	University of Coimbra/Beira Interior University, Portugal
Vaibhav Anu	Montclair State University, USA
Doo-Hwan Bae	Korea Advanced Institute of Science and Technology, South Korea
Petra Bago	University of Zagreb, Croatia
Claudio Baptista	Universidade Federal de Campina Grande, Brazil

Óscar Mortágua Pereira	University of Aveiro, Portugal
Azah Muda	Universiti Teknikal Malaysia Melaka, Malaysia
Hiroyuki Nakagawa	Osaka University, Japan
Jørgen Nilsson	Technical University of Denmark, Denmark
Alex Norta	Tallinn University of Technology, Estonia
Carlos Periñán-Pascual	Universitat Politècnica de València, Spain
Dimitris Plexousakis	FORTH, Greece
Mihail Popescu	University of Missouri-Columbia, USA
Claudia Raibulet	University of Milano-Bicocca, Italy
Amar Ramdane-Cherif	University of Versailles Saint-Quentin-en-Yvelines, France
Domenico Redavid	University of Bari "Aldo Moro", Italy
Thomas Risse	University Library Johann Christian Senckenberg, Germany
Mariano Rodríguez Muro	Google LLC, USA
Oscar Rodriguez Rocha	Teach on Mars, France
Colette Rolland	Université Paris 1 Panthéon-Sorbonne, France
Viera Rozinajova	Slovak University of Technology in Bratislava, Slovakia
Fabio Sartori	University of Milano-Bicocca, Italy
Meng Sun	Peking University, China
Gerson Sunye	University of Nantes, France
Orazio Tomarchio	University of Catania, Italy
Petr Tucnik	University of Hradec Kralove, Czech Republic
Manolis Tzagarakis	University of Patras, Greece
Rafael Valencia-Garcia	Universidad de Murcia, Spain
Hironori Washizaki	Waseda University, Japan
Bingyang Wei	Texas Christian University, USA
Lai Xu	Bournemouth University, UK
Gian Zarri	Sorbonne University, France
Ying Zhao	Naval Postgraduate School, USA
Nianjun Zhou	IBM, USA
Qiang Zhu	University of Michigan–Dearborn, USA
Eugenio Zimeo	University of Sannio, Italy

KEOD Additional Reviewers

Kevin Angele	University of Innsbruck, Austria
Kongtao Chen	University of Pennsylvania, USA
Rajesh Kumar Gnanasekaran	Towson University, USA
Oleksandra Panasiuk	Semantic Technology Institute Innsbruck, Austria

KMIS Program Committee

Samia Aitouche	Université de Batna 2, Algeria
Hamed Alhoori	Northern Illinois University, USA
Michael Arias	Universidad de Costa Rica, Costa Rica
Ana Azevedo	Polytechnic Institute of Porto, Portugal
Giuseppe Berio	University of South Brittany, France
Kelly Braghetto	University of São Paulo, Brazil
Malgorzata Bugajska	Swisscom Schweiz AG, Switzerland
Cindy Chen	University of Massachusetts Lowell, USA
Dickson Chiu	University of Hong Kong, Hong Kong
Ritesh Chugh	Central Queensland University, Australia
Nour El Mawas	Université de Lille, France
Madjid Fathi	University of Siegen, Germany
Michael Fellmann	Universität Rostock, Germany
Joan-Francesc Fondevila-Gascón	CECABLE/Universitat Pompeu Fabra/Universitat Ramon Llull/EU Mediterrani/Universitat Oberta de Catalunya, Spain
Annamaria Goy	University of Turin, Italy
Michele Grimaldi	University of Cassino, Italy
Gabriel Guerrero-Contreras	University of Cádiz, Spain
Anne Håkansson	KTH, Sweden
Jennifer Harding	Loughborough University, UK
Mounira Harzallah	LS2N, Polytech Nantes, University of Nantes, France
Vincent Homburg	Erasmus University Rotterdam, The Netherlands
Anca Ionita	Politehnica University of Bucharest, Romania
Radoslaw Katarzyniak	Wroclaw University of Science and Technology, Poland
Helmut Krcmar	Technische Universität München, Germany
Tri Kurniawan	Universitas Brawijaya, Indonesia
Christine Lahoud	Université Française d'Egypte, Egypt
Dominique Laurent	ETIS Laboratory, CY Cergy Paris University, ENSEA, CNRS, France
Michael Leyer	University of Rostock, Germany
Kecheng Liu	University of Reading, UK
Xiaoyue Ma	Xi'an Jiaotong University, China
Carlos Malcher Bastos	Universidade Federal Fluminense, Brazil
Federica Mandreoli	University of Modena and Reggio Emilia, Italy
Jouni Markkula	University of Oulu, Finland
Nada Matta	University of Technology of Troyes, France
Brahami Menaouer	National Polytechnic School of Oran, Algeria
Michele Missikoff	ISTC-CNR, Italy

Luis Molina Fernández	University of Granada, Spain
Jean-Henry Morin	University of Geneva, Switzerland
Parth Nagarkar	New Mexico State University, USA
Ravi Patnayakuni	University of Alabama in Huntsville, USA
Wilma Penzo	University of Bologna, Italy
Filipe Portela	University of Minho, Portugal
Colette Rolland	Université Paris 1 Panthéon-Sorbonne, France
Irina Rychkova	Université Paris 1 Panthéon-Sorbonne, France
Maria Sapino	Università di Torino, Italy
Meenu Singh	Murray State University, USA
Scott Spangler	IBM Watson Health, USA
Malgorzata Sterna	Poznan University of Technology, Poland
Mani Subramani	University Minnesota, USA
Goce Trajcevski	Northwestern University, USA
Shu-Mei Tseng	I-Shou University, Taiwan, China
Costas Vassilakis	University of the Peloponnese, Greece
Martin Wessner	Darmstadt University of Applied Sciences, Germany
Qiang Zhu	University of Michigan–Dearborn, USA

KMIS Additional Reviewers

Sara Balderas-Díaz	University of Cadiz, Spain
Omid Jafari	New Mexico State University, USA

Invited Speakers

Alexander Smirnov	SPC RAS, Russia
Manfred Reichert	Ulm University, Germany
Frank van Harmelen	The Hybrid Intelligence Center/Vrije Universiteit Amsterdam, The Netherlands
Stefan Decker	RWTH Aachen University, Germany

Contents

A Novel Semi-supervised Clustering Algorithm: CoExDBSCAN

Benjamin Ertl[1,2]($\boxtimes$) (iD), Matthias Schneider[2] (iD), Jörg Meyer[1] (iD), and Achim Streit[1] (iD)

[1] Steinbuch Centre for Computing (SCC), Karlsruhe Institute of Technology (KIT), Karlsruhe, Germany
{benjamin.ertl,joerg.meyer2,achim.streit}@kit.edu

[2] Institute for Meteorology and Climate Research (IMK-ASF), Karlsruhe Institute of Technology (KIT), Karlsruhe, Germany
matthias.schneider@kit.edu

Abstract. Cluster analysis helps to better understand the inherent structure of data by grouping similar data points together. Typically this similarity is expressed in terms of distance between data points, either in full value space or value subspaces or in terms of correlations among attributes. However, distance-based clustering algorithms suffer the curse of dimensionality, where points tend to become equidistant from one another as the dimensionality increases. Subspace and correlation clustering algorithms overcome these issues but still face challenges when data points have complex relations or clusters overlap. Semi-supervised clustering algorithms can significantly improve the results of any cluster analysis that encounters such problems by incorporating a priori knowledge into the clustering process. This paper presents a novel semi-supervised clustering algorithm, CoExDBSCAN, that is based on the original DBSCAN algorithm and combines traditional, density-based clustering with techniques from subspace, correlation and constrained clustering methods. The correctness and usefulness of the algorithm, specifically for spatio-temporal data, is demonstrated on a synthetic dataset and a real-world dataset in the domain of climatology.

Keywords: Data mining · Machine learning · Pattern recognition · Clustering · Correlation clustering · Constrained clustering · DBSCAN · Spatio-temporal data · Climate research

1 Introduction

1.1 Motivation

An increasing amount of high-dimensional data is available today through new technologies, higher processing power, bigger storage capacities and data-driven research. Mining such datasets can reveal interesting patterns and dependencies often caused by complex correlations. Unsupervised cluster analysis is a common approach to extract such dependencies. However, distance-based clustering algorithms suffer the curse of dimensionality, where points tend to become equidistant from one another as the dimensionality increases [23]. Subspace and correlation clustering algorithms have been introduced to overcome this issue. These algorithms extend traditional clustering algorithms

© Springer Nature Switzerland AG 2022
A. Fred et al. (Eds.): IC3K 2020, CCIS 1608, pp. 1–21, 2022.
https://doi.org/10.1007/978-3-031-14602-2_1

to detect correlations in subsets of features [3,4]. Correlation algorithms like CASH [1] or 4C [11] can find arbitrarily oriented subspace clusters and local subgroups of data points sharing arbitrarily complex correlations. However, the complexity of these algorithms is high, and they do not provide the flexibility to align the outcome with the expectations of the analysis; for example, a cluster analysis of spatio-temporal data is expected to identify geographically close structures that are not necessarily correlated in spatial space but expected to be correlated in value space. Therefore, there has been a growing interest in semi-supervised clustering methods, where additional information or domain knowledge is included into the clustering process [8,15,33] to align the cluster analysis outcome with the expected result.

This paper presents a novel semi-supervised density-based clustering algorithm with constrained cluster expansion, CoExDBSCAN, that combines different techniques from subspace, correlation and constrained clustering. The CoExDBSCAN algorithm was initially presented at the Knowledge Discovery and Information Retrieval 2020 (KDIR'20) conference and published in the conference proceedings [17]. Compared to the original paper, this extended version provides corrections for the algorithm itself, an updated constraint formulation for correlated structures, a more challenging synthetic dataset, an comprehensive comparison with semi-supervised algorithms for the synthetic dataset and finally, an extended analysis of the real-world dataset.

The proposed algorithm uses DBSCAN [21] to find density-connected clusters in a defined subspace of features and restricts the expansion of clusters to a priori constraints. The correctness and usefulness of the algorithm, specifically for spatio-temporal data, is demonstrated on a synthetic dataset and a real-world dataset in the domain of climatology. The provided results of our experimental studies on synthetic and real-world datasets demonstrate that CoExDBSCAN is especially suited for spatio-temporal data, where one subspace of features defines the spatial extent of the data and another subspace correlations between features.

The extensions to the original DBSCAN algorithm can be summarised as follows:

- Two additional user-defined parameters are introduced, one to define the subspace dimensions to be used to discover density-based clusters and one to define the dimensions of the subspace to be used to apply constraints to the cluster expansion of DBSCAN.
- The cluster expansion step in the original DBSCAN algorithm is modified to be restricted to user-defined constraints.
- A generic constraint to discover correlated structures in large datasets is evaluated on the synthetic and real-world data.

The remainder of the paper is organised as follows: This section continues with relevant background knowledge in literature and theory. Section 2 presents the CoExDB-SCAN algorithm in detail. Section 3 shows the verification, evaluation and runtime analysis of the algorithm on a synthetic and real-world climatology dataset of satellite observations. In Sect. 4, we give a discussion on the results and provide the conclusions and outlooks.

1.2 Background

Various clustering algorithms exist today for different purposes, for example, in the areas of density-based clustering, correlation clustering or constrained clustering. Anil K. Jain provides a well-received survey of the field in his article "Data Clustering: 50 Years Beyond K-Means" [28]. This section focuses on the most related and relevant work to our proposed approach.

CoExDBSCAN is based on the original DBSCAN algorithm and combines traditional, density-based clustering with techniques from subspace, correlation and constrained clustering methods. The DBSCAN algorithm was presented by Martin Ester et al. in 1996 as a density-based clustering algorithm for discovering clusters in large spatial databases with noise [21]. With the introduction of this new algorithm, the authors established further a new notion of clusters based on the density of their surrounding neighbours. The algorithm can be summarised as follows. For all data points, if the distance from an initial point to at least a $minPts$ defined number of other points is smaller than a defined distance ϵ, these points form a cluster. The initial point is considered a core point, and the remaining points are the ϵ-neighbourhood of that point. This cluster is then expanded by applying the initial step to all points in the ϵ-neighbourhood. If the initial point has less than $minPts$ neighbours, the point is considered a noise point, and the algorithm moves to the next point in the dataset. If a noise point is density-reachable from some other point, this point can become a border point and, therefore, belong to a different cluster later in the process. DBSCAN has two parameters, $minPts$ and ϵ, that determine the outcome of the algorithm. The purpose of the $minPts$ parameter is to smooth the density estimate and is recommended to be chosen according to the dimensionality of the dataset. The purpose of the radius parameter ϵ depends on the distance function and should ideally be based on domain knowledge, according to Schubert et al. [38].

Schubert et al. further discuss the advantages and disadvantages of DBSCAN and state that DBSCAN continues to be relevant even for high-dimensional data but becomes difficult to use:

"Independent of the algorithm, the parameter ϵ of DBSCAN becomes hard to choose in high-dimensional data due to the loss of contrast in distances [10, 26, 44]. Irrespective of the index, it therefore becomes difficult to use DBSCAN in high-dimensional data because of parameterization; other algorithms such as OPTICS and HDBSCAN*, that do not require the ϵ parameter are easier to use, but still suffer from high dimensionality".

The mentioned OPTICS [5] and HDBSCAN* [12] algorithms are DBSCAN variants that focus on finding hierarchical clustering results [38]. CoExDBSCAN is based on the original DBSCAN algorithm, however it is not restricted to it and can be used in combination with any variant where the cluster expansion step can be restricted to user-defined constraints.

Related algorithms in the area of subspace clustering and correlation clustering have attracted more and more attention recently [1]. For example, CLIQUE [4] for axis-parallel subspaces or ORCLUS [3] and CASH [1] for arbitrarily oriented subspaces.

The CASH algorithm was introduced as an efficient and effective method to find arbitrarily oriented subspace clusters. The algorithm transforms every data point from data space to the space of all possible subspaces based on the Hough transformation [16,25]. This approach maps every data point in data space onto the corresponding sinusoidal curve in parameter space. By splitting the parameter space into hypercuboids, intersecting sinusoidal curves within the same hypercuboid indicate points in data space that are located on, or near, a common hyperplane, and therefore are considered to form a subspace cluster [1]. According to the authors, CASH can find subspace clusters of different dimensionality even if they are sparse or are intersected by other clusters within a noisy environment. Moreover, CASH outperforms other correlation clustering algorithms such as ORCLUS or 4C [11] on datasets with highly overlapping clusters [1], which is the case for our synthetic and real-world datasets.

However, CASH lacks the exploitation of available a priori knowledge, known as constrained or semi-supervised clustering and has been the subject of extensive research recently [15]. Much of early work in semi-supervised clustering focused on extending feature-based clustering methods regarding to two types of semi-supervision, pointwise semi-supervision and pairwise semi-supervision [2]. The notion of using constraints that express information about the underlying class structure in the clustering process was introduced by Wagstaff and Cardie [42] following the semi-supervised approach of pairwise constraints or instance-level constraints. This approach considers two general types of constraints, (1) *must-link* constraints that specify that two instances have to be in the same cluster and (2) *cannot-link* constraints that specify, that two instances cannot be in the same cluster.

Two algorithms in the domain of semi-supervised clustering algorithms are the constraint K-means algorithm (CK-means) and the pairwise constraint K-means algorithm (PCK-means). CK-means uses partially labelled data to initialise the cluster centres and also uses the seed labels in the subsequent K-means algorithm, i.e. the seed labels are kept unchanged, and only the labels of the non-seed data are re-estimated [6]. The labels can be derived from pairwise constraints by labelling points with cannot-link constraints differently and points with must-link constraints with the same label. Basu et al. further showed that the pairwise constrained clustering problem could be solved by finding the Hidden Markov Random Field (HMRF) configuration with the highest posterior probability, i.e. minimising its energy, and proposed the PCK-means algorithm for solving this problem [7].

Another relevant algorithm in the area of constraint clustering is the C-DBSCAN algorithm by Ruiz et al. [36]. C-DBSCAN extends the original DBSCAN in three steps. First, the data space is partitioned into dens partitions by applying a k-d tree [9]; second, local clusters are created under the cannot-link constraints; third, local clusters are merged under the must-link and cannot-link constraints. In their paper, the authors chose a random percentage of points under the must-link constraint and derived the cannot-link constraint interdependently. They could demonstrate that even those randomly chosen constraints improve the clustering quality substantially, notably on datasets where the original DBSCAN performs poorly [36].

Compared to the introduced methods, our approach does not follow the method of instance-level constraints expressed as must-link and cannot-link constraints. Our modifications to the original DBSCAN restricts the cluster expansion to user-defined constraints, which has been proven to be very flexible and is explained in detail in the next section, after establishing necessary definitions based on the definitions of the original DBSCAN algorithm in the following.

1.3 Definitions

Martin Ester et al. presented in the original DBSCAN paper six main definitions essential for the algorithm [21] that are recapitulated in the following.

Definition 1. *ϵ-neighbourhood of a point*
Let DB be a database of points. The ϵ-neighbourhood of a point p, denoted by $N_\epsilon(p)$, is defined by

$$N_\epsilon(p) = \{q \in DB | dist(p, q) \leq \epsilon\}$$

Definition 2. *Directly density-reachable*
A point p is directly density-reachable from a point q wrt. ϵ and $minPts$ if

1. *$p \in N_\epsilon(q)$ and*
2. *$|N_\epsilon(q) \geq minPts|$ (core point condition).*

Definition 3. *Density-reachable*
A point p is density-reachable from a point q wrt. ϵ and $minPts$ if there is a chain of points $p_1, ..., p_n, p_1 = q, p_n = p$ such that p_{i+1} is directly density-reachable from p_i.

Definition 4. *Density-connected*
A point p is density-connected to a point q wrt. ϵ and $minPts$ if there is a point o such that both, p and q are density-reachable from o wrt. ϵ and $minPts$.

Definition 5. *Cluster*
A cluster C wrt. ϵ and $minPts$ is a non-empty subset of DB satisfying the following conditions:

1. *$\forall p, q$: if $p \in C$ and q is density-reachable from p wrt. ϵ and $minPts$, then $q \in C$. (Maximality)*
2. *$\forall p, q \in C$: p is density-connected to q wrt. ϵ and $minPts$. (Connectivity)*

Definition 6. *Noise*
Let $C_1, ..., C_k$ be the clusters of the database DB wrt. parameters ϵ_i and $minPts_i$, $i = 1, ..., k$. Then we define the noise as the set of points in the database DB not belonging to any cluster C_i, i.e. noise = $\{p \in DB | \forall i : p \notin C_i\}$

In summary, the DBSCAN algorithm extracts clusters that comprise points with at least a specific number of other points ($minPts$) within a specific distance (ϵ) or otherwise, points are considered to be noise. DBSCAN can find clusters of arbitrary shape, but with the global density parameter ϵ, DBSCAN can not identify clusters with different densities. While the ϵ and $minPts$ parameters can be fine-tuned, for example, based on a k-distance graph proposed in the original paper [21], finding suitable, global parameters becomes even more challenging for high-dimensional data. Ertöz et al. [20] demonstrate specifically why the Euclidean distance does not work well in high-dimensional data. Additionally, as long as points are density-connected, DBSCAN will group them into the same cluster. With overlapping clusters, DBSCAN will either merge clusters or consider the lesser dense true cluster points as noise. CoExDBSCAN addresses these problems by modifying the original DBSCAN algorithm as described in the following section.

2   CoExDBSCAN

2.1   Algorithm

CoExDBSCAN, our density-based clustering algorithm with Constrained Expansion, modifies the original DBSCAN clustering algorithm as follows. First, a user-defined parameter can be defined to restrict the discovery of density-based clusters to a possible subspace. Second, the cluster expansion step in the DBSCAN algorithm is restricted to user-defined constraints, applied to a user-defined subspace of the dataset.

The ϵ-neighbourhood definition from the original DBSCAN algorithm introduced in the previous section, Definition 1, can be adjusted accordingly.

Definition 7. *CoExDBSCAN ϵ-neighbourhood of a point*
Let DB be a set (database) of points. The CoExDBSCAN ϵ-neighbourhood of a point p, denoted by $CoExN_\epsilon(p)$, is defined by

$$CoExN_\epsilon(p) = \{q \in DB | dist(p_\varsigma, q_\varsigma) \leq \epsilon \wedge constraints(p_\rho, q_\rho)\}$$

where p_ς, q_ς are the subspace representations of point p and q of the user-defined spatial subspace ς, p_ρ, q_ρ are the subspace representations of point p and q of the user-defined constraint subspace ρ and the constraints function evaluates true for each constraint Γ_i in a user-defined set of constraints $\Gamma = \{\Gamma_1, \Gamma_2, ..., \Gamma_m\}$.

A pseudo-code representation of the CoExDBSCAN algorithm is given in Algorithm 1. This representation has been adopted from the pseudo-code representation of the original DBSCAN algorithm by Schubert et al. [38]. Modifications to the algorithm are coloured red and marked by a star (*). The algorithm can be described as follows.

DBSCAN and CoExDBSCAN label each data point as noise, if the core point condition is violated, see Definition 2, i.e. if there are not at least $minPts$ points in the ϵ-neighbourhood, and if the point has not been processed already. If there are at least $minPts$ points in the ϵ-neighbourhood of the point under consideration, the point is labelled as core point. This point forms a new cluster while iteratively expanding and adding the core point neighbours to the cluster.

The first modification of the DBSCAN algorithm is in the `RangeQuery` function in line 3 and line 14 (Algorithm 1). The modified version accepts a user-defined parameter $sDim$ that allows defining the dimensions of the space for the range query. In the original DBSCAN algorithm, the range query is always executed on the full space of the dataset unless the algorithm operates on a precomputed distance matrix that takes

---

Algorithm 1: Pseudocode of the CoExDBSCAN Algorithm.

    input : dataset D
    input : radius ϵ
    input : density threshold $minPts$
    input : distance function $dist$
    input : spatial dimensions $sDim$ *
    input : user-defined constraints $cFunc$ *
    input : constraint dimensions $cDim$ *
    output: point labels $label$ initially $undefined$

1 **foreach** *point p in dataset D* **do**
2   **if** $label(p) \neq undefined$ **then continue;**
3   Neighbours $N \leftarrow$ RangeQuery$(D, dist, sdim, p, \epsilon)$ *;
4   **if** $|N| < minPts$ **then**
5         $label(p) \leftarrow Noise$;
6   **continue;**
7     $c \leftarrow$ next cluster label;
8     $label(p) \leftarrow c$;
9   Seed set $S \leftarrow N \setminus \{p\}$;
10   **foreach** *q in S* **do**
11   **if** $label(q) = Noise$ **then** $label(q) \leftarrow c$;
12   **if** $label(q) \neq undefined$ **then continue;**
13   **if** PointConstraint$(cFunc, cDim, q)$ *is false* **then continue** *;
14   Neighbours $N \leftarrow$ RangeQuery$(D, dist, sdim, q, \epsilon)$ *;
15       $label(q) \leftarrow c$;
16   **if** $|N| < minPts$ **then continue;**
17   **foreach** *s in N* **do**
18          $S \leftarrow S \cup s$;

---

these restrictions into account. However, the parametrisation of the spatial dimensions makes these restrictions more explicit and more straightforward understandable to the user. Especially for data with explicit spatial dimensions, excluding specific dimensions or all non-spatial dimensions from the range query can improve the clustering quality.

The second modification of the DBSCAN algorithm restricts the cluster expansion step in line 13 (Algorithm 1). The original DBSCAN algorithm expands a cluster by starting at one core point and adding all of its neighbours to a set of seeds that are iteratively expanded on if they satisfy the core point condition itself. The PointConstraint function in line 13 of the pseudo-code takes a set of user-defined constraints in the form of functions and returns true if all of the constraints can be satisfied or false otherwise. This modification allows for additional user-defined constraints to be considered before adding points to a cluster and as potential new seeds. One or multiple constraints ($cFunc$) as well as the dimensions ($cDim$) that the constraints should be applied to can be provided to the algorithm. This approach can significantly improve the clustering quality and allows incorporating a priori knowledge into the clustering process expressed in sub- or full-space constraints.

The behaviour of the `PointConstraint` function can be relaxed, for example, by applying a threshold of the number of constraints that need to be satisfied instead of the all-true behaviour.

2.2 Constraint

Finding reasonable constraints is challenging, depending on the data to analyse, the analysis to be conducted, and the expected outcome. The following constraint is formulated specifically to evaluate linear correlations in the synthetic dataset and real-world dataset. This constraint allows restricting the expansion of clusters to a defined margin around the linear regression of existing cluster points.

Definition 8. *A Point p_i belongs to a cluster $C = p_1, ..., p_n$, according to Definition 5, with n number of cluster points iff*

$$(Y_{C \cup p_i} - \hat{Y}_{C \cup p_i})^2 < \delta \cdot \frac{1}{n} \sum_{C \setminus p_i} (Y_{C \setminus p_i} - \hat{Y}_{C \setminus p_i})^2 \tag{1}$$

where Y and $\hat{Y}$ are the dependent variable and fitted value of the linear regression respectively, fitted to the user-defined subspace of features.

According to Definition 8, a point p_i is added to an existing cluster C only if the squared residuals of the linear regression of all cluster points, including p_i, is smaller than the mean squared residuals of all cluster points without p_i times a specific threshold δ. The linear regression is fitted to the user-defined constraint subspace, see Definition 7, and the threshold parameter δ provided by the user as well. Experiments have shown that this constraint is a suitable constraint that expresses the a priori knowledge of correlated structures in the dataset generic and allows the algorithm to expand clusters on arbitrarily correlated structures with changing correlations up to a certain degree.

3 Cluster Analysis

3.1 Verification

This section provides a comparison between CoExDBSCAN, the original DBSCAN algorithm as a baseline approach, the CK-means and PCK-means algorithms as a comparison to existing semi-supervised clustering algorithms, and the CASH algorithm as a state-of-the-art comparison in the field of correlation clustering. The CASH algorithm significantly outperforms other correlation clustering algorithms such as the ORCLUS algorithm or the 4C algorithm on datasets with highly overlapping clusters in terms of robustness and effectiveness. The comparison is carried out on a self-generated synthetic dataset. A self-generated dataset allows us to control the properties of the clusters fully and allows us to create a dataset that is especially challenging for density-based clustering methods and subspace and correlation clustering methods. Since the true labels of the synthetic dataset are known, we use the Rand index adjusted for chance (ARI) [27,34] to evaluate our clustering results and the clustering accuracy (ACC) [35]. The Rand index is a measure of similarity between two data clusterings and can be computed as follows [34]:

Definition 9. *Rand index*

Given a set of n elements $S = \{o_1, ..., o_n\}$, a partition $X = \{X_1, ..., X_r\}$ of S into r subsets and a partition $Y = \{Y_1, ..., Y_s\}$ of S into s subsets, the Rand index is:

$$R = \frac{a+b}{n(n-1)/2} \tag{2}$$

with a, the number of pairs of elements in S that are in the same subset in X and Y, with b, the number of pairs of elements in S that are in the same subset in X and in different subsets in Y, and the total number of pairs $\binom{n}{2}$ in the denominator.

The adjusted Rand index, bounded above by one and takes on the value of zero when the index equals its expected value $\mathbf{E}(R)$, can be expressed in the general form of an index corrected for chance the following [27]:

Definition 10. *Adjusted Rand index*

$$ARI = \frac{R - \mathbf{E}(R)}{max(R) - \mathbf{E}(R)} \tag{3}$$

The clustering accuracy finds the best match between the actual labels and the cluster labels; the higher the clustering accuracy, the better the clustering performance.

Definition 11. *Clustering accuracy (ACC)*

$$ACC(y, \hat{y}) = \max_{perm \in P} \frac{1}{n} \sum_{i=0}^{n-1} 1(perm(\hat{y}_i) = y_i) \tag{4}$$

where P is the set of all permutations in $[1; K]$ where K is the number of clusters. The set of all permutations can be efficiently computed using the Hungarian algorithm [31].

Our synthetic dataset contains 2,000 points in total with three overlapping clusters. Compared to our initially presented work, the number of data points in one cluster has been reduced to generate inhomogeneous clusters. Figure 1 illustrates the synthetic dataset in three-dimensional space (Fig. 1a) and two-dimensional projection (Fig. 1b). The values for the x and y variables of the cluster with label zero, blue colour in Fig. 1, are generated by sampling the random uniform distribution in the half-open interval $[0, 1)$; the values for the z variable are computed using the linear equation $0.1x + 0.1y$. For the cluster with label one, orange colour in Fig. 1, the values for the x and y variables are generated by sampling the random uniform distribution in the half-open interval $[0, 1)$; the values for the z variable are computed using the linear equation $0.4x + 0.2y$. The green coloured cluster with label two in Fig. 1 is generated by evenly spaced x values in the closed interval $[0, 1]$ and the values for the y and z variables following the linear equation $-0.5x + 0.2 + \xi$, where ξ is some random variation with $\xi \sim \mathcal{N}(0, 0.01)$.

The scikit-learn Python package [32] provides an implementation of the DBSCAN algorithm, and the active-semi-supervised-clustering Python package [41] provides implementations of the constraint k-means algorithm (CK-means) and the pairwise constraint k-means algorithm (PCK-means). The ELKI data mining software written in

Java [39] provides an implementation of the CASH algorithm. We provide our implementation of the CoExDBSCAN algorithm in Python [17].

The CoExDBSCAN and DBSCAN algorithm are evaluated for an ϵ range of $[0.01, 0.20]$ with a step size of 0.01 and a $minPts$ range of $[10, 70]$ with a step size of 10; range and step size have been chosen to cover the main variability of the number of clusters and the cluster accuracy. The δ threshold parameter for the constraint formulated in Definition 8 is evaluated for three values $[3, 4, 5]$ that yield the best accuracy score on a given set of parameters. The spatial and constraint subspace for the CoExDBSCAN algorithm is set to the x and z dimensions, based on empirical analysis. The full value space has been provided for the DBSCAN, CK-means, PCK-means and CASH algorithm, resulting in higher accuracy scores in general.

The results after applying the CoExDBSCAN algorithm to the synthetic dataset range from zero to 26 clusters. The ARI score is between 0 and 0.60 and the ACC ranges from 0.32 to 0.82, depending on the ϵ and $minPts$ parameters of the original DBSCAN algorithm and the δ threshold parameter. The parameter set with the second highest accuracy ($\sim$80%), with $\epsilon = 0.09$, $minPts = 20$ and $\delta = 4$, however, yields a better result in terms of the number of noise points, which can be validated visually as well, see Fig. 2.

With the DBSCAN algorithm the results range from zero to 24 clusters. The ARI score is between 0 and 0.52 and the ACC ranges from 0.50 to 0.74, depending on the ϵ and $minPts$ parameters. The clustering result with the highest accuracy produces only one cluster. The clustering result with the highest accuracy ($\sim$70%) and correct number of clusters does not correctly represent the true structure of the clusters An example for a clustering result that better captures the true structure of the data is given in Fig. 3.

The CK-means algorithm can be applied to the synthetic data with partially labelled data, while for the PCK-means algorithm, the true labels have to be transformed into pairwise constraints. For the must-link constraints, all pairwise combinations for each point within each cluster are generated, and for the cannot-link constraints, all pairwise combinations between cluster points have to be generated. With the fraction of labels being randomly sampled from all true labels without replacement, it can be observed that providing around 55% of the true labels results in the same accuracy of the CK-

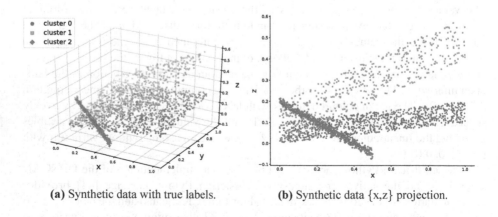

(a) Synthetic data with true labels.   (b) Synthetic data {x,z} projection.

Fig. 1. Synthetic dataset for the evaluation of the CoExDBSCAN algorithm.

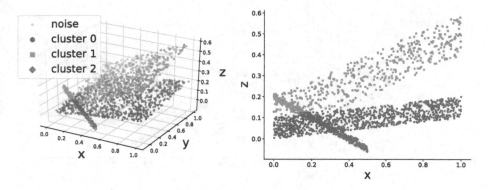

Fig. 2. CoExDBSCAN clustering result with the second highest accuracy ($\sim$80%), $\epsilon = 0.03$, $minPts = 20$ and $\delta = 5$.

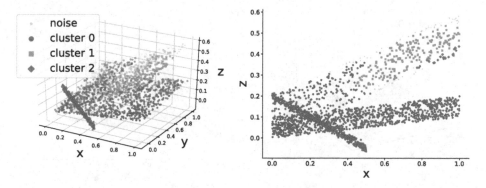

Fig. 3. Example DBSCAN clustering result with a better visually verifiable representation of the true clusters; cluster accuracy $\sim$60%, $\epsilon = 0.14$ and $minPts = 30$.

means clustering algorithm as the accuracy of the CoExDBSCAN algorithm. For the PCK-means algorithm, providing around $2,200$ constraints, $1,100$ must-link and $1,100$ cannot-link constraints, results in the same accuracy as the CoExDBSCAN algorithm.

Figure 4 visualises an example clustering result of the synthetic data applying the CK-means algorithm with 55% of the true labels randomly sampled provided to the algorithm. With around half of the true labels provided in addition to the true number of clusters $k = 3$, the clusters identified by the CK-means algorithm show overlapping areas with different inherent correlation structures. This can be observed, for example for cluster 0 (blue colour) and cluster 1 (orange colour) in the $x - z$ projection for x values greater 0.6.

Figure 5 visualises an example clustering result of the synthetic data applying the PCK-means algorithm with $2,200$ constraints based on the true labels randomly sampled provided to the algorithm. With $2,200$ constraints, $1,100$ must-link and $1,100$ cannot-link constraints respectively, provided in addition to the true number of clusters $k = 3$, the PCK-means algorithm shows a qualitative better result than the CK-means clustering algorithm, where the overlap of identified clusters is visibly smaller.

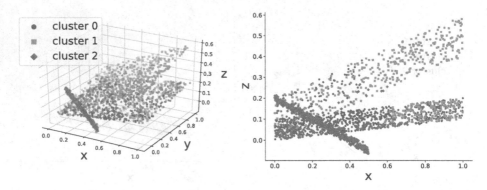

Fig. 4. Example constraint k-means clustering result; cluster accuracy ∼80%, number of true clusters given $k = 3$ and 55% of true labels provided.

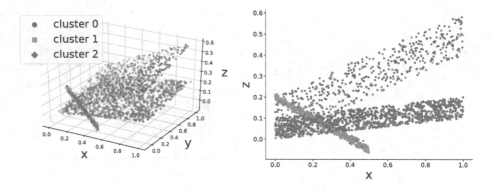

Fig. 5. Example pairwise constraint k-means clustering result; cluster accuracy ∼78%, number of true clusters given $k = 3$ and $2,200$ constraints based on the true labels provided.

The parameters for the CASH algorithm as a state-of-the-art comparison that need to be defined are first the minimum number of sinusoidal curves that need to intersect a hypercuboid in the parameter space such that this hypercuboid is regarded as a dense area [1]. The transformation from data space to parameter space is done following an approach based on the Hough transformation [16]. According to [1], this parameter represents the minimum number of points in a cluster. Second, the maximum number of splits along a search path in parameter space has to be given that controls the maximally allowed deviation from the hyperplane of the cluster in terms of orientation and jitter. Third, the jitter parameter has to be defined to allow a certain degree of deviation from exact intersections of sinusoidal curves due to discretising the parameter space into grid cells. The parameter space has been evaluated for the minimum number of curves in the interval $[1, 1000]$ with a step size of one, the maximum number of splits for 5, 10 and 20 and the jitter values 0.1, 0.15 and 0.2. The range for each parameter has been chosen to cover the main variability in cluster accuracy.

The parameter space exploration shows that CASH reaches its highest cluster accuracy (∼77%) for $minPts = 460$, $maxSplit = 20$ and $jitter = 0.2$. Figure 6 visualises an example clustering result of the synthetic data applying the CASH algorithm

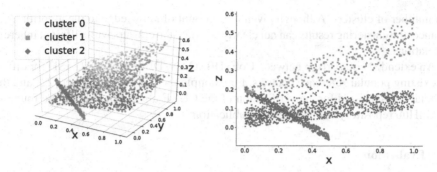

Fig. 6. Example CASH clustering result; cluster accuracy $\sim$77%, $minPts = 460$, $maxSplit = 20$ and $jitter = 0.2$.

$minPts = 460$, $maxSplit = 20$ and $jitter = 0.2$. The number of true clusters has been correctly identified; further, the algorithm demonstrates its capability to find subspace clusters with correlated structures even other clusters intersect them. However, the CASH algorithm can not entirely separate overlapping areas with different inherent correlation structures similar to the results with the CK-means algorithm, for example, cluster 0 (blue colour) and cluster 1 (orange colour) that are noticeable in the 3D view and the x-z projection for x values smaller 0.4.

Table 1 summarises the clustering results for the synthetic data applying the CoExDBSCAN algorithm, the DBSCAN algorithm the CK-means and PCK-means algorithms and the CASH algorithm. Without the prior knowledge of the true number of clusters or partially labelled data, CoExDBSCAN is outperforming the original DBSCAN algorithm as a baseline approach and the state-of-the-art CASH algorithm in terms of cluster accuracy (ACC), ARI and the ability to separate clusters with different inherent correlated structures. To reach a similar accuracy as the CoExDBSCAN algorithm, the semi-supervised algorithms CK-means and PCK-means require around half of the true labels known a priori or around 2,000 pairwise constraints in addition to the

Table 1. Summary of clustering results for the synthetic data using the adjusted Rand index (ARI) and Cluster Accuracy (ACC) metrics.

	ϵ	$minPts$	δ	Noise	Cluster	ARI	ACC
CoExDBSCAN	0.03	20	5	435	3	0.60	0.82
	0.09	20	4	**20**	3	0.59	**0.80**
DBSCAN	0.03	20	-	405	1	0.37	0.70
	0.02	10	-	428	3	0.37	0.70
	0.08	50	-	21	3	0.20	0.61
	k	Known labels			Cluster	ARI	ACC
CK-means	3	55%			3	0.49	0.80
PCK-means	3	2,200			3	0.46	0.78
	maxSplit	minPts	Jitter		Cluster	ARI	ACC
CASH	20	460	0.2		3	0.44	0.77

true number of clusters. Although given this amount of knowledge to the algorithms in advance, the clustering results can not clearly separate the clusters with different inherent correlations.

An extended comparison between CoExDBSCAN, DBSCAN and CASH for different existing popular reference datasets, for example the Iris flower dataset [22] and the artificial datasets used for the verification of the CURE algorithm [24] can be found in the GitHub repository[1] of the original publication.

3.2 Evaluation

To evaluate the proposed CoExDBSCAN algorithm on a real-world dataset, we applied CoExDBSCAN, DBSCAN and CASH to a dataset within the domain of spatio-temporal data and climate research. The dataset consists of spectral data gathered from Metop-A and Metop-B satellites that have been processed for the water vapour H_2O mixing ratio and water isotopologue δD depletion for air masses at 5 km height with most sensitivity [14]. The paired analysis of water vapour H_2O mixing ratio and water isotopologue δD depletion allows to identify different processes in the atmosphere, which leave a distinctive isotopologue fingerprint [37], for example, air mass mixing, precipitation and condensation [30]. Cluster analysis allows a data-driven method to identify and analyse such processes for a better understanding of atmospheric water transport and to evaluate the moisture pathways as simulated by different state-of-the-art atmospheric models. These methods and algorithms have to scale and cope with the amount of data continuously produced by the remote sensing instruments on board the satellites, where global measurements of our data for one year aggregate to 20 Terabytes.

Our dataset in this example comprises 2,898 satellite observations with geographical coordinates and spectral data. The spectra are processed for the water vapour H_2O mixing ratio and water isotopologue δD depletion; this corresponds to measurements for one global morning overpass of both satellites in a region of interest over the Atlantic and West Africa, filtered for highest quality observations (e.g. cloud free, fit quality). The feature space for the clustering algorithms consists of the latitude and longitude values as well as the natural logarithm of the H_2O values and the natural logarithm of the δD values divided by 1,000 plus one, $\ln(\frac{\delta D}{1000} + 1)$, assuming a linear correlation between $\ln(H_2O)$ and $\ln(\frac{\delta D}{1000} + 1)$. This assumption is expected to be verifiable by correlated structures in the $\{H_2O, \delta D\}$ value space. All features have been standardised by removing the mean and scaling to unit variance to avoid individual features dominating the distance calculations.

Evaluating the DBSCAN algorithm in the parameter space $\epsilon \in [0.05, 0.5]$ with a step size of 0.05 and $minPts \in [10, 50]$ with a step size of 1 results in zero up to 21 clusters, with the number of clusters peak at ϵ around 0.3 and $minPts$ around 10. To compare the selected algorithms on the same level of granularity for the number of clusters, the parameter set that produces 20 clusters has been chosen, i.e. $\epsilon = 0.35$ and $minPts = 12$. The first row of Fig. 7 shows the clustering result for the DBSCAN algorithm on the defined and standardised feature space of the real-world data snapshot

---

[1] https://github.com/bertl4398/kdir2020.

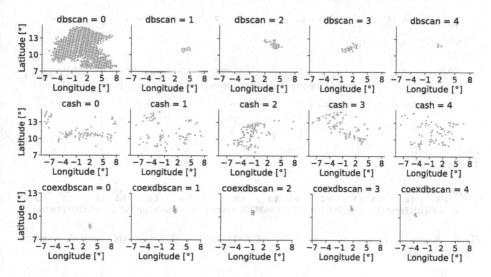

Fig. 7. Example cluster for DBSCAN, CASH and CoExDBSCAN in geo-referenced space {Longitude, Latitude}.

with the selected parameter set in the geo-referenced latitude and longitude space. The result shows mostly spatial discrete and concise clusters, except the first large cluster; points that do not belong to any cluster (noise) are not shown. The same pattern can be observed in the $\{H_2O, \delta D\}$ feature space, see the first row of Fig. 8, which shows primarily discrete and concise clusters, except for the first large cluster. However, there are no particular correlated structures recognisable.

In comparison, the CASH algorithm can produce clustering results with the same level of granularity, i.e. the same number of clusters, with the parameters $minPts = 80$, $maxSplit = 5$ and $jitter = 0.20$, that have been determined via grid search on the parameter space $minPts \in [10, 100]$, $maxSplit \in \{5, 10, 20\}$ and $jitter \in \{0.10, 0.15, 0.20\}$. The clusters in the geo-referenced latitude and longitude space for the CASH algorithm illustrated in the second row of Fig. 7 are not as concise and spatial discrete as the clusters identified by the DBSCAN algorithm. However, in the $\{H_2O, \delta D\}$ feature space, the clusters found by the CASH algorithm exhibit noticeably more of the correlated structures than the clusters found by the DBSCAN algorithm, see the second row in Fig. 8.

The CoExDBSCAN clustering results with the same level of granularity can be achieved with the parameter set $\epsilon = 0.25$, $minPts = 10$ and $\delta = 2.0$. These parameters have been determined via grid search on the parameter space $\epsilon \in [0.20, 0.50]$ with a step size of 0.01, $minPts \in [10, 20]$ with a step size of 5 and $\delta \in [1.0, 3.0]$ with a step size of 0.5. The clusters in the geo-referenced latitude and longitude space for the CoExDBSCAN algorithm illustrated in the third row of Fig. 7 are very concise and spatial discrete; further, the clusters exhibit the correlated structures to a high degree in the $\{H_2O, \delta D\}$ feature space, see the third row in Fig. 8. In comparison to the clusters found by DBSCAN, the clusters found by CoExDBSCAN are spatially separated as well and better represent the a priori assumed linear correlation in the $\{H_2O, \delta D\}$ feature space. Compared to the clusters found by CASH, some represented correlations

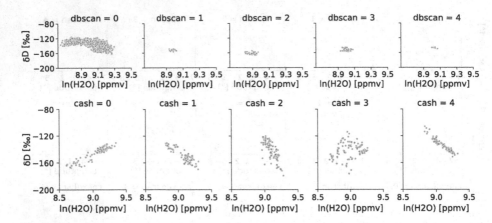

Fig. 8. Example cluster for DBSCAN, CASH and CoExDBSCAN in value space $\{\ln(H_2O), \delta D\}$.

are not as strong and significant as the CASH clusters' represented correlations by looking at the Pearson correlation coefficient and the corresponding p-values. However, the spatial coherence outweighs this fact for the objective of the analysis to identify correlated structures that are geographically close and that are expected to follow theoretical assumptions.

3.3 Runtime

For the runtime analysis, we consider the average complexity of the original DBSCAN algorithm with the additional complexity of user-defined constraints. The average runtime complexity of DBSCAN is $O(n \log n)$ [21]. Since distance queries can be supported efficiently by spatial access methods such as *R*-trees* with an average search complexity of $O(\log n)$, and because for each of n points only one query has to be executed, the average run time complexity for DBSCAN is consequently $O(n \log n)$.

Schubert et al. [38] argue that the DBSCAN runtime complexity can be $\Theta(n^2 \cdot D)$, with cost D of computing the distance of two points, if the range query is implemented as a linear scan. In general, however:

"[...] DBSCAN remains a method of choice even for large n because many alternatives are in $\Theta(n^2)$ or $\Theta(n^3)$. [...] In the general case of arbitrary non-metric distance measures, the worst case remains $O(n^2 \cdot D)$ [...]"

Adding a set of constraints $\Gamma = \{\Gamma_1, \Gamma_2, ..., \Gamma_m\}$ to the expansion step of the DBSCAN algorithm adds the complexity of $O(n \cdot max(K_i))$, with K_i the cost of computing the constraint Γ_i, to check the set of constraints for each point. This additional complexity can vary greatly, for example, from hash table searches with average time complexity $O(1)$ [13] to linear regression complexity $O(w^2 n + w^3)$ for n number of observations and w number of weights [29], as in Definition 8. The runtime complexity of CoExDBSCAN depending on the user-defined constraints can therefore be formulated as the average runtime complexity of DBSCAN plus the maximum complexity of the user-defined constraints:

$$O(n \cdot max(K_i) + n \cdot \log n) \tag{5}$$

4 Summary

4.1 Conclusion

This article presents a new density-based clustering algorithm with constrained cluster expansion, CoExDBSCAN, in an extended version to the original paper. CoExDBSCAN uses DBSCAN to find density-connected clusters in a defined subspace of features and restricts the expansion of clusters to a priori constraints. Incorporating a priori knowledge into the clustering process can significantly improve the clustering results and align the outcome of the clustering process with the objective of the data analysis. CoExDBSCAN combines different techniques from subspace, correlation and constrained clustering. Specifically, we introduce two user-defined parameters to the original DBSCAN algorithm, one to define the subspace dimensions to be used to discover density-based clusters and one to define the subspace dimensions to be used to apply constraints to the cluster expansion. The cluster expansion step in the original DBSCAN algorithm is restricted to the provided user-defined constraints.

In the presented verification, CoExDBSCAN outperforms the original DBSCAN algorithm and the CASH algorithm in terms of cluster accuracy and adjusted rand score on the synthetic dataset. To achieve a similar accuracy with the semi-supervised clustering algorithms CK-means and PCK-means on the synthetic dataset, around 55% of true labels or around 2, 200 pairwise constraints have to be provided a priori. In addition, the CK-means and PCK-means algorithms need to know the number of clusters to form in advance, whereas the CoExDBSCAN algorithm can explore the given dataset without this kind of restriction.

The evaluation of our real-world climatological dataset demonstrates CoExDBSCAN is especially suited for spatio-temporal data, where one subspace of features defines the spatial extent of the data and another correlations between features. In the presented evaluation, CoExDBSCAN is better suited to identify correlated structures that are geographically close than the original DBSCAN algorithm and the CASH algorithm.

Beyond the presented low-dimensional verification and evaluation, CoExDBSCAN remains relevant even for high-dimensional data. This derives from Schubert's evaluation of the DBSCAN algorithm for high-dimensional data [38] shows that DBSCAN continues to be relevant even for high-dimensional data. However, the parameter ϵ of DBSCAN becomes hard to choose in high-dimensional data due to the loss of contrast in distances. To overcome the loss of contrast in distances, CoExDBSCAN can utilise a user-defined subspace for the distance measure.

4.2 Outlook

To allow users to constrain the expansion of clusters in specific subspaces of the data can significantly improve the clustering results, as demonstrated in Sect. 3.1 and Sect. 3.2 for synthetic and real-world data. However, finding and expressing suitable constraints is a challenging task. We applied mainly generic constraints throughout multiple experimental runs that allow the algorithm to expand clusters for arbitrarily correlated data points. With generic constraints overfitting the clustering algorithm can be avoided, i.e.

constraining the cluster expansion to the generating process. With specially tailored constraints, for example, if we express the information about the functions that generate the dependent y and z variables in our synthetic data example as constraints, we can achieve a perfect match to the accurate label of the dataset. However, we would lose the generality of the algorithm.

A future step is to evaluate different constraints in terms of their feasibility and added overhead compared to the improvement of the clustering results, as well as propose a machine learning based selection of suitable constraints, according to the inherent structure of the data. To simplify the process of defining constraints, methods from the field of active learning could be included into the data analysis workflow [40,43] that provide appropriate constraints to the CoExDBSCAN algorithm.

Besides the challenge of finding and expressing suitable constraints, finding the correct parameters for the algorithm remains another challenge, especially for high-dimensional data. In addition to the parameters of the DBSCAN algorithm, the dimensions for the spatial- and constraint-subspace have to be determined by the user. For the parameters of the DBSCAN algorithm, one can rely on hyperparameter optimisation techniques, for example, grid search, while varying the selected dimensions based on domain knowledge and the expected outcome of the analysis. We expect to provide more general guidance on selecting parameters with future cluster analysis findings based on CoExDBSCAN.

The successful adaptation of the CoExDBSCAN algorithm for time-point clustering [18] and trajectory segmentation [19] demonstrates the applicability to different domains and problem formulations. However, an optimised implementation of the algorithm should be provided in the future to provide additional runtime measurements and detailed comparison studies with other algorithms in the field of subspace, correlation and constrained clustering.

References

1. Achtert, E., Böhm, C., David, J., Kröger, P., Zimek, A.: Robust clustering in arbitrarily oriented subspaces. In: Proceedings of the 2008 SIAM International Conference on Data Mining, pp. 763–774. ICDM 2008, Society for Industrial and Applied Mathematics, Philadelphia, PA (2008). https://doi.org/10.1137/1.9781611972788.69, https://epubs.siam.org/doi/abs/10.1137/1.9781611972788.69
2. Aggarwal, C.C., Reddy, C.K.: Data Clustering: Algorithms and Applications, 1st edn. Chapman & Hall/CRC, Boca Raton (2013)
3. Aggarwal, C.C., Yu, P.S.: Finding generalized projected clusters in high dimensional spaces. In: Proceedings of the 2000 ACM SIGMOD International Conference on Management of Data. pp. 70–81. SIGMOD 2000, ACM, New York, NY, USA (2000). https://doi.org/10.1145/342009.335383, https://doi.acm.org/10.1145/342009.335383
4. Agrawal, R., Gehrke, J., Gunopulos, D., Raghavan, P.: Automatic subspace clustering of high dimensional data for data mining applications. In: Proceedings of the 1998 ACM SIGMOD International Conference on Management of Data. pp. 94–105. SIGMOD 1998, ACM, New York, NY, USA (1998). https://doi.org/10.1145/276304.276314, https://doi.acm.org/10.1145/276304.276314

5. Ankerst, M., Breunig, M.M., Kriegel, H.P., Sander, J.: OPTICS: ordering points to identify the clustering structure. SIGMOD Rec. **28**(2), 49–60 (1999). https://doi.org/10.1145/304181. 304187

6. Basu, S., Banerjee, A., Mooney, R.J.: Semi-supervised clustering by seeding. In: Proceedings of 19th International Conference on Machine Learning (ICML-2002), pp. 19–26 (2002). https://www.cs.utexas.edu/users/ai-lab?basu:ml02

7. Basu, S., Banerjee, A., Mooney, R.J.: Active semi-supervision for pairwise constrained clustering. In: Proceedings of the 2004 SIAM International Conference on Data Mining (SDM-2004), April 2004. https://www.cs.utexas.edu/users/ai-lab?basu:sdm04

8. Basu, S., Davidson, I., Wagstaff, K.: Constrained Clustering: Advances in Algorithms, Theory, and Applications. CRC Press, Boca Raton, Florida (2008)

9. Bentley, J.L.: Multidimensional binary search trees used for associative searching. Commun. ACM **18**(9), 509–517 (1975). https://doi.org/10.1145/361002.361007

10. Beyer, K., Goldstein, J., Ramakrishnan, R., Shaft, U.: When is "Nearest Neighbor" meaningful? In: Beeri, C., Buneman, P. (eds.) ICDT 1999. LNCS, vol. 1540, pp. 217–235. Springer, Heidelberg (1999). https://doi.org/10.1007/3-540-49257-7_15

11. Böhm, C., Kailing, K., Kröger, P., Zimek, A.: Computing clusters of correlation connected objects. In: Proceedings of the 2004 ACM SIGMOD International Conference on Management of Data, SIGMOD 2004, pp. 455–466. ACM, New York, NY, USA (2004). https://doi.org/10.1145/1007568.1007620, https://doi.acm.org/10.1145/1007568.1007620

12. Campello, R.J.G.B., Moulavi, D., Sander, J.: Density-based clustering based on hierarchical density estimates. In: Pei, J., Tseng, V.S., Cao, L., Motoda, H., Xu, G. (eds.) PAKDD 2013. LNCS (LNAI), vol. 7819, pp. 160–172. Springer, Heidelberg (2013). https://doi.org/10.1007/978-3-642-37456-2_14

13. Cormen, T.H., Leiserson, C.E., Rivest, R.L., Stein, C.: Introduction to Algorithms. MIT Press, Cambridge (2009)

14. Diekmann, C.J., et al.: The MUSICA IASI H2O, δD pair product. Earth Syst. Sci. Data Discuss. **2021**, 1–27 (2021). https://doi.org/10.5194/essd-2021-87, https://essd.copernicus.org/preprints/essd-2021-87/

15. Dinler, D., Tural, M.K.: A survey of constrained clustering. In: Celebi, M.E., Aydin, K. (eds.) Unsupervised Learning Algorithms, pp. 207–235. Springer, Cham (2016). https://doi.org/10.1007/978-3-319-24211-8_9

16. Duda, R.O., Hart, P.E.: Use of the Hough transformation to detect lines and curves in pictures. Commun. ACM **15**(1), 11–15 (1972). https://doi.org/10.1145/361237.361242, https://doi.org/10.1145/361237.361242

17. Ertl, B., Meyer, J., Schneider, M., Streit, A.: CoExDBSCAN: Density-based Clustering with Constrained Expansion. In: Proceedings of the 12th International Joint Conference on Knowledge Discovery, Knowledge Engineering and Knowledge Management - Volume 1, KDIR, pp. 104–115. INSTICC, SciTePress (2020). https://doi.org/10.5220/0010131201040115

18. Ertl, B., Meyer, J., Schneider, M., Streit, A.: Semi-supervised time point clustering for multivariate time series. In: Proceedings of the Canadian Conference on Artificial Intelligence, June 2021. https://doi.org/10.21428/594757db.9fa1eff5, https://caiac.pubpub.org/pub/a3py333z

19. Ertl, B., Schneider, M., Diekmann, C., Meyer, J., Streit, A.: A Semi-supervised Approach for Trajectory Segmentation to Identify Different Moisture Processes in the Atmosphere. In: Paszynski, M., Kranzlmüller, D., Krzhizhanovskaya, V.V., Dongarra, J.J., Sloot, P.M.A. (eds.) ICCS 2021. LNCS, vol. 12742, pp. 264–277. Springer, Cham (2021). https://doi.org/10.1007/978-3-030-77961-0_23

20. Ertöz, L., Steinbach, M., Kumar, V.: Finding clusters of different sizes, shapes, and densities in noisy, high dimensional data. In: Society for Industrial and Applied Mathematics, Philadelphia, PA, pp. 47–58 (2003). https://doi.org/10.1137/1.9781611972733.5, https://epubs.siam.org/doi/abs/10.1137/1.9781611972733.5

21. Ester, M., Kriegel, H.P., Sander, J., Xu, X.: A density-based algorithm for discovering clusters a density-based algorithm for discovering clusters in large spatial databases with noise. In: Proceedings of the Second International Conference on Knowledge Discovery and Data Mining, KDD 1996, pp. 226–231. AAAI Press, Palo Alto, California (1996)

22. Fisher, R.A.: The use of multiple measurements in taxonomic problems. Ann. Eugen. **7**(2), 179–188 (1936). https://doi.org/10.1111/j.1469-1809.1936.tb02137.x, https://onlinelibrary.wiley.com/doi/abs/10.1111/j.1469-1809.1936.tb02137.x

23. Friedman, J.H.: An overview of predictive learning and function approximation. In: Cherkassky, V., Friedman, J.H., Wechsler, H. (eds.) From Statistics to Neural Networks. NATO ASI Series, vol. 136, pp. 1–61. Springer, Heidelberg (1994). https://doi.org/10.1007/978-3-642-79119-2_1

24. Guha, S., Rastogi, R., Shim, K.: Cure: an efficient clustering algorithm for large databases. Inf. Syst. **26**(1), 35–58 (2001). https://doi.org/10.1016/S0306-4379(01)00008-4, https://www.sciencedirect.com/science/article/pii/S0306437901000084

25. Hough, P.V.: Method and means for recognizing complex patterns (18 December 1962). US Patent 3,069,654

26. Houle, M.E., Kriegel, H.-P., Kröger, P., Schubert, E., Zimek, A.: Can shared-neighbor distances defeat the curse of dimensionality? In: Gertz, M., Ludäscher, B. (eds.) SSDBM 2010. LNCS, vol. 6187, pp. 482–500. Springer, Heidelberg (2010). https://doi.org/10.1007/978-3-642-13818-8_34

27. Hubert, L., Arabie, P.: Comparing partitions. J. Classif. **2**(1), 193–218 (1985). https://doi.org/10.1007/BF01908075

28. Jain, A.K.: Data clustering: 50 years beyond K-means. Pattern Recogn. Lett. **31**(8), 651–666 (2010). https://doi.org/10.1016/j.patrec.2009.09.011, https://www.sciencedirect.com/science/article/pii/S0167865509002323. (award winning papers from the 19th International Conference on Pattern Recognition (ICPR))

29. Mohri, M., Rostamizadeh, A., Talwalkar, A.: Foundations of Machine Learning. MIT Press, Cambridge, Massachusetts (2012)

30. Noone, D.: Pairing measurements of the water vapor isotope ratio with humidity to deduce atmospheric moistening and dehydration in the tropical midtroposphere. J. Clim. **25**(13), 4476–4494 (2012)

31. Papadimitriou, C.H., Steiglitz, K.: Combinatorial Optimization: Algorithms and Complexity. Courier Corporation (1998)

32. Pedregosa, F., et al.: Scikit-learn: machine learning in Python. J. Mach. Learn. Res. **12**, 2825–2830 (2011)

33. Pourrajabi, M., Moulavi, D., Campello, R.J.G.B., Zimek, A., Sander, J., Goebel, R.: Model selection for semi-supervised clustering. In: Amer-Yahia, S., Christophides, V., Kementsietsidis, A., Garofalakis, M.N., Idreos, S., Leroy, V. (eds.) Proceedings of the 17th International Conference on Extending Database Technology, EDBT 2014, Athens, Greece, March 24–28, 2014. pp. 331–342. OpenProceedings.org, Konstanz (2014). https://doi.org/10.5441/002/edbt.2014.31

34. Rand, W.M.: Objective criteria for the evaluation of clustering methods. J. Am. Statist. Assoc. **66**(336), 846–850 (1971). https://doi.org/10.1080/01621459.1971.10482356, https://www.tandfonline.com/doi/abs/10.1080/01621459.1971.10482356

35. Role, F., Morbieu, S., Nadif, M.: CoClust: a python package for co-clustering. J. Statist. Softw. Articles **88**(7), 1–29 (2019). https://doi.org/10.18637/jss.v088.i07, https://www.jstatsoft.org/v088/i07

36. Ruiz, C., Spiliopoulou, M., Menasalvas, E.: C-DBSCAN: density-based clustering with constraints. In: An, A., Stefanowski, J., Ramanna, S., Butz, C.J., Pedrycz, W., Wang, G. (eds.) RSFDGrC 2007. LNCS (LNAI), vol. 4482, pp. 216–223. Springer, Heidelberg (2007). https://doi.org/10.1007/978-3-540-72530-5_25

37. Schneider, M., et al.: MUSICA MetOp/IASI $H_2O,\delta D$ pair retrieval simulations for validating tropospheric moisture pathways in atmospheric models. Atmos. Measur. Techn. **10**(2), 507–525 (2017). https://doi.org/10.5194/amt-10-507-2017, https://www.atmos-meas-tech.net/10/507/2017/

38. Schubert, E., Sander, J., Ester, M., Kriegel, H.P., Xu, X.: DBSCAN Revisited, revisited: why and how you should (Still) use DBSCAN. ACM Trans. Database Syst. 42(3), 1–21 (2017). https://doi.org/10.1145/3068335

39. Schubert, E., Zimek, A.: ELKI: A large open-source library for data analysis - ELKI release 0.7.5 "Heidelberg", pp. 1–134. CoRR abs/1902.03616 (2019). https://arxiv.org/abs/1902.03616

40. Settles, B.: Active learning literature survey. University of Wisconsin-Madison Department of Computer Sciences, Technical report (2009)

41. Svehla, J.: Active-semi-supervised-clustering (2018). https://github.com/datamole-ai/active-semi-supervised-clustering

42. Wagstaff, K., Cardie, C.: Clustering with instance-level constraints. In: Proceedings of the Seventeenth International Conference on Machine Learning, pp. 1103–1110. ICML 2000, Morgan Kaufmann Publishers Inc., San Francisco, CA, USA (2000)

43. Zhu, X.J.: Semi-supervised learning literature survey. University of Wisconsin-Madison Department of Computer Sciences, Technical report (2005)

44. Zimek, A., Schubert, E., Kriegel, H.P.: A survey on unsupervised outlier detection in high-dimensional numerical data. Statist. Anal. Data Mining ASA Data Sci. J. **5**(5), 363–387 (2012). https://doi.org/10.1002/sam.11161, https://onlinelibrary.wiley.com/doi/abs/10.1002/sam.11161

Amharic Semantic Information Retrieval System

Tilahun Yeshambel[1]([⊠]), Josiane Mothe[2], and Yaregal Assabie[3]

[1] IT PhD Program, Addis Ababa University, Addis Ababa, Ethiopia
`tilahun.yeshambel@uog.edu.et`
[2] INSPE, Univ. de Toulouse, IRIT, UMR5505 CNRS, Toulouse, France
`Josiane.Mothe@irit.fr`
[3] Department of Computer Science, Addis Ababa University, Addis Ababa, Ethiopia
`yaregal.assabie@aau.edu.et`

Abstract. Amharic is the official language of Ethiopia, currently having a population of over 118 million. Developing effective information retrieval (IR) system for Amharic has been a challenging task due to limited resources coupled with complex morphology of the language. This paper presents the development of Amharic semantic IR system using query expansion based on deep neural learning model and WordNet. In order to optimize the retrieval result, we propose Amharic text representation using root forms of words applied for stopword identification, indexing, term matching and query expansion. Comparisons are made with the conventional stem-based text representation for information retrieval, and we show that using the root forms of words is better for both resource construction and system development. The effectiveness of the proposed Amharic semantic IR system is evaluated on Amharic *Adhoc* Information Retrieval Test Collection (2AIRTC).

Keywords: Semantic information retrieval · Query expansion · Complex morphology · Amharic IR resources

1 Introduction

Searching information on a huge corpus is one of the common tasks nowadays. Information Retrieval (IR) focuses mainly on the process of matching user queries terms to index terms in order to locate relevant documents from Web or corpus. Matching query terms with index terms is one of the main challenges of IR in many languages [1]. Linguistic variation of a natural language and term mismatch affects the effectiveness of IR system. As a result of linguistic variation, some relevant documents for a user need will be omitted from a search result. Natural language processing (NLP) has significant role in many languages IR systems for extracting index and query terms. It is applicable to reduce the space required for indexing and maximizing the retrieval effectiveness by conflating variants of words to a common form [2]. Stemming is one of the typical NLP techniques to handle morphological variants in many languages and is still an active research topic specifically for under resourced languages [3, 4]. Furthermore, NLP techniques are employed to handle term matching for semantically related concepts.

© Springer Nature Switzerland AG 2022
A. Fred et al. (Eds.): IC3K 2020, CCIS 1608, pp. 22–44, 2022.
https://doi.org/10.1007/978-3-031-14602-2_2

Semantic text matching in IR is the task of finding semantic similarity between query and document text. Sometimes, since a user information need is imprecise, incomplete and semantically ambiguous, a retrieval system cannot retrieve relevant documents to a query. Query expansion is the task of adding semantically related terms to a given query for improving the performance of IR system. Different approaches have been proposed for expanding query terms such as relevance feedback [5], the use of Wikipedia [6], or resources like thesauri or WordNet [7], and neural network (NN) to capture semantic relationships between words [8].

Research and development on Amharic IR lags behind because of morphological complexity of the language, lack of usable NLP tools, resources, and test collection. Despite many works on IR for many languages, few researches have been conducted on Amharic IR. The existing Amharic IR systems face challenges in searching relevant documents because of the morphological complexity and semantic richness of the language. Amharic exhibits complex morphology that poses challenges in NLP and IR [9, 10]. The base of Amharic word can be stem or root. The morphological structure (root or stem) one should choose for indexing, matching, and resource construction is an open question in Amharic IR. Relevant documents for an Amharic query may not be retrieved as a result of term mismatch between index terms and query terms. Amharic stem-based indexing and term matching misses some relevant documents because multiple stems exist for variants. For example, the variant ፈለገ /fələgə/, ፈላጊ /fəlagi/, ፍላጋ /filəga/, እንፈሊግ /ʔinifəligi/, and አፋለገ /ʔəfaləgə/ have the stems ፈለግ /fələgi/, ፈላግ /fəlagi/, ፍላግ /filəgi/, ፈልግ /fəligi/, and ፈልግ /fələgi/, respectively. On the other hand, a document can possibly be relevant to a user query even if they share semantically similar terms that may even be different variants. For example, ህብረት /hibirəti/ 'union'/, አንድነት /ʔənidinəti/ 'unity'/, አብሮነት /ʔəbironəti/ 'fellowship'/, ቅንጅት /k'inidʒiti/ 'coalition'/, ትብብር /tibibiri/ 'cooperation'/ and ጥምረት /t'imirəti/ 'collaboration'/ are semantically related words. Both cases, i.e. same variants with different stems and similar semantics with different variants, lead to poor IR performance as relevant documents are missed. Therefore, Amharic retrieval system needs to identify optimal representative of variants and reformulate a user query by expanding initial user query in order to retrieve more relevant documents. In this paper, we investigate the characteristics of the language and suggest root forms of words to handle morphological variations to increase the quality of indexing and the probability of matching between index and query terms. Furthermore, we investigate the impact of query expansion on Amharic semantic IR using word embedding and WordNet.

The rest of this paper is organized as follows. Section 2 briefly describes the characteristics of Amharic language. Section 3 discusses related work. Section 4 presents the design of Amharic semantic IR system whereas Sect. 5 presents Amharic resources that we constructed. Experimental results are discussed in Sect. 6. Finally, conclusion and future research directions are forwarded in Sect. 7.

2 Amharic Language

Amharic is the official language of Ethiopia that has a population of over 118 million at present [11]. It has been used as a working language of the government of the country for a long time. As a result, its rich literary heritage has endowed the language with huge written resources and it serves as a *lingua franca* of the country. Amharic belongs to Semitic language families and has its own script which has alphabet, numbers and punctuations. The alphabet has 33 basic characters and each of them has 7 different forms representing consonant-vowel combination. The vowels are ኧ /ʔə/, ኡ /ʔu/, ኢ /ʔi/, ኣ /ʔa/, ኤ /ʔe/, እ /ʔɨ/, and ኦ /ʔo/. For example, consonant-vowel combination of the base character ከ /kə/ has the following modifications: ኩ /ku/, ኪ /ki/, ካ /ka/, ኬ /ke/, ክ /kɨ/, and ኮ /ko/. Furthermore, the alphabet has labialized characters such as ሏ /lʷa/, ሟ /mʷa/, ሷ /sʷa/, and ቋ /qʷa/. Their structure is consonant-vowel-vowel combinations.

Amharic is morphologically rich and complex agglutinative language. It is considered as one of the most prolific languages [9]. Clitics such as prepositions, articles, conjunctions, and pronouns are glued to nouns, verbs, and adjectives. The internal structure of a word may include the base (i.e. stem or root), affixes, and patterns. Amharic word may contain many affixes which are attached in complex rules. An Amharic word can represent a sentence in another language. For example, ሰበረቻቸው /səbərətʃatʃəwi 'she broke them'/ is an agglutination of the verbal stem (ሰበር /səbəri 'broke'/), subject marker pronoun (ኧች /ʔətʃi/), and object marker pronoun (ኣቸው /ʔatʃəwi/). Amharic words can be classified as *derived* and *non-derived*. Derived words are formed from other word classes through derivational process. The word formation in both cases usually involves change in one or more characters of a stem or root. The change arises as a result of making a word for case, gender, number, tense, person, mood, etc.

3 Related Work

3.1 Conventional Information Retrieval

Although Amharic is widely used in Ethiopia, the status of IR system development for the language is relatively at rudimentary level. The retrieval effectiveness of stem-based and root-based text representations on Amharic language are studied in [12]. Experiments were carried out by running 40 queries on 548 documents using OKAPI system and the study concluded that stem-based retrieval is slightly better than root-based one. Amharic search engine was developed using stems and tested by running 11 queries on 75 news documents [13]. The average precision and recall values were 0.65 and 0.95, respectively using OR operator for query terms, and 0.99 and 0.52, respectively using AND operator. Arabic is a Semitic language for which relatively more IR research is conducted. For example, Al-Hadid *et al.* [14] developed a neural network-based model where documents and queries are represented using stems and their similarity is computed using cosine similarity. The effectiveness of Arabic word-based, stem-based, and root-based representation of documents and queries was investigated by Musaid [15].The word-based and stem-based representations miss relevant documents while root-based one retrieves non-relevant documents. The effects of stem and root on Arabic search engine was also compared by Moukdad [16].The results indicated that stemming is more effective than root. A comparison between stem-based and root-based Arabic retrieval was made by Larkey *et al.* [17]. The finding indicates that light stemmer outperforms root analyzer and other stemmers which are based on detailed morphological analysis. Ali *et al.* [18] investigated the effect of morphological analysis on Arabic IR.

A rule-based stemmer was used to extract the root/stem of words to be used as indexing and searching terms. The results showed slight improvement on IR effectiveness due to the stemmer. Hebrew is one of the Semitic languages spoken mainly in Israel. Ornan [19] designed Hebrew search engine by applying a rule-based morphological analysis. The design of the search engine takes into account the construction of a morphological, syntactic and semantics analyzer. Words unsuited for the syntax and the semantic of a sentence were removed.

3.2 Semantic Information Retrieval

Amharic semantic-based IR using BM25 was developed [20]. Documents and queries were processed by a stemmer. The system was evaluated by running 10 queries on 8,759 documents and performed an average recall and precision of 0.84 and 0.23, respectively. Fang [21] developed and evaluated English semantic retrieval system using WordNet and dependency-thesaurus on TREC test collections. Query terms are expanded considering term relationships and synset definition of a word in the WordNet and mutual information in the collection. The retrieval results indicated that significant improvement was achieved after query expansions using both methods. Better retrieval result was obtained using synset definition of terms. Retrieval based on thesaurus is less effective than definition-based retrieval. The impact of integrating word embedding and entity embedding with and without interpolation within the *adhoc* document retrieval task was studied and evaluated on TREC collections (ClueWeb'09B and 100 ClueWeb'12B) [22]. The authors reported that word embedding do not show competitive performance to any of the baselines (relevance model, sequential dependence model and entity query feature expansion) even after interpolation. CBOW method showed better performance than skip-gram for the *adhoc* document retrieval task. Entity-based embedding performed better than word-based embedding.

3.3 Evaluation of Amharic IR Corpora, Resources and NLP Tools

Few studies have been conducted to develop NLP tools and create Amharic corpora resources although IR test collections are required for automatic evaluation of IR system. We can quote a few such studies. Demeke and Getachew [23] created Walta Information Center news corpus; Yeshambel *et al.* [24] built 2AIRTC; and Yeshambel *et al.* [10] created stem-based and root-based morphologically annotated Amharic corpora semi-automatically. The sizes of corpora created by Demeke and Getachew [23], Yeshambel *et al.* [24] and Yeshambel *et al.* [10] are 1,065, 12,586, and 6,069 documents, respectively. Mindaye *et al.* [13] and Samuel and Bjorn [25] created Amharic word-based stopword list whereas Alemayehu and Willett [26] built stem-based stopwords list. NLP tools such as stemmer and morphological analyzer have crucial role for processing text documents and user information need. Alemayehu and Willett [26] and Alemu and Asker [27] developed rule-based Amharic stemmers. Sisay and Haller [28] and Amsalu and Gibbon [29] developed Amharic morphological analyzers using Xerox Finite State Tools (XFST) method. Gasser [30] developed rule-based morphological analyzer for Amharic, Tigrignya and Afaan Oromo languages. Mulugeta and Gasser [31] also developed a morphological analyzer using supervised machine learning approach whereas Abate and Assabie [9] developed morphological analyzer using memory-based supervised machine learning approach.

In this work, we assess the accessibility, quality, and usability of the existing accessible Amharic IR corpora, resources and tools with the purpose of highlighting the status of Amharic language processing applications. The majority of them are not accessible and have limited functionality and size. They are also inconvenient to use or to integrate in Amharic IR experiments. The existing Amharic NLP tools are not full-fledged systems as they are under prototype stages. For example, the stemmer developed by Alemayehu and Willett [26] and Gasser's morphological analyzer [30] over-stem and under-stem many words. Moreover, these NLP tools extract basic stems of some words and derived-stems of other words. We tested them using a dataset that contains 200 words from different word classes. The stemmer and the analyzer performed 41.4% and 47.6%, respectively. From our experiments, we observed that the performance of Amharic NLP tools on verbs is less than on other word types. Many of the existing test collections are simply sets of documents without topics and relevance judgment. Furthermore, they are small in size compared to test collections created for other languages. Consequently, they would not be used for accurately testing the performance of IR techniques. In our previous work [24], we developed an Amharic IR test collection that consists in a corpus, topic set and the associated relevance judgment. It allows researchers to evaluate retrieval system automatically though the size is still small relative to standard test collections. The test collection is accessible freely at https://www.irit.fr/AmharicResources/.

4 Design of Amharic Semantic IR System

Considering the morphological characteristics of the language, we propose a design for Amharic semantic IR system. In the proposed design, the morphological analysis is carried out before stopword removal (see Fig. 1). Morphological analysis is among the key tasks in our IR system as it helps to select index and query terms from documents and queries.

4.1 Preprocessing

Preprocessing includes character normalization as well as tag removal and punctuation mark removal. Character normalization is made to represent various characters having similar pronunciation using a single grapheme. The characters ሐ /hə/, ሕ /hə/, ኸ /hə/ and their modifications are normalized to their corresponding modifications of ሀ /hə/. The character ሠ /sə/ and its modifications are normalized to their corresponding modifications of ሰ /sə/. The character ፀ /ts'ə/ and its modifications are normalized to their corresponding modifications of ጸ /ts'ə/. The character ዐ /ʔə/ and its modifications are normalized to their corresponding modifications of አ /ʔə/. The fourth orders ሃ /ha/, ሓ /ha/, ኋ /ha/ and ኻ /ha/ are normalized to ሀ /ha/ whereas the fourth orders ኣ /ʔa/ and ዓ /ʔa/ are normalized to አ /ʔa/. After character normalization, we segment sentences and tokenize words. Sentence segmentation is carried out using punctuation marks used for marking sentence boundaries whereas word tokenization is performed using space, tags and punctuation marks. Tags and punctuation marks are removed after sentence segmentation and tokenization.

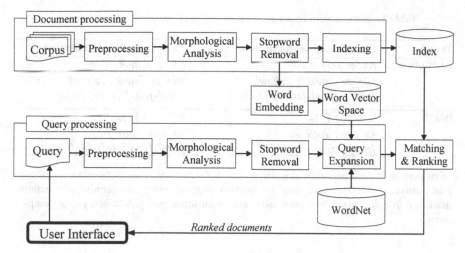

Fig. 1. Design of Amharic semantic IR system.

4.2 Morphological Analysis

Documents and user information need should be represented appropriately using terms that will be used later for matching query with documents. It is to be noted that indexing terms are weighted based on the word frequency. In IR, most often, the variants of a word are conflated during indexing into a single form. It has the advantage of making the calculation of indexing term frequency straightforward. Therefore, in this research, we study the feasibility of stem-based and root-based document representation with respect to their effectiveness for Amharic IR. Since well-designed Amharic stemmer and morphological analyzer are not available yet, we design a semi-automatic morphological processor to segment words into their morphemes so that the base of words (i.e. stem and root) could be extracted easily and quickly. The two morphological analyses performed in this work are stem-based and root-based morphological analysis using lexicons created by Yeshambel *et al.* [10]. The lexicons are constructed from a corpus. The stem-based morphological process segments stem of a word from the rest of morphemes whereas the root-based morphological process segments root from the rest of morphemes of a word. For example, the stem-based and root-based morphological segmentation of the verb ሲላታወቃፀዋ /silətawək'atʃəwɨ/ and the noun ከሰዎች /kəsəwotʃu/ are presented in Table 1. The morphological annotation of different word classes is further presented in Sect. 5.1.

In Amharic, roots are the base of stems. Multiple verbal stems can be generated from an Amharic verbal root (see Table 2). The stems are generated by using different patterns that insert different vowels between root radicals. However, variants of words that are not derived from verbal roots have only one stem which has the same representation as its root. The stems and roots of words are extracted from stem-based and root-based morphologically annotated corpora, respectively, using Algorithm 1.

Table 1. Sample stem-based and root-based morphological segmentation.

Word	Stem-based segmentation	Root- based segmentation
ስለታወቃቸው·	ስለ_ተ_አወቅ_አቸው·	ስለ_ተ_አ-ው-ቅ_አቸው·
	silə_tə_ʔawək'i_ʔətʃəwi	silə_tə_ʔ-w-k'_ʔətʃəwi
	[pre[1]]-[pas]-[stem]-[3,pl]	[pre]-[pas]-[root]-[3,pl]
ከሰዎቹ	ከ_ሰው·_አች_ኡ	ከ_ሰው·_አች_ኡ
	kə_səwi_ʔotʃi_ʔu	kə_səw_ʔotʃi_ʔu
	[pre]-[stem]-[pl]-[def]	[pre]-[root]-[pl]-[def]

[1] *1*: first person, *3*: third person, *s*: singular, *p*: plural, *f*: feminine, *pre*: preposition, *foc*: focus, *pas*: passive, *nom*: nominative, *conj*: conjunction, *neg*: negative, *gen*: genitive, *def*: definite marker, *adj*: adjectivizer, *pos*: possessive, *acc*: accusative, *pal*: palatalizer, *comp*: complement.

Algorithm 1. Extracting stem and root from corpus.

```
Input:   Affix lists and Annotated corpora
Output:  Stem-based and root-based Corpora
Step 1:  Open affix lists and annotated corpora
Step 2:  For each document in the annotated corpus:
             For each word in a document:
                 Segment a word into morphemes using '_'
                 If a morpheme is in affix lists
                     Delete from an annotated document
                 End if
             End for
         End for
```

4.3 Stopword Removal

Stopwords are words that evenly occur in many documents and serve as purpose rather than content. Thus, as they are non-content bearing terms, they are removed from documents and queries in IR systems. As shown in our proposed design (Fig. 1) Amharic stopwords are removed after morphological analysis is carried out on documents and queries, which is different from the design of IR for morphologically simple languages. In morphologically simple languages like English, stopword identification and removal is made before stemming by using stopword list. The conventional trend applied so far for removing Amharic stopwords is also to use a stopword list, and it is carried out before stemming or morphological analysis. However, taking the characteristics of the language into consideration, this is certainly not the most appropriate way. Indeed, Amharic stopwords are characterized by the following three morphological features: (*i*) they do not necessarily exist as standalone words; (*ii*) they can accept prefixes and suffixes; and (*iii*) they may exist as part of Amharic words and serve as prefix or suffix. For these

Table 2. Sample of Amharic verbal roots and basic stems of variants.

Root	Stem	Variant	Concept
ጥ-ቅ-ም	ጠቀም	ጠቀሙ, ጠቀሙኝ, ሲጠቀም, እንዲጠቀም, etc.	Use
	ጢቃም	ጢቃሚ, የጢቃሚው, ተጢቃሚ, ጢቃሚያችን, etc.	
	ጠቀም	ሲጠቀም, ይጠቀም, ሊጠቀም, ጠቅሞኛል, etc.	
	ጥቀም	ጥቀሙን, ከጥቅሜ, ለጥቀማቸው, etc.	
	ጥቀም	ጥቀሙ·, መጥቀሙ, እንጥቀም, etc.	
ም-ረ-ም-ር	መረመር	መረመረ, መረመሩ, ስመረመር, ተመረመረች, etc.	Investiga-tion
	መራመር	ተመራመረች, አመራመረ, ተመራመረችሁ, etc.	
	ምርምር	ምርምሩ, የምርምራቸውን, በምርምሬ, etc.	
	መርማር	መርማሪ, ከመርማሪው·, መርማሪዋ, etc.	
	መርምር	እንመርምር, ይመርምሩ, ተመርምሬ, etc.	
	መርምር	ይመርምር, ትመርመር, እንመርመር, ልመርመር, etc.	
	መረምር	እንመረምራለን, ሲመረምር, ይመረምራሉ, ስትመረምር, etc.	

reasons, it is not possible to find and remove all Amharic stopwords unless the morphological structure of words is known. For example, the stopwords ስለ /silə 'about'/, ከ /kə 'from'/, and አል /ʔəli 'not'/ do not appear as a standalone word as shown in the following sample words. The word ስላመጣ /silaməṭ'a 'since he brought'/, ከልብ /kəlibi 'from heart'/, አልመጣ /ʔəliməṭ'a 'did not come'/ are equivalent to ስለ+አመጣ, ከ+ልብ, and አል+መጣ, respectively. As there could be several sequences of affixes representing various linguistic functions, words can appear in various morphological structures. As a result, Amharic stopwords usually have many variants. For example, the stopword ሌላ /lela 'other'/ has variants የሌላ /jəlela/, ሌሎች /lelotʃi/, በሌላኛው· /bəlelaɲawi/, etc. This indicates that stopword identification and term representation in Amharic IR demands a different consideration than the conventional trend. It means that one could not work with the surface forms of words to identify and remove stopwords. Therefore, we removed them after applying morphological analysis on documents and queries using a stopword list. The stopword list itself is constructed from a corpus after applying morphological analysis. We removed stopwords from stem-based and root-based corpora using our stem-based and root-based stopword lists, respectively.

4.4 Indexing

In our system, document processing involves text preprocessing, morphological analysis, stopword removal and indexing. As a result of these processes, we obtain indexed documents. To test the impact of morphological analysis on Amharic IR, word-based, stem-based and root-based indexes were created using Lemur[1] toolkit. The stem-based index was created using basic stems of words while the root-based index was created using the root of words. The number of root-based index terms is less than or equal to stem-based index terms. However, the frequency of a root is greater than or equal to the frequency of the corresponding stem as root form conflates all variants of a word to a single common form. Accordingly, the frequency of terms accurately computed

---

[1] http://www.lemurproject.org.

using root forms, which means that index term selection could be appropriately made by making use of the root forms of words.

4.5 Word Embedding

One of the main objectives of this work is to create an efficient model on a large Amharic dataset and investigate the impact of query expansion using term embedding on Amharic IR retrieval effectiveness. To this effect, we propose four neural network models using word2vec: stem-based with Continuous Bag of Words (CBOW), stem-based with skip-gram algorithm, root-based with CBOW and root-based with skip-gram algorithm. Accordingly, four vector space models are generated, which are used for expanding stem-based and root-based query terms based on semantic similarity of words in stem-based and root-based corpora, respectively. The similarity *sim* between a query term *q* and a corpus word *d* is computed using cosine similarity as shown in Eq. (1).

$$sim(q, d) = \frac{\sum_i qi.di}{\sqrt{\sum_i qi^2 \sum_i di^2}} \tag{1}$$

where qi is vector representation of the ith query term and di is the vector representation of the ith word in the corpus. The top 5 most related terms are used to expand query terms.

4.6 Query Expansion

The root-based morphological analysis addresses variation among word variants during exact matching between Amharic documents and queries. However, matching only keywords may not accurately reveal the semantic similarity between a query and a document. To resolve this issue and optimize Amharic IR system, we performed query expansion using vector space model and WordNet. Semantically related terms to each non-stopword of user query are identified based on the word vector space and WordNet. Since there is no publicly available Amharic WordNet, we build the resource to be used only for the title of the topics from 2AIRTC [24]. The WordNet is organized to include terms' synonyms, hypernyms, and hyponyms relationships. The stem-based and root-based morphological analyses are carried out on words included in the WordNet and a user query. For query expansion, the stem or root of semantically related words from the WordNet are added to the original set of query term(s).

4.7 Matching and Ranking

Query term vector for searching is constructed after a query is subjected to preprocessing, morphological analysis, and stopword removal. Here, we applied both semantic-based and exact vocabulary term matching. The system searches documents that contain query terms and semantically related words (i.e. expanded terms). Searching for relevant documents is carried out by matching query terms (representing information need of users) with index terms (representing documents). As documents and query terms are represented using stem and root forms of words, the stem-based query terms are matched against stem-based index terms whereas root-based query terms are matched against root-based index terms. In IR, a given user information need does not uniquely identify one document in the corpus. Instead, many documents might match a query but with different degree of relevancy. For a given query Q and a collection of retrieved documents D, the Lemur toolkit ranks retrieval results based on their possible relevance. The document length and number of matching query terms are taken into consideration. OKAPI BM25 score ranks documents based on Eq. (2).

$$score\,(D, Q) = \sum\nolimits_{i=1}^{n} IDF(qi). \frac{f(qi, D).(k1 + 1)}{f(qi, D) + k1.\left(1 - b + b.\frac{|D|}{avgdl}\right)} \tag{2}$$

where $f(qi,D)$ is qi's term frequency in the document D, $|D|$ is the length of the document D in words, and $avgdl$ is the average document length in the text collection from which documents are drawn. The variables $k1$ and b are free parameters whereas $IDF(qi)$ is the inverse document frequency weight of the query term qi. For language modeling, the similarity between a document D and a query Q is measured by the Kullback-Leibler (KL) divergence between the document model $D\theta$ and the query model $Q\theta$. The KL divergence ranking function captures the term occurrence distributions and it is computed using Eq. (3) as:

$$KL\,(Q\theta, D\theta) = \sum\nolimits_{w \in V} p(w|Q\theta) \log \frac{p(w|Q\theta)}{p(w|D\theta)} \tag{3}$$

where w is word, v is word vector, $p(w|Q\theta)$ is estimated query term, $p(w|D\theta)$ is the smoothed probability of a term seen in the document. The ranking of the results of the proposed IR system was evaluated by precision, recall, mean precision and normalized discounted cumulative gain (NDCG). *Precision* is used to measure how many of retrieved documents are relevant and it is computed as:

$$Precision = \frac{relevant\ item\ retrieved}{retrieved\ items} \tag{4}$$

Recall measures the ability of an IR system to retrieve all relevant items and it is computed as:

$$Recall = \frac{relevant\ item\ retrieved}{relevant\ items} \tag{5}$$

Mean Average Precision (MAP) indicates a single-figure measure of quality across multiple queries. The *MAP* value is obtained by taking the mean of the Average Precision *Pav(qi)* over all the queries in the set Q and it is computed as:

$$MAP = \frac{1}{|Q|} \sum\nolimits_{qi \in Q} Pav(qi) \tag{6}$$

Normalized Discounted Cumulative Gain (*NDCG*) is used to measure the position of relevant documents in the retrieval set. It is calculated as:

$$NDCG = \frac{DCG}{IDCG} \tag{7}$$

where *DCG* is discount cumulative gain, *IDCG* is the ideal discounted cumulative gain and it is the maximum possible value. These measures are valued between 0 and 1.

5 Construction of Amharic IR Resources

5.1 Context-Based Morphologically Annotated Corpora

Segmenting a word into its morphemes and extracting its base is crucial in many applications. In this work, Amharic surface words are segmented into their morphemes by analyzing the internal structure of words and their contexts. The annotation is made semi-automatically using Amharic lexicons built by Yeshambel *et al.* [10]. For comparison of stem-based and root-based text representations, we created the stem-based and root-based corpora from the same document collection. Words are morphologically segmented into affixes and basic stems or roots. The general annotation structure for a word W is represented as:

$$[p\_]^* w[\_s]^*$$

where p is a prefix morpheme, '_' is a morphological segment marker, w is the root or stem of W, s is a suffix morpheme, [...] denotes optionality, and * denotes the possibility of multiple occurrence. For example, the word ስማቸው /simatʃəwi/ can be annotated as follows.

$$\underbrace{ስም}_{w}\ \underbrace{አቸው}_{s}$$

A single word may have multiple annotations when annotated with a single base form. However, among multiple annotations, only one of them could be relevant in a given context. For example, the root-based annotation of the word ስማቸው /simatʃəwi/ could be ስም_አቸው /simi_ʔatʃəwi 'their name'/, ስማቸው /simatʃəwi 'a person having a name 'Simachew'/, ስ-ም_አ_አቸው /s-m_ʔə_ʔatʃəwi 'you listen them'/, and ስ-ሰ-ም_አ_አቸው /s-ʃ-m_ʔə_ʔatʃəwi 'having that she kissed them'/. This may lead to incorrect retrieval results. Thus, we identify the context of the word in a sentence during the annotation process. We annotate each word in the corpus with a single annotation by taking the context into consideration and context-based morphologically annotated corpora is constructed for stem-based and root based text representation. Depending on morphological structures, Amharic words can be categorized as derived and non-derived from verbs. Words derived from verbs may have various word classes, but they are morphologically generated from verbal stems or roots. The root forms of such words are represented only by radicals. On the other hand, words that are non-derived from verbs have root forms that contain radicals and vowels. The process of context-based morphological annotation of different word classes is presented as follows.

Stem-Based Morphologically Annotated Corpus. The stem-based morphological annotation segments word forms into more general representation known as basic stem and affixes. The majority of Amharic words are composed of stems and attached affixes. IR systems use the stems of words during indexing and term matching, and thus, we segment the stems of words from the rest of morphemes.

Stem-Based Annotation of Words Derived from Verbs: The base of many verbs, nouns, adjectives, and adverbs are verbal roots. Stems can be generated from a single verbal root and many words can be generated from a single stem by attaching affixes. For example, the verb ስላልፈጠኑ /silalifət'ənu 'since they haven't been fast'/, the noun ከፍጥነታችን /kəfit'inətatʃini 'from our speed'/, the adjective እንደፈጣኖቹ /ʔinidəfət'anotʃu 'like the fast ones'/ and the adverb በፍጥነት /bəfit'inəti 'quickly'/ are derived from the verbal root ፍ-ጥ-ን /f-t'-n/. These words are generated from three stems (ፈጠኒ /fət'əni/, ፈጣን /fət'ani/ and ፍጥን /fit'ini/) and their stem-based annotation is shown below.

ስላልፈጠኑ	ከፍጥነታችን
ስለ_አል_ፈጠን_ኡ	ከ_ፍጥን_እት_አችን
silə_ʔəli_fət'əni_ʔu	kə_fit'ini_ʔəti_ʔətʃini
[pre]-[neg]-[stem]-[3,pl]	[pre]-[stem]-[nom]-[1,pl,pos]
እንደፈጣኖቹ	በፍነት
እንደ_ፈጣን_አች_ኡ	በ_ፍጥን_እት
ʔinidə_fət'ani_ʔotʃi_ʔu	bə_fit'ini_ʔəti
[pre]-[stem]-[pl]-[def]	[pre]-[stem]-[nom]

Stem-Based Annotation of Words Not Derived from Verbs: Amharic words may also be generated from primary nouns, adjectives, adverbs and functional words. Such words are not formed from verbal roots, and their stem representation is different from that of verbal stems as variants of words that are not derived from verbal stems have a single common basic stem. For example, words derived from the primary noun ሀገር /hagəri 'country'/ include ለሀገራችን /ləhagəratʃini 'for our country'/, ስለሀገሪቱ /siləhagəritu 'about the country'/, ሀገራዊ /hagərawi 'national'/, etc. The stem-based annotations of these words are presented as follows.

ለሀገራችን	ስለሀገሪቱ	ሀገራዊ
ለ_ሀገር_አችን	ለ_ሀገር_ኢት_ኡ	ሀገር_አዊ
lə_hagəri_ʔətʃini	lə_hagəri_ʔəti_ʔu	hagəri_ʔəwi
[pre]-[stem]-[1,pl,pos]	[pre]-[stem]-[ʃ]-[def]	[stem]-[adj]

Root-Based Morphologically Annotated Corpus. Root-based morphological annotation segments the roots of words from other affixes. The annotation helps to investigate the impact of root-based text representation on Amharic IR. The root annotation process for verbal words differs from that of others as presented below.

Root-Based Annotation of Words Derived from Verbs. Verbal words are words derived from verbal roots by inserting new character, palatalizing one or more characters, changing the shape of one or more characters, or adding affixes. For example, the verb ስላልፈጠኑ /silalifət'ənu 'since they haven't been fast'/, the noun ከፍጥነታችን /kəfit'inətatʃini 'from our speed'/, the adjective አንደፈጣኞቹ /ʔinidəfət'anotʃu 'like the fast ones'/ and the adverb በፍጥነት /bəfit'inəti 'quickly'/ are derived from the verbal root ፍ-ጥ-ን /f-t'-n/. The root-based annotations are shown below.

ስላልፈጠኑ
ስለ_አል_ፍ-ጥ-ን_ኡ
silə_ʔəli_f-t'-n_ʔu
[pre]-[neg]-[root]-[3,pl]

ከፍጥነታችን
ከ_ፍ-ጥ-ን_ኤት_አችን
kə_f-t'-n_ʔəti_ʔətʃini
[pre]-[root]-[nom]-[1,pl,pos]

አንደፈጣኞቹ
አንደ_ፍ-ጥ-ን_አች_ኡ
ʔinidə_f-t'-n_ʔotʃi_ʔu
[pre]-[root]-[pl]-[def]

በፍጥነት
በ_ፍ-ጥ-ን_ኤት
bə_f-t'-n_ʔəti
[pre]-[root]-[nom]

Root-Based Annotation of Words Not Derived from Verbs: The root and stem forms are the same for words that are generated from primary nouns, adjectives, adverbs and functional words. The root forms may contain vowel in addition to radicals. For example, the words ለሀገራችን /ləhagəratʃini 'for our country'/, ስለሀገሪቱ /siləhagəritu 'about the country'/, ሀገራዊ /hagərawi 'national'/, etc. are derived from the primary noun ሀገር /hagəri 'country'/. The root-based annotations of these words are presented as follows.

ለሀገራችን
ለ_ሀገር_አችን
lə_hagəri_ʔətʃini
[pre]-[root]-[1,pl,pos]

ስለሀገሪቱ
ለ_ሀገር_ኢት_ኡ
lə_hagəri_ʔəti_ʔu
[pre]-[root]-[ʃ]-[def]

ሀገራዊ
ሀገር_አዊ
hagəri_ʔəwi
[root]-[adj]

5.2 Stopword List Construction

We remove Amharic stopwords from the vocabulary using a predefined list constructed based on stem and root forms. For the sake of comparison between stem-based and root-based text retrieval, both types of stopword lists were created from the annotated corpora based on morpheme statistics involving frequency, mean, variance, and entropy. The values of frequency, variance, entropy and mean of each morpheme in the corpus were used while constructing the stopword list. The top 250 morphemes based on the values of frequency, variance, entropy and mean are selected to create corpus-based stopword lists. However, the final stopword list also contains a few words which were selected manually from other sources considering the nature of the language. In total, 222 morphemes are included in each stopword list. The identified stopwords include prepositions (e.g. ወደ /wədə 'to'/, ስለ /silə 'about'/, እስከ /ʔiskə 'up to', በ /bə 'by'/, ከ /kə 'from'/, etc.), conjunctions (e.g. እና /ʔina 'and'/, ይሁን እንጅ /yihuni ʔinidʒi 'however'/, እዚህ /ʔizihi 'here'/, etc.), negation markers (አል...ም /ʔəli...mi 'not'/), indefinite articles (አንድ /ʔənidi 'an'/), auxiliary verbs (አ-ል /ʔ-l 'say'/, ን-በ-ር /n-b-r 'was'/, etc.), ወዘተ /wəzətə 'and so on'/, etc. The stem-based stopword list may contain multiple stems for variants of a word while the root-based list contains only one root form for variants of a word.

6 Experiment

6.1 Implementation

We carried out different experiments on 2AIRTC collection [24]. Python was used to implement preprocessing tasks whereas Lemur toolkit was used for indexing and retrieval. The retrieval effectiveness was evaluated automatically using *trec_eval* tool which can compute many evaluation measures[2]. LM and BM25 models were used as retrieval models.

6.2 Experimental Results

Retrieval with LM and BM25. LM is a popular model for the development of IR systems, but it has not been used in previous Amharic IR ones. Many of them are rather based on vector space model [13, 20, 32, 34]. Here, we investigated the effect of LM model on Amharic IR and compared it with BM25. As shown in Table 3, LM performs slightly better than BM25 model. This is potentially because of the capability of LM to capture term dependency and estimate the probability distribution of a query in each document. This means LM is more suitable retrieval model for Amharic language.

Table 3. Comparison of LM and BM25.

Model	Average precision	R-precision	NDCG	Bpref
BM25	0.67	0.64	0.83	0.64
LM	0.70	0.65	0.86	0.66

The Effect of Stopword Removal on Amharic IR. Experiments were conducted to investigate the effect of morpheme-based stopword removal on Amharic IR. The retrieval effectiveness of stem-based and root-based text representations with and without stopwords are shown in Table 4. As shown in the table, removing stopwords has a positive impact both in stem-based and root-based retrieval using LM.

Retrieval Without Query Expansion. The retrieval effectiveness of the proposed Amharic IR model without query expansion using LM is presented in Table 5. As shown in the table, root-based retrieval is better than stem-based retrieval as the root-based text

---

[2] http://trec.nist.gov/trec_eval.

Table 4. Stem-based and root-based retrieval with and without stopwords on 2AIRTC.

Metrics	Stem-based		Root-based	
	With stopword	Without stopword	With stopword	Without stopword
AMP	0.14	0.51	0.24	0.70
NDCG	0.37	0.71	0.50	0.86
Bpref	0.15	0.48	0.27	0.66
R-prec	0.17	0.49	0.29	0.65

representation maps all variants to a single common form and can reject non-relevant documents better than stem-based and word-based text representations. The word-based and stem-based methods miss more relevant documents since they cannot handle some morphological variations. The retrieval effectiveness of the three text representations decreases from precision @5 documents to precision @20 due to scarcity of relevant documents in the test collection.

Table 5. Retrieval effectiveness based on the three text representations.

Text representation	Precision					NDLG
	P@5	P@10	P@15	P@20	MAP	
Word	0.56	0.49	0.44	0.40	0.43	0.47
Stem	0.62	0.53	0.47	0.43	0.57	0.71
Root	0.79	0.70	0.61	0.55	0.70	0.86

The overall recall and precision values of stem-based and root-based text representations are shown in Fig. 2 which has been taken from our previous study [33]. The blue line depicts the root-based retrieval effectiveness whereas the red line represents the stem-based retrieval results without query expansion. It can be seen that the retrieval effectiveness of root-based representation outperforms stem-based one.

Semantic Retrieval Using Word Embedding. CBOW and skip-gram learning algorithms were trained by adjusting the parameter settings into the following same values: *vector size* (300), *min_count* (7), *iter* (400), *alpha* (0.05) and *negative* (20). By experiment, we found that the best performing window size of CBOW (resp. skip-gram) are 3 (resp.7). Recall and precision of semantic retrieval using word embedding technique on stem-based and root-based corpora are shown in Figs. 3 and 4. The green curve depicts stem-based (Fig. 3) and root-based retrieval (Fig. 4) without query expansion and the remaining are after query expansion using word embedding with CBOW and skip-gram algorithms. The retrieval effectiveness of stem-based query expansion based on both algorithms are almost similar. In the case of root-based representation, CBOW

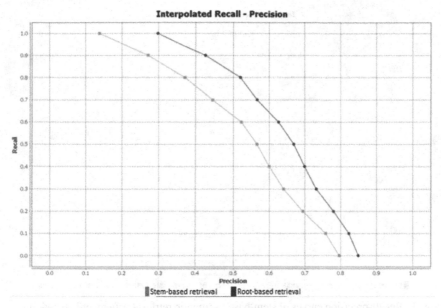

Fig. 2. Recall-precision curves of stem-based and root-based retrieval [33].

model slightly outperforms skip-gram method. However, the retrieval effectiveness after query expansion is reduced in stem-based and root-based representation. A statistical test is made for root-based query expansion using CBOW and Skip-gram models (see Table 6).

Table 6. Statistical test for root-based query expansion using CBOW and Skip-gram models.

Statistical test	Average precision	R-precision	NDCG	Bpref	P@5	P@10	P@20
t-test	0.7123	0.9564	0.7711	0.7778	0.6487	0.8413	0.9282
Randomized test	0.7043	0.9597	0.7643	0.7763	0.6647	0.8443	0.9345
Sign test	0.5270	0.9924	0.7718	0.9183	0.6847	0.7576	0.8356

Semantic Retrieval Using WordNet. The retrieval effectiveness of stem-based and root-based text representations are investigated with the application of query expansion using WordNet. Experimental results are shown in Figs. 5 and 6. The red curve is retrieval without query expansion and the others are semantic retrieval with query expansion using WordNet.

6.3 Discussion

Comparison of Root and Stem for Retrieval. Both stem-based and root-based text representations improve Amharic retrieval effectiveness in comparison to word-based

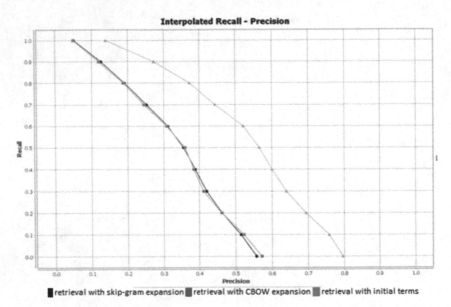

Fig. 3. Recall-precision curves of stem-based semantic retrieval using word embedding.

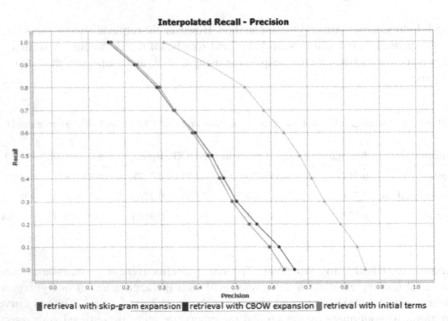

Fig. 4. Recall-precision curves of root-based semantic retrieval using word embedding.

text representation. Root-based retrieval is better than stem-based possibly due to the following three reasons.

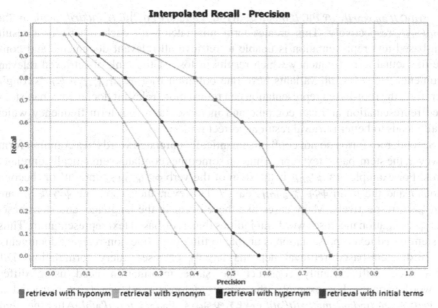

Fig. 5. Recall-precision curves of stem-based retrieval using WordNet.

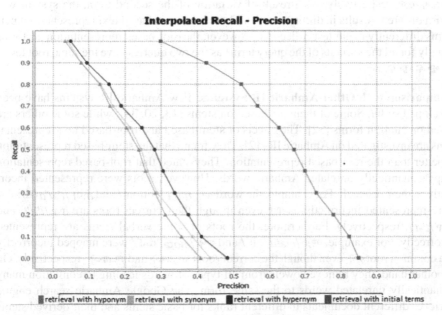

Fig. 6. Recall-precision curves of root-based retrieval using WordNet.

First, variants of a word have a single common root but might have more than one stem. For example, the stems of morphological variants ጠነከረ /t'ənəkərə/, ጥንካሬ /t'inikare/, ጠንካራ /t'ənikara/, እንጥንክሪ /ʔinit'ənikiri/ and አጠነከረ /ʔət'ənəkərə/

are ጠንካሪ /t'ənəkəri/, ጥንካሪ /t'inikari/, ጠንካሪ /t'ənikari/, ጠንካሪ /t'ənikiri/ and ጠናካሪ /t'ənakəri/, respectively. This creates term mismatch with each other. As a result, stem-based text representation is unable to retrieve all relevant documents and compute the actual term frequency which results in loss of the rank of retrieved relevant documents. However, all variants have one common root ጥ-ን-ከ-ር /t'-n-k-r/ 'strong'/. Therefore, the root-based representation can return more relevant documents than stem-based representation and can compute and increase the actual term frequency which usually leads to better retrieval result at correct rank.

Second, root forms do not conflate semantically unrelated words to a common form. However, the stem-based text representation sometimes conflates semantically unrelated words. For example, ቀን /k'əni/ is the stem of the verb ቀና /k'əna 'upright' or 'become jealous'/ and the noun ቀናት /k'ənati 'days'/. However, their roots are ቅ-ን /k'-n/ and ቀን /k'əni/, respectively. Many cases like these occur in the language, and stem-based text representation increases word ambiguities than root-based text representation. Thus, the stem-based text representation is unable to filter out some non-relevant documents.

Third, stem-based retrieval depends largely on user query formulation. Different users will certainly construct the same information need using different word variants. For example, the query 'deforestation' can be constructed as የደን መጨፍጨፍ /jədəni mətʃ'əfitʃ'əfi/ or የደን ጭፍጨፋ /jədəni tʃ'ifitʃ'əfa/. After the stem-based morphological analysis, the two queries have stem terms ደን ጨፍጨፍ and ደን ጭፍጨፍ, respectively. As a result of variation of the second term, the system will return different results in different ranks. Therefore, stem-based text representation performs differently in our test collection. However, the root-based representation performs equally for all the variants of the query terms as the two queries have the same root terms ደን ጭ-ፍ-ጭ-ፍ.

Comparison with Other Amharic IR Systems. Few Amharic IR systems have been developed so far. Some of them are based on stems [13, 20, 34]; while some others are based on citation forms [32]. The effects of stem-based and root-based text representations are investigated on Amharic IR [12]. They found that the stem-based representation is better than the root-based representation. They stated that root-based representation maps semantically unrelated Amharic words. However, roots were represented incorrectly in their research. For example, the word ጥጥ /t'it'i 'cotton'/ and ጠጣ /t'ət'a 'drink'/ were represented incorrectly as ጥጥ even though their correct roots are ጥጥ /t'it'i/ and ጥ-ጥ /t'-t'/, respectively. Furthermore, the roots of some verbal stems are represented incorrectly. For example, መታ /məta 'hit'/ and ሞተ /mota 'die'/ were mapped incorrectly to a common root ምት even though the correct roots are ም-ት and ም-ው-ት, respectively. On the other hand, they remove vowels from all types of words leading to conflation many semantically unrelated words to the same form. The Google Amharic search engine retrieves different documents in different ranks for basic stems and their derived stems though they are morphological variants. For example, Google search results of the queries ስብራት /sibirati 'being broken'/ and መሰበር /məsəbəri 'the process of being broken'/ are different though the same concept is expressed via these two variants. In our work, on the contrary, the stem-based text representation considers only basic stems and provides the same retrieval results for both basic stems and derived stems. We use root-based text representation as it conflates all variants of words to a single common form. In summary, previous studies that recommended the use of stems made their conclusions without thorough investigation on the applicability of roots. Many of them suggested stem-based as the best option. However, due to the complexity of the language stem-based representation does not work well. In this work, we have shown that the roots are better than stems for Amharic IR. This is a new finding which was not looked at in previous work.

Comparison of Conventional and Semantic Amharic IR. Even though the proposed morphological analysis (i.e. root-based) has positive impact on Amharic IR, query expansion using word embedding and WordNet does not improve the performance of the system due to term ambiguity. Ambiguous terms are prevalent in the language due to its complex morphology. For example, the term አለሙ /ʔaləmu/ can mean 'the world', 'they targeted', 'they dreamed', 'they developed' or a person with the name 'Alemu'. Accordingly, the term አለሙ /ʔaləmu/ needs to be expanded based on the context of the term in a given query. This affects the retrieval effectiveness of the proposed Amharic IR system. Since Amharic word sense disambiguator is not available yet, we did not integrate disambiguator into our proposed semantic retrieval system. Moreover, stem-based representation may not expand query terms though its semantically related words are in the WordNet. This is because a word can have several stems but there could be only one form representing the word in the WordNet. In this case, the plausible way to organize Amharic WordNet is to make use of root form as it can represent all variants of a word by a single common form. This could not be achieved by stem-based representation. Thus, root-based expansion could work well if word sense disambiguator was integrated in this work. Moreover, the case of word embedding, variants of a given word in the corpus might co-occur with variants of a given semantically related word in different forms. For example, the word ደን /dəni/ might co-occur with ጽፍጨፋ /tʃʼifitʃʼəfa/, መጨፍጨፍ /matʃʼəfitʃʼəfi/, ጨፍጨፊ /tʃʼəfitʃʼafi /, and ጨፍጭፍ /tʃʼəfitʃʼifi / within a specified window size. As these words have different stems, the actual co-occurrence frequency based on stem could not be computed correctly. As a result, the similarity between a query term and its semantically related word is lower which affects stem-based semantic retrieval. Furthermore, some expanded terms are related to a query term syntactically rather than semantically. For instance, the expanded terms for the proper noun በቀለ /bak'ələ/ are ጥላሁን /t'ilahun/, አበራ /ʔəbəra/, መስፍን /masifin/, ማሞ /mamo/ and ንጉሴ /niguse/ where their meanings are completely different. Consequently, retrieval using expanded terms sometimes returns more non-relevant documents than the original query retrieval. The overall retrieval effectiveness using expanded terms is lower than retrieval with only original query terms. The other possible reason for lower performance could be the small size of the corpus. However, a promising result was reported in previous Amharic IR research even using stems [20].

Comparison of Our Stopword List with Others. Few researches were conducted to build Amharic stopwords. However, classical methods that have been used in many morphologically simple languages such as English are applied without considering the characteristics of Amharic. For example, stopword lists constructed by Mindaye *et al.* [13] and Samuel and Bjorn [25] contain variants of a word. However, it is challenging to list all the variants of stopwords. Alemayehu and Peter [26] created stopword list based on stem. Though stems are better than word forms to construct Amharic stopwords, it is not the plausible way because of the existence of multiple stems for variants of a stopword. In our case, all the variants of stopword have a single common form. For example, the stopword list created by Alemayehu and Peter [26] would contain two stems (ነበር /nabari/, ነበር /nabari/) which are variants of a single word. However, in our case all variants of the stopword are represented by single root ን-በ-ር /n-b-r/ 'was'/.

7 Conclusion

Amharic has complex morphology which poses tremendous challenges for NLP and IR. In this work, we evaluate the existing Amharic NLP tools and resources, and investigate the implications of the morphological complexity on Amharic IR. After analyzing the gaps, we constructed standard resources and proposed a new Amharic IR system that takes the morphology of the language into consideration. The resources that we constructed are Amharic stopword list and context-based morphologically annotated corpora. They are made publicly accessible to the research community. Furthermore, stem-based and root-based morphological features were considered to construct resource, corpora, and develop Amharic IR system. Our findings indicate that root is the optimal form of word representation for Amharic IR development and resource construction. We also investigated semantic-based query expansion based on word embedding and Word-Net. We exploited the deep learning models (i.e. CBOW and Skip-gram) and WordNet to deal with term mismatch in Amharic IR though negative results were obtained due to prevalent term ambiguity. Further research on Amharic IR needs to be conducted by integrating Amharic word sense disambiguation so that only relevant terms are considered during query expansion of words having multiple interpretations.

References

1. Xu, J., Croft, W.: Query expansion using local and global document analysis. In: Proceedings of the 19th Annual International ACM SIGIR Conference on Research and Development in Information Retrieval, pp. 4–11. ACM (1996)
2. Ben, W., Karaa, A.: A new stemmer to improve information retrieval. Int. J. Netw. Secur. Appl. (IJNSA) 5(4), 143–154 (2013)
3. Coustié, O., Mothe, J., Teste, O., Baril, X.: Meting: a robust log parser based on frequent n-gram mining. In: 2020 IEEE International Conference on Web Services (ICWS), pp. 84–88 (2020)
4. Jabbar, A., Iqbal, S., Tamimy, M.I., Hussain, S., Akhunzada, A.: Empirical evaluation and study of text stemming algorithms. Artif. Intell. Rev. 53(8), 5559–5588 (2020). https://doi.org/10.1007/s10462-020-09828-3
5. Lavrenko, V., Croft, W.: Relevance based language models. In: SIGIR 2001, New Orleans, Louisiana, USA, pp. 260–267 (2001)
6. Xu, Y., Jones, G.J., Wang, B.: Query dependent pseudo-relevance feedback based on Wikipedia. In: SIGIR 2009, Boston, MA, USA, pp. 59–66 (2009)
7. Harb, H., Fouad, K., Nagdy, N.: Semantic retrieval approach for web documents. Int. J. Adv. Comput. Sci. Appl. 2(9) (2011)

8. El-Mahdaouy, A., Ouatik, S., Gaussier, E.: Semantically enhanced term frequency based on word embedding for Arabic information retrieval. In: 4th IEEE International Colloquium Information Science and Technology (CiSt), pp. 385–389 (2016)

9. Abate, M., Assabie, Y.: Development of Amharic morphological analyzer using memory-based learning. In: Przepiórkowski, A., Ogrodniczuk, M. (eds.) NLP 2014. LNCS (LNAI), vol. 8686, pp. 1–13. Springer, Cham (2014). https://doi.org/10.1007/978-3-319-10888-9_1

10. Yeshambel, T., Mothe, J., Assabie, Y.: Morphologically annotated Amharic text corpora. In: Proceedings of 44th ACM SIGIR Conference on Research and Development in Information Retrieval, Online Conference, Canada, pp. 2349–2355 (2021)

11. Countrymeters: Ethiopian population (2021). https://countrymeters.info/en/Ethiopia. Accessed 02 Aug 2021

12. Alemayehu, N., Willett, P.: The effectiveness of stemming for information retrieval in Amharic. Program Electron. Libr. Inf. Syst. **37**(4), 254–259 (2003)

13. Mindaye, T., Redewan, H., Atnafu, S.: Design and implementation of Amharic search engine. In: Proceedings of the 5th International Conference on Signal Image Technology and Internet Based Systems, pp. 318–325 (2010)

14. Al-Hadid, Afaneh, S., Al-Tarawneh, H., Al-Malahmeh, H.: Arabic information retrieval system using the neural network model. Int. J. Adv. Res. Comput. Commun. Eng. **3**(12), 8664–8668 (2014)

15. Musaid, S.: Arabic information retrieval system-based on morphological analysis (AIRSMA): a comparative study of word, stem, root and morpho-semantic methods. Ph.D. dissertation,Computer and Information Science, De Montfort University, United Kingdom (2000)

16. Moukdad, H.: A comparison of root and stemming techniques for the retrieval of Arabic documents. Ph.D. dissertation, Graduate School of Library and Information Studies, McGill University, Montreal (2002)

17. Larkey, L.S., Ballesteros, L., Connell, M.E.: Light stemming for Arabic information retrieval. In: Soudi, A., Bosch, A.V., Neumann, G. (eds.) Arabic Computational Morphology, pp. 221–243. Springer, Dordrecht (2007). https://doi.org/10.1007/978-1-4020-6046-5_12

18. Ali, A., Mosa, E., Abdullah, B.: An intelligent use of stemmer and morphology analysis for Arabic information retrieval. Egypt. Inform. J. **21**(4), 209–217 (2020). https://doi.org/10.1016/j.eij.2020.02.004

19. Ornan, U.: A morphological, syntactic and semantic search engine for Hebrew texts.In: Proceedings of the ACL-2002 Workshop on Computational Approaches to Semitic Languages, Philadelphia, Pennsylvania, USA, pp. 1–10 (2002)

20. Getnet, B., Assabie, Y.: Amharic information retrieval based on query expansion using semantic vocabulary. In: Delele, M.A., Bitew, M.A., Beyene, A.A., Fanta, S.W., Ali, A.N. (eds.) ICAST 2020. LNICSSITE, vol. 384, pp. 407–416. Springer, Cham (2021). https://doi.org/10.1007/978-3-030-80621-7_29

21. Fang, H.: A re-examination of query expansion using lexical resources. In: Proceedings of ACL-2008: HLT, Columbus, Ohio, USA, pp. 139–147 (2008)

22. Bagherid, E., Ensane, F., Al-Obeidat, F.: Neural word and entity embeddings for Ad hoc retrieval. J. Inf. Process. Manag. **54**, 657–673 (2018)

23. Demeke, G., Getachew, M.: Manual annotation of Amharic news items with part-of-speech tags and its challenges. ELRC Working Papers **2**(1), 1–16 (2006)

24. Yeshambel, T., Mothe, J., Assabie, Y.: 2AIRTC: the Amharic Adhoc information retrieval test collection. In: Arampatzis, A., et al. (eds.) CLEF 2020. LNCS, vol. 12260, pp. 55–66. Springer, Cham (2020). https://doi.org/10.1007/978-3-030-58219-7_5

25. Samuel, E., Bjorn, G.: Classifying Amharic news text using self-organizing maps. In: Proceedings of the ACL Workshop on Computational Approaches to Semitic Languages, Michigan, USA, pp. 71–78 (2005)

26. Alemayehu, N., Willett, P.: Stemming of Amharic words for information retrieval. J. Lit. Linguistic Comput. **17**(1), 1–17 (2002)
27. Alemu, A., Asker, L.: An Amharic stemmer: reducing words to their citation forms. In: Proceedings of the 2007 Workshop on Computational Approaches to Semitic Languages: Common Issues and Resources, Prague, Czech Republic, pp. 104–110. Association for Computational Linguistics (2007)
28. Sisay, F., Haller, J.: Application of corpus-based techniques to Amharic texts. In: Proceedings of MT Summit IX Workshop on Machine Translation for Semitic Languages (2003)
29. Amsalu, S., Gibbon, D.: Finite state morphology of Amharic. In: 5th Recent Advances in Natural Language Processing, pp. 47–51 (2006)
30. Gasser, M.: HornMorpho: a system for morphological processing of Amharic, Oromo, and Tigrinya. In: Conference on Human Language Technology for Development, Alexandria, Egypt, pp. 94–99 (2011)
31. Mulugeta, W., Gasser, M.: Learning morphological rules for Amharic verbs using inductive logic programming. In: Workshop on Language Technology for Normalisation of Less-Resourced Languages (SALTMIL8/AfLaT2012), Istanbul, Turkey, pp. 7–12 (2012)
32. Argaw, A.A., Asker, L.: Amharic-English information retrieval. In: Peters, C., et al. (eds.) CLEF 2006. LNCS, vol. 4730, pp. 43–50. Springer, Heidelberg (2007). https://doi.org/10. 1007/978-3-540-74999-8_5
33. Yeshambel, T., Mothe, J., Assabie, Y.: Amharic document representation for adhoc retrieval. In: Proceedings of the 12th International Joint Conference on Knowledge Discovery, Knowledge Engineering and Knowledge Management - KDIR, pp. 124–134 (2020). https://doi.org/ 10.5220/0010177301240134. ISBN 978-989-758-474-9; ISSN 2184-3228
34. Munye, M., Atnafu, S.: Amharic-English bilingual Web search engine. In: Proceedings of the 4th ACM International Conference on Management of Emergent Digital EcoSystems (MEDES 2012), Addis Ababa, Ethiopia, pp. 32–39 (2012)

Semantic Similarity Analysis for Entity Set Expansion

Weronika T. Adrian(✉) ⓘD, Kornel Wilk, Marek Adrian ⓘD, Krzysztof Kluza ⓘD,
and Antoni Ligęza ⓘD

AGH University of Science and Technology, al. A. Mickiewicza 30, 30-059 Krakow, Poland
{wta,madrian,kluza,ligeza}@agh.edu.pl

Abstract. Grouping objects into a common, initially unknown, category under-
lies several important tasks, such as query suggestion or automatic lexicon generation. However, while coming up with more things "of the same kind" is easy for
humans, it is not trivial for Artificial Intelligence. This task is commonly known
as the Entity Set Expansion (ESE) problem, and has been studied in different
branches of AI and NLP. In this paper, we review different similarity metrics and
techniques that could be applied to the ESE problem. Moreover, we decompose
the problem into phases and demonstrate how to use several approaches together.
In particular, we combine semantic similarity metrics with Meta Path algorithm
for knowledge graphs. We discuss the results and show that the presented setting
can be reused in further research into hybrid approaches to the ESE problem.

Keywords: Knowledge representation · Semantic similarity · Knowledge
graphs · Entity set expansion · Knowledge integration · Knowledge processing

1 Introduction

The ability to categorize objects is an ability that most humans learn at a very young
age. It is fundamental to our intellectual development and by the time we are adults it
is so natural that we are capable of doing it without a conscious effort. When we see a
set of words like "cat", "dog", "hamster", the word "animal" or "pet" will easily pop
into our mind. But the ability to do something with ease is not the same as describing
how we achieve it in a computational manner. The latter of course is necessary, if we
would want to create an Artificial Intelligence with similar categorizing capabilities to
our own. This however has proven itself to be difficult, and so the task of categorization
has been broken down to smaller problems that can be studied in greater detail.

One of such problems is the Entity Set Expansion problem, in which we are searching for more elements similar initial set. Of course the word "similar" may be seen
as ambiguous. After all, word senses can be similar, but also words, phrases, or even
whole documents can be similar, and it is not obvious, that recognizing those similarities would use the same computational methods for all of the mentioned cases. In fact
throughout the years several new methods for each of these cases have been proposed
and still new metrics appear every year.

This paper is supported by AGH UST.

One of the aforementioned methods of describing similarity, discussed in works like "Dimensions of Similarity" [3] associates similarity with a geometrical representation of the concepts characteristics, using the mathematical distance measuring methods to quantify the result. Similarity, in this sense, estimates how "close" the considered things are according to some defined dimensions. We can say that for example *cat* is similar to *dog*, because they are both *animals*. But how do we actually compute that? The method was signaled in the example. If two species of animals are similar, because they are animals, we can use the *classes of objects* and their *associations* to determine how similar they are. In order to define the range of a class, we either do it extensionally, using numerous examples of the concept, or intensionally, by defining some class constraints. In order to calculate similarity between any "entities", we usually attach to each entity some sort of a virtual *representation* derived from its semantics. These representations could be vectors in some space, or nodes in large connected graph. Then we can calculate distances in the space or paths and other measurements in the graph to determine similarity.

This paper is an extended version of the paper [1] presented at IC3K/KEOD 2020 conference. It has been significantly revised, such that the analysis is now geared towards application of similarity metrics for Entity Set Expansion problem. The problem of Entity Set Expansion [21] is the problem of finding similar elements for given small seed set. Example of such a problem can be expanding set of [London, Berlin, Warsaw], because as we can see all of those entities are capitals of European countries. In this case, some of the entities which we can expand our set can be Athens, Budapest, Oslo and many more. We can see that from human way of thinking one of the solutions for this problem is to find the common class or some defining features of the elements, which then is used to evaluate potential candidates. Those candidates are for example found by determining some neighbourhood or superclass of those entities. Other approach can be determining set of common features among the elements and then finding entities with same set of common features.

In this paper, we analyze the stages of the ESE problem, and point out in which phases, similarity metrics can be applied. The proposed solution is one of possible options and we show how to combine different solutions for a hybrid approach. We hope that this outline of the ESE stages will help structure the research and experiments of other methods applied to this problem. Thus, the original contributions of this papers can be stated as follows:

– We review the semantic similarity metrics, with a particular focus on methods that assume a graph-based knowledge representation;
– We analyze the Entity Set Expansion problem in terms of its sub-problems and outline the stages for which particular similarity metrics may be applied;
– We provide a solution proposal that uses similarity metrics and (parts of) the Meta Path [22] algorithm and works online using the Web semantic resources.

The paper is organized as follows: in Sect. 2, we review existing approaches to semantic similarity analysis. Then in Sect. 3, we outline the Entity Set Expansion problem phases and reflect on the metrics described in Sect. 2. Following is the Sect. 4, in which we combine different semantic similarity metrics in a single algorithm. We present and discuss the results in Sect. 6, and conclude the paper in Sect. 7.

2 Semantic Similarity Analysis: Overview of Methods

Semantic Similarity is quite interesting concept to implement in a computer system, as the similarity is based on human natural language and associations of concepts. To calculate semantic similarity of words we need some representations and data on which we base the calculation. Such data can be obtained either from large amount of texts, which are processed to create some representations of words and concepts which then can be compared and used to calculate similarity, or from other representations such as knowledge graphs in which we also can have the hierarchical structure of the concepts.

2.1 Corpus-Based Methods

The corpus based methods try to determine similarity of entities based on large data. The similarity is based on statistics, examples of those methods are normalised google distance, which is working on concept associations [7], or by representing entities as a high-dimensional vectors, such as Explicit Semantic Analysis [6], or finally vectorisation algorithms which give low-dimension vectors as an output. Such algorithms are quite recent, for example word2Vec and similar algorithms, which are able to create vector representations of such things as words in sentences, nodes in graphs and even such high-level structures as RDF graphs or OWL ontologies. Such representations are created using machine learning methods especially neural networks, to create vectors based on the surroundings of the entity. From the resulting representation we can easily calculate similarity as a distance between each vector.

Interesting fact about such methods is that though they originate from calculating similarity based on large amount of sentences, we can also use them on other representations. For example basing on the word2vec algorithm the family of other "2vec" algorithms was created. All of those are based on the concept of creating word or entity embeddings, which are vectors representing them, calculated from the input data. In those algorithms we either create CBOW - continuous bag of words, in which we can find the middle word based on the sourroundings, or skip-gram, in which for given word we get probable sourrounding. The examples of those are:

1. word2vec [14] - Word2Vec is an algorithm for generating word embeddings - vector representations for words. The algorithm bases on the assumption that if we have some neighbourhood, for example "While on the walk [word] found a stick". We can predict a word in the middle, which in this case could be a dog. Also it could be the other way and based on the word we could guess it's surroundings. Those two types of embeddings are CBOW and Skip-gram and they can be calculated from some corpora of words using neural networks and machine learning.
2. node2vec [8] - it is an algorithm for generating embedding of nodes in a single graph. The whole graph is our corpus, while edges mean neighbourhood and nodes are words. Then we can make random walks through the graph, which will give us the equivalent of sentences. Now we have our large corpus generated from the graph and we can use any method which was created for texts with sentences l ike word2Vec. The random walks here are the core of transforming the graph to the corpora on which we further implement algorithm.

3. RDF2Vec [18] - This algorithm is based on RDF graphs. In the same fashion as in node2vec from the RDF graph we generate random walks. This time not only nodes are parts of the equivalents of sentences, but also names of edges are considered. Once we generate the sequences of nodes and edges, which are RDF objects, subjects and predicates we can treat this collection of sequences as our corpora for further learning. On this set we run algorithm such as word2vec, which generates vector embeddings.

4. OWL2Vec [5] - This algorithm is similar to RDF2Vec in this way, that it is concerned mainly in transferring data in OWL format to format which can be used in word2Vec. This time though we do not have only the graph to get our knowledge from, as the OWL introduces labels and descriptions which could be used in better way than as a nodes in the graph. We create three corporas of sequences in this algorithm. One which is just same as in RDF2Vec, one which takes every sequence from output of RDF2Vec part and transfers it to its labels. Then sequences are split by the words. The last document is the mix of the first two linking structural data with lexical mixing labels and resources in same document. Those three create our new corpora.

2.2 Knowledge-Based Methods

Knowledge based methods use structured knowledge representation expressed for instance in variouse *semantic resources*, such as knowledge graphs, ontologies, lexical databases etc. A graph-based knowledge representation is very useful when using such metrics as the length of the path between the nodes, lowest common ancesor of the nodes (or Least Common Subsumer concept in Description Logic ontologies) and distance of path to it, depth in the graph, or Information content [19] which is the measure of information which is carried by some concept. The broader the concept, the less information it carries, and the narrower the concept, the more information content it has. For example the concept plant carries many information, but much less than concept oak tree, which gives us all information which are given by the concept plant and then more by the information about oak tree. This is because the oak tree is the subconcept of the plant. In such case, the lower the concept is in the hierarchy of concepts the higher is its information concept.

For two entities c_i and c_j the exemplary metrics which can be used are [23]:

1. simple measurement of path between entities, which was created by R. Rada, H. Mili, E. Bicknell, and M. Blettner in "Development and application of a metric on semantic nets" in 1989 [16]:

$$sim(c_i, c_j)_{path} = \frac{1}{1 + length(c_i, c_j)} \tag{1}$$

2. non linear function with maximum depth(D) of the concept. Created by C. Leacock and M. Chodorow in "Combining local context and WordNet similarity for word sense identification" in 1998 [10]

$$sim(c_i, c_j)_{lch} = -\log\left(\frac{length(c_i, c_j)}{2 * D}\right) \tag{2}$$

3. the depths of entities and their Least Common Subsumer. Created by Z. Wu and M. Palmer in "Verbs semantics and lexical selection" in 1994 [20]

$$sim(c_i, c_j)_{wup} = \frac{2depth(c_{lcs})}{depth(c_i) + depth(c_j)} \tag{3}$$

4. combined shortest path length and LCS depth. Where α and β are the parameters, created by Y. Li, Z. Bandar, and D. Mclean in "An approach for measuring semantic similarity between words using multiple information sources" in 2003 [12]

$$sim(c_i, c_j)_{li} = e^{-\alpha length(c_i, c_j)} \frac{e^{\beta depth(c_{lcs})} - e^{\beta depth(c_{lcs})}}{e^{\beta depth(c_{lcs})} + e^{\beta depth(c_{lcs})}} \tag{4}$$

5. information content of entities LCS, for wich we use the corpus Formulated by P. Resnik in "Using information content to evaluate semantic similarity in a taxonomy" in 1995 [17]

$$sim(c_i, c_j)_{res} = IC_{corpus}(C_{lcs}) \tag{5}$$

6. function of IC of LCS and each entity, formulated by D. Lin in "An information-theoretic definition of similarity," in 1998 [13]

$$sim(c_i, c_j)_{lin} = \frac{2IC_{corpus}(c_{lcs})}{IC_{corpus}(c_i) + IC_{corpus}(c_j)} \tag{6}$$

7. reverse of the distance calculated as sum of differences between IC of entities and their LCS, which was formulated by J. J. Jiang and D. W. Conrath in "Semantic similarity based on corpus statistics and lexical taxonomy," in 1997 [9]

$$sim(c_i, c_j)_{jcn} = \frac{1}{1 + IC_{corpus}(c_i) + IC_{corpus}(c_j) - 2IC_{corpus}(c_{lcs})} \tag{7}$$

8. weighted path length where weight is calculated based on the IC of the LCS and parameter k

$$sim(c_i, c_j)_{wpath} = \frac{1}{1 + length(c_i, c_j) * k^{IC(lcs)}} \tag{8}$$

2.3 Analysis of Similarity Metrics

When comparing corpus-based and knowledge-based methods, we can say that the former can be very useful, but they are less explainable, as they need a lot of statistical data and use complicated mathematical calculations to determine representations, and from this we can calculate distances between new representations and use them to measure similarity. The advantage of such methods as word2vec, RDF2vec or OWL2vec is that we can use them to get either most probable surrounding of the entity, or find entity which suits the sequence the most by just using those algorithms. The latter type which is the knowledge based approach covers multiple metrics, but all share that they are able to calculate similarity between two known concepts with simple equations which are explainable and we can show why exactly the two concepts are similar.

From the knowledge-based methods, we can see that the most straightforward are 1 and 2. The ones which take into account the conceptual structure of the graph and the depth of concepts and their LCS are 3 and 4. They have advantage over first two, as even concepts with same path length which are on the different depth will have different similarity. Still there are some cases when there will be same similarity between concepts. The three measurements based on IC (5, 6, 7) are also interesting, as they are operating on the important property of the entities, but we lose information about the path between concepts. The last one 8 is weighted path, which can take into account information about IC and LCS.

3   Towards Semantic Similarity Analysis for Entity Set Expansion

The aim of the Entity Set Expansion problem is to find the entities which are "similar" to the seed set of entities. An important factor is that those similarities should be understandable and reasonable for humans. The input to the problem consists of initial set of entities, called the "seed set", and some data from which we can search for the entities. We should search the data in order to find entities belonging to the same category and *as similar as possible* to the initial set.

As an example, consider a knowledge base shown in Fig. 1. The problem is stated as follows: "Find expansion of the set [Martin Williams, John Smith].". In the Figure, we can see the seed set marked in green. The common properties of the seed set - [owns, name]. By traversing the graph by the connections or going and

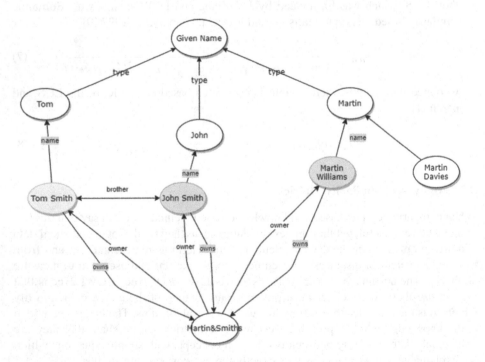

Fig. 1. An example of the ESE problem and its solution.

returning by the properties, we can find some candidate entities, such as Tom Smith, or Tom, or Martin Davies. We can see that `Tom Smith` entity shares most of the properties with our seed set. Thus, the expanded set is "`[John Smith, Martin Williams, Tom Smith]`."

3.1 Steps in Solving the Entity Set Expansion

Let us now decompose the ESE problem into subproblems to be solved and steps that need to be performed (see Fig. 2).

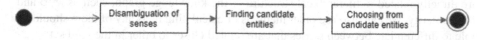

Fig. 2. Steps in solving Entity Set Expansion.

Word Sense Disambiguation. The first problem concerns the seed set itself. When we got the seed set, such as (Australia, United States, Monaco, Russia) we can have a problem determining in which sense those words are used here. For example Australia can be a country, or a continent, Monaco can be a country or a city. And this problem will occur probably in many cases, so we need some way of determining the most suiting sense for each of these words. Once we do this, we should have the (set of) senses which are the most appropriate in the given context.

Finding Candidate Entities. The second problem concerns the size of the datasource. As processing large knowledge bases is not practical, we should find the *candidate* entities which will be connected to seed entities in some way which will maximise their potential similarity to them. As the input here, we have the seed set with their "best" senses. In this step, we should find some sort of a superset or some set which will be suitable to search for similar entities to those from seed set. Once we do this, we will have probably quite a large set of candidate entities for the expansion.

Choosing from Candidates. At the beginning of this step, we have already prepared set of candidate entities which will be considered. Now we have to find those which are most suitable to expand our seed set. To do this, we should choose some way of ranking them and based on this we will be able to determine the best entities to include to our set. Having done this we can just return our seed set expanded by those entities and this will be our final result.

3.2 Existing Solutions that Can Be Used for ESE

Existing solutions to this problem are based either on the structure of the knowledge graph and hierarchy of classes and concepts, or on the similarity of entities, which can be calculated in many different ways. The approaches which are based on similarity are mainly using textual patterns or co-occurrence as the measure on which we will add new entities. There are also knowledge based approaches using Knowledge Graphs, for example Meta Path, which uses the structure of the graph [22] to find the entities which will expand the initial seed set.

A Class-Based Solution. One of the solution for the problem is pretty straightforward. It is based on the classes of the entities, as defined in Knowledge Graph. To use this solution we should first find the set of most similar senses. Then we try to find the Least Common Subsumer [4]. This should be in some way constrained, so we should not search too high in the hierarchy of concepts. Once we got the class which connects all entities in the seed set we expand our seed set by all the elements of this class.

Semantic Similarity Metrics. We can use similarity metrics to determine the senses of seeds which we should use for the expansion [2]. We can chose similarity metrics which are directly related to hierarchical structure of the knowledge graph, such as wup and li similarity. We can also use other methods of calculating it, as any of them should be able to differentiate between senses that are related closer to other in the seed set.

The other part of Entity Set Expansion problem where we can use semantic similarity is to verify which entities found are the most similar to the current entities in the set. Both those problems need checking the similarity of one entity to the set of entities. The solution for this can be creation of function which will be able to calculate some average similarity. We can do it by calculating mathematical mean of calculated similarities for each of the entities in set. If we use similarity measure which has values between 0 and 1 the mean of those values will be in this range.

Sematch[1] is a tool developed to easily calculate semantic similarity using multiple different methods. The tool is implemented in Python and the knowledge graphs of YAGO or DBpedia data. Just using the knowledge graph, we can calculate measures which are not based on information content. To use the measures with IC we have to give additional file, in which we will provide the information content of the entities whose similarity we are calculating. The API gives also methods of calculating similarity of words based on Wordnet.

Meta Path Algorithm [22]. is an algorithm which gets the initial seed set and processes it to give the set of Paths which connect the seed entities and are ranked in relevance. To do it, it creates the tree which is gradually expanding from the root. Nodes consist of list of entity pairs, where one is element of seed set and the other current end of the path, the value Q which is 1 if we have a connection between two different seed entities and the set of visited entities. As we expand the tree, we visit further entities connected by some relation R, saving them in the sets of visited, and expanding the list. If we encounter some of the other seed entity the value Q in this element of the list is set to 1.

We create separate node for each relation R and the nodes are valued in the length of source set – how many source entities have such path of relations, and in SC which is the sum of value of parent SC and sum of Q values in this node. We always choose the node with the longest source set and from those we choose one with the minimum number of tuples in the list. The resulting tree structure can be seen on the Fig. 3. At the end, we have the node with paths which are common to most of the seed entities and connect them. From this we can derive our candidate entities.

---

[1] See https://github.com/gsi-upm/sematch.

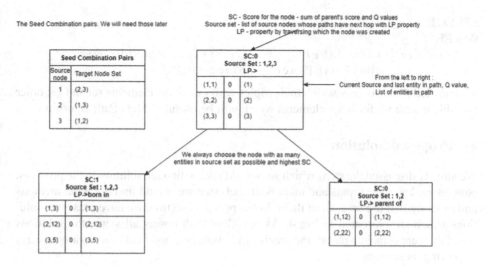

Fig. 3. Elements of Meta Path algorithm tree after one iteration.

This algorithm, as proposed in its original paper, covers all steps of the Entity Set Expansion. However, as we have clearly defined the sub-problems of ESE, together with its input and output, we can also use a part of the whole algorithm to part of the ESE problem.

Online Semantic Resources. The semantics of words and relationships among objects are explicitly defined in various online semantic resources, most prominent of which we will now describe.

Wordnet [15] is a lexical database of English that contains nouns, verbs, adverbs and adjectives. They are organized into sets of cognitive synonyms (so-called "synsets"). The synsets are linked to each other by semantic and lexical relations, which creates large linked database of most of the words in English. The database can be accessed via tools or can be downloaded as the database. The data in this database is mainly connected as synonyms and super-subordinate relations, so it is interesting to use it in finding and calculating semantic similarity. This tool is also one of the tools used in the implementation of the Sematch tool.

DBPedia [11] is one of the largest sources of data in the form of linked graph. It consists of many concepts and entities. It is also linked to other resources in the linked data, which makes it quite interesting tool and database. Furthermore the DBPedia has easy way of accessing data, as it has its own SPARQL endpoint which allows us to create even elaborated queries to search the database. The queries are based on the structure of DBpedia, to we can use some RDF triples, or ask for elements with some properties. If we want for example get all entities labeled as Cristiano Ronaldo, and find his birthplace, we can run following query:

```
SELECT  *
WHERE  {
    ?athlete    rdfs:label         "Cristiano Ronaldo"@en  ;
                dbo:birthPlace    ?place  . }
```

We can also create a query which finds triples with one of the elements set and get other possible matchings for other elements which will be useful in Meta Path algorithm.

4   Proposed Solution

We already discussed the steps which we should take to find the solution to the problem. Now as we know the inputs and outputs of each step we should find out what methods and tools we will use on each of them. In the previous section, we have presentes solutions which are presented in Fig. 4. As the Meta Path covers all steps, the solutions based on it are at the top part of the graph, while bottom consists of other example ways of solving those steps

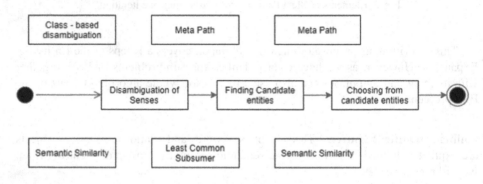

Fig. 4. Steps in solving Entity Set Expansion with a range of possible methods.

4.1   Disambiguation of Senses

This is the step where we are determining the most suitable senses. To do this, we can use either semantic similarity and find such a combination of senses which will have the maximum similarity, or find such combination of senses which have the most specific common class. We will use the similarity-based disambiguation, as we want to get the results which will be most closely connected in terms of similarity. This should give us the initial senses which are also similar to humans, as the semantic-based similarity metrics are usually close to human understanding of the similarity.

To use this similarity on the entities of the DBPedia data base we need to consider that not all of the elements of the DBPedia are concepts and also every object can have multiple concepts connected with it. Also, we are not interested in similarity between two entities, but average similarity between *all* the seed set elements. To calculate it, we can first collect concepts connected with the objects from seed set, then do the pairwise similarity calculation, get the maximum value between each of the entities and finally get the mean of those values as the similarity for the whole set.

4.2   Finding Candidate Entities

In this step, we have to find the entities which will be most promising in the context of finding new elements to expand our set. We can do it by simply finding all entities under the same LCS, or we can use more complex methods such as Meta Path Generation [22], which will give us the set of paths with their relevance. We will choose the second option, and use the part of the Meta Path to extract the candidate entities. This will give us quite large amount of candidate entities. Those entities will also share same features and paths of properties, because of the specification of Meta Path.

The implementation of this part of Meta Path starts with the seed set, or in further iterations from the set of entities which we connected with the seed set using the Path currently in consideration. Then we need to find all the properties which are available for further expansion of the path. Once we do this we will have all the possible properties. We split them to sets connected with the seed properties which have the path with such property. Now to narrow the field of the search we extract those properties which have the best chance of becoming next hop for the algorithm. As we already know the algorithm chooses ones with largest seed set, which in other words means that this property has to have at least one path for each of the seed set elements which can be archived. In such case we begin our search from those which have such path for all of the seed. To find those all we need to do is find the intersection of previously created sets of properties:

$$NewProperties = \bigcap_{i=1}^{n} PropertiesForSeedSet(i) \tag{9}$$

where i is index used to iterate through seed set.

Then if no property fulfilling this is found we have to search for less strict criteria. In the nest step we create the set of properties which are not yet considered and are in any of intersections of combinations of all seed set elements but one, then all but two and so on. This step is done twice. In the first one we search for properties in which the lase element of already archived path is subject and the second one is where those elements are the target of the triple with the property.

Once we have found which properties we will consider, we have to find which one is best – which one has the smallest number of paths created. To achieve this, we create new sets which are images of currently considered set by the function defined by each of the properties which we have found. From the size of those sets, we decide which property should be our next and create new set by traversing graph through this property.

The algorithm goes up to three such steps when if no connection is found between any of the seed set elements then we reverse the path to get back to the beginning. To do this during execution we are saving which is the current path and now we get the set at the last branch and with it doing same steps, but in reverse we return to the beginning, but now we should have more elements in set than just in seed set. This is our list of proposed expansions. If during the steps we encounter connection between elements of seed set, we end the algorithm and the list of proposed expansions is the list of entities at the end of all paths in the ending branch.

4.3   Choosing from Candidates

The final step is to choose which from candidate entities are the best. In the first step we used semantic similarity to find the best candidates, so in this step we can also use the semantic similarity to determine which candidates are the best. This way we will have consistent decision, which in case of second iteration will with high probability give same senses and avoid "concept drift".

The implementation will work similar to the sense disambiguation, but this time we will just calculate similarity of the seed set expanded by each of the proposed entities, then sort them by their similarity with the seed set and finally choose some of them to add to the seed set.

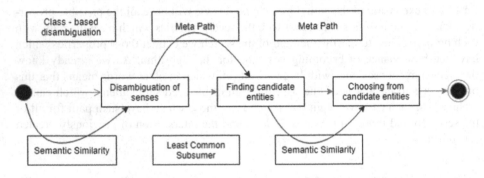

Fig. 5. Selected methods applied to stages of ESE.

The whole process of solving the ESE problem is depicted in Fig. 5.

5   Implementation

In this Section, we provide the technical details of the implementation of the proposal.

5.1   Word Sense Disambiguation

The first step of the program is to find the seed set senses. Input for the algorithm is list of words, which then after this step should be converted to most coherent list of DBpedia URIs. To do this we will need two elements. First is a way to find URIs connected with words. Second is to calculate similarities between those URIs. The first step is implemented as creating list of URIs for each of words from seed set. To get them we use DBPedia lookup service. This returns the data in the form of xml file, which can be easily processed. The following function returns such list for given sense:

```
def GetSenses(entity):
    SensesURIs = []
    with urlopen(\
        "https://lookup.dbpedia.org/api/search.asmx/
```

```
        KeywordSearch?QueryString="+\
        entity + "&MaxHits=" + str(MaxHits)) as url:
        QueryResult = url.read()
        tree = ET.fromstring(QueryResult)
        results = tree.getchildren()
        for r in results:
            SensesURIs.append(r.getchildren()[1].text)
    return SensesURIs
```

When we have the senses for each word we should evaluate them and choose those most appropriate. Those in this solution are interpreted as those which give highest similarity score. Choosing them is implemented in a greedy way, to improve performance. If we calculate each and every combination then our algorithm will have complexity of k^n where n is number of words in seed set and k is number of senses for each seed which we got from DBPedia lookup. As such complexity will have negative impact on performance we decided to switch it to less complex. Generally if a person tries to create a set of similar entities, the first few are probably those connected the most, while other are those which are thought of after creating first few. In this context, we decided to search from the first word. We choose mostly connected pair of entities, then from this expand it by most similar sense from third word senses and so on. At the end we have list of URIs of most similar senses from those which we collected.

5.2 Finding Candidates

Second step in the algorithm is finding entities which are potential candidates for expansion of the seed set. We decided on using Meta Path algorithm to do so. The Meta Path algorithm uses list of tree branches where each branch has the structure:

```
Branch = {}
Branch["SC"] = RootInFunction["SC"]
Branch["source_set"] = set()
Branch["elements"] = []
Branch["property"] = ""
```

Where source set is the part of source set which have at least one instance of path of properties leading to this branch, property is the property used to get to this branch from earlier, SC is weight of the branch, which is the same as number of paths connecting elements of seed set in this and any previous branch and finally we have list of elements which uses following structure:

```
Branch["elements"][-1]["pair"] = []
Branch["elements"][-1]["pair"].
append(PreviousBranch["elements"]["pair"][0])
Branch["elements"][-1]["pair"].
append(NewElementAddedByTraversingProperty)
Branch["elements"][-1]["list"] =
PreviousBranch["elements"]["list"] +
    NewElementAddedByTraversingProperty
```

Each element represents one of instances of path which begins in one of the seed set elements, which is the first element in both pair and list, element which was just added by traversing the tree, and list of the all elements in path.

The algorithm begins with the seed set. Then we use following SPARQL query to find all senses for each of the elements of currently used set:

SELECT DISTINCT ?p **WHERE**
{ <el["pair"][1]> ?p ?o. }

The query is invoked using SPARQLWrapper connected to DBPedia endpoint.

```
queryString = "SELECT DISTINCT ?p WHERE
{ <" + el["pair"][1] + "> ?p ?o. }"
sparql = SPARQLWrapper("https://dbpedia.org/sparql")
sparql.setReturnFormat(JSON)
sparql.setQuery(queryString)
ret = sparql.query()
```

In the implementation "el["pair"][1]" is the element at the end of the path from one of the elements in source set. Query is executed for each of such elements and then the results of this query are summed. The result of single query is the python dictionary. To get the bindings for our variable ?p we need to use the following code:

```
for result in ret.convert()["results"]["bindings"]:
    print(result["p"]["value"])
```

This way we will print all the values which were assigned to ?p. As we follow all the results of this query we sum them to one set of all possible properties which we can use to expand the Path.

In the implementation next step of finding the appropriate property is done by creating the list of python sets where each set is connected with the seed set element. Then using intersection or sum of the sets we create appropriate sets.

Next step of evaluating properties is done by first by querying DBPedia for the elements which this property connects to the path. To do this we use following queries, first for normal direction of traversing the graph, second for reverse direction:

```
#For normal direction
queryString = "SELECT DISTINCT ?o WHERE
{ <" + el["pair"][1] + "> <" + prop + "> ?o. }"
#For reversed direction
queryString = "SELECT DISTINCT ?o WHERE\
{ ?o <" + prop + "> <" + el["pair"][1] + ">. }"
```

Where el["pair"][1] is the element at the end of path and prop is property currently considered.

We do this in the loop until length of the created path reaches three, because in experiments longer paths did not finish in desired time. Then we try to reverse by implementing going through the tree by the properties from current path, but in reverse direction. If during any of steps we encounter path connecting two different elements of the seed set we finish creating new set and exit the loop early.

5.3   Evaluating Candidates and Expanding the Seed Set

At this step we have our seed set and the set of potential expansions. From those expansions we need to find those which are most appropriate. We calculate similarity of seed set with each of this proposed expansions and then sort them in a list from one with the best similarity to one with the smallest. Then we choose the most suitable and add them to the seed set. The resulting set is the output of our algorithm.

The choice of the most suitable can be done in different ways. In this algorithm we decided to choose only those elements which do not decrease the internal similarity of the set by more than ten percent. This way we avoid unnecessary drop in similarity while still giving some space for elements. Also to make the results clearer we will not add to much elements stopping at double of original source set length.

6   Results and Discussion

In this Section, we illustrate the results of example instances of the problem with different parameters used to solve them. The main parameters of the problem are:

- depth of the Meta Path tree which we will consider
- metric which we will use for calculating semantic similarity

For this experiment, we have chosen to use trees of the depth two and three, as the deeper we go the larger the data and there are limited resources which we can use. Furthermore, from the article about Meta Path [22] we know that paths longer than four are usually not as relevant. In our implementation, even tree of depth two can create path of length four, as we use the created path to return to source set if no viable end of algorithm is reached. In this case, path of length two and three should be enough to get good results. The second parameter of the program is the metric. We have chosen three: the simplest metric – path [16], the metric with the depths of elements and their Least Common Subsumer [20] and finally li which uses powers of e [12].

6.1   Results

The results are found by executing the program created based on the method defined in the previous Section. This program searches the DBpedia, so all the results are from this database. Every result is the URI in form "http://dbpedia.org/resource/NAME\discretionary-OF\discretionary-RESOURCE". To increase readability of the data, we have shortened it by deleting the "http://dbpedia.org/resource/" prefix and replacing "" with space. As sense disambiguation is independent of Meta Path tree depth, we will first present the results of sense disambiguation for each used metric and then we will present the entities found by algorithm to expand the seed set.

The sense disambiguation is the first part of the algorithm. It takes words from initial set and searches for their URIs. Based on DBPedia lookup service it gets URIs and finds the best ones. The results of this search and comparison are presented in the Table 1. Each row is the set of results for other data set, where columns represent different metrics used to determine similarity.

Table 1. Sense disambiguation results.

source set	li	wup	path
Moscow	Moscow	Moscow	Moscow
Warsaw	Warsaw	Warsaw	Warsaw
Washington	Washington D.C.	Washington D.C.	Washington D.C.
Beijing	Beijing	Beijing	Beijing
London	London	London	London
Einstein	Albert Einstein	Albert Einstein	Albert Einstein College of Medicine
Boris Podolsky	Boris Podolsky	Boris Podolsky	Bell's theorem
Isaac Newton	Isaac Newton	Isaac Newton	Isaac Newton Institute
Galileo	Galileo Galilei	Galileo Galilei	Galileo (spacecraft)
Stefan Banach	Stefan Banach	Stefan Banach	Polish Mathematical Society
Methane	Atmospheric methane	Atmospheric methane	Methane
ethane	1,2-Bis (diphenylphosphino)ethane	1,2-Bis (diphenylphosphino)ethane	Ethane
fluoroethane	2-Fluoroethanol	1,1-Dichloro-1-fluoroethane	2-Fluoroethanol
ethanol	Ethanol fuel	Ethanol fuel	Ethanol fuel

Then, the algorithm is applied to the data sets for which we already have determined senses. The senses of those data sets are in the first column, while the elements which are used to expand the seed set are in columns appropriate for the metric used. Tables 2, 3 and 4 are representing the results of the algorithm for Meta Path tree with depth two. Those are the results of shorter paths. What are the result of the longer paths can be seen in Tables 5, 6 and 7.

6.2   Discussion

As we can see in the sense disambiguation (Table 1), we mostly got as results the same words. The first data set with is intended as the data set of cities is probably the easiest, as all the measures gave the results same as the cities intended in the seed set. As cities have many similar properties, it was easy for any of the metrics to give proper results.

The more interesting results are in the two other data sets. In the one with scientists "li" and "wup" measures give the same results which are the scientists themselves, but "path" gives element's connected to science, such as theorems and institutes. We can see that if we use too simple metric and very specific data, such as people of specific occupation, we can end up with the collection of elements which are connected to them and have some closer relations in this simple metric.

The last one is also quite interesting, as the closest results are the ones given by "path" metric. In the context of previous result we would assume that for entities such

Table 2. ESE results for first set with tree depth two.

source set		
	li	Lakeshore-Ontario
		Sebastopol-Cali-fornia
		French-River-Ontario
		Amherstburg
		Smithers-British-Columbia
		Kingsville-Ontario
		Red-Lake-Ontario
		Fort-Saskatchewan
		Fairview-Alberta
		Tianjin
Moscow	wup	Lillooet
Warsaw		Victoria-British Columbia
Washington		Runnymede-Toronto
Beijing		CityPlace-Toronto
London		Cuyo-Palawan
		New-Toronto
		Fort St. John-British-Columbia
		Fort Vermilion
		Haldimand County
		San Francisco-Cebu
	path	Auburn-California
		Detroit
		Taytay-Palawan
		San Rafael-California
		Purvis-Mississippi
		Mullingar
		San Luis Potosí
		Zacatecas
		Guanajuato
		Martinez-California

specific as chemical substances the more complex "li" and "wup" metrics would be better. Analysing the senses given by those measures we can see that the URIs are even more specific than the chemical substances, those entities are either the substances in some specific conditions, such as atmospheric methane, or some other substances which have some connection to the substances intended.

Summarising the sense disambiguation results we can observe that simpler metric such as path is better at finding more general ideas and classes, but in case of very specific entities it can generalise too much.

Tables 2, 3, 4, 5, 6 and 7 present the results of the whole Entity Set expansion algorithm. In the first one, we can see that for the first data set the results of all the tree

Table 3. ESE results for second set with tree depth two.

source set		
	li	Killer Kowalski
		Antoni Paweł Sułkowski
		Stefan Frankowski
		Georgios Papadopoulos
		Bolko von Richthofen
		Lucius Curtis
		Jerzy Andrzejewski
		St. John Richardson Liddell
		Luis Merlo de la Fuente
		August Thiele
source set	wup	Ryckman Park
Einstein		Le Plessis-Hébert
Boris Podolsky		Mr Joe B. Carvalho
Isaac Newton		Thuit-Hébert
Galileo		Sobieski (vodka)
Stefan Banach		Saint-Guiraud
		Pont-Hébert
		Saint-Martin-le-Hébert
		Galani
		Xanthi
		Dalzell House
	path	Minkowski inequality
		Gagliardo– Nirenberg interpolation inequality
		Clarkson's inequalities
		Cauchy–Schwarz inequality
		Cotlar–Stein lemma
		Fatou's lemma
		Interpolation inequality
		Ladyzhenskaya's inequality
		Leggett–Garg inequality
		Hanner's inequalities

depths and similarity metrics are similar. Even more, for both lengths of the path the resulting sets are the same. From that we can infere that in the path there was already some property traversed both in normal and reverse way. Furthermore, the first data set for all similarity measures gives also other cities. The seed set had only capital cities, but in the expanded set we got just normal cities. Either way the algorithm was able to catch similar entities.

The second set consists of scientists. Already on the sense disambiguation we got quite large difference between "path" measure and the others, so that is no surprise that

Table 4. ESE results for third set with tree depth two.

source set		
Methane ethane fluoroethane ethanol	li	Iodobenzene dichloride (Z)-Stilbene MPTP Phenylpiracetam DIOP Troparil Hippuric acid Phenyllithium Benzal chloride Phenylsulfinic acid
	wup	Tetraphenylporphyrin Phenylsulfinic acid Peroxybenzoic acid Vesamicol Iodobenzene dichloride Trans-2-Phenyl-1-cyclohexanol Benzal chloride Clotrimazole Phanephos Nirvanol
	path	Fuel surrogate Fuel factor Starting fluid Dimethyl ether Coal Alternative fuel Natural gasoline Charcoal lighter fluid Ultra-low-sulfur diesel P-series fuels

there are big differences in the final results. For "path" measure in both depths of the tree we got similar mixture of scientific institutions and scientific formulas. As for "li" similarity with depth of two we got people, most of whom are not scientists, but people from roughly nineteen and twenty century and large part of them are connected to some form of military, which is not exactly close to our firstly intended set of scientists. But as we proceed to tree depth three we can see drastic shift. Now nearly every person added to the set has higher university education and most of them are from nineteen and twenty century. The last metric, "wup" for the tree depth of two is completely of the mark. It gave pleces, alcohol and some other data which is very loosly related. For

Table 5. ESE results for first set with tree depth three.

source set		
	li	Tianjin
		Sebastopol-California
		Fort Saskatchewan
		Fairview-Alberta
		Smithers-British-Columbia
		Amherstburg
		Lakeshore-Ontario
		Red Lake-Ontario
		French River-Ontario
		Kingsville-Ontario
source set	wup	CityPlace-Toronto
Moscow		Lillooet
Warsaw		San Francisco-Cebu
Washington		New Toronto
Beijing		Haldimand-County
London		Cuyo-Palawan
		Runnymede-Toronto
		Fort Vermilion
		Fort St. John-British Columbia
		Victoria-British Columbia
	path	San Luis Potosí
		Purvis-Mississippi
		Detroit
		Taytay-Palawan
		Guanajuato
		Zacatecas
		Mullingar
		San Rafael-California
		Martinez-California
		Auburn-California

the same metric if we use tree depth three we got better results consisting of more people, but there are still elements such as murder cases.

The last most specific data set consisted of chemical substances. From the results using "li" and "wup" metrics we got also chemical substances, interestingly for "li" we got some degradation as for path of length three resulted only in one element added. On the other hand "path" metric gave us not only chemical substances, but also elements connected to fuel industry, which is also good category, as most of elements in the seed set can be used as fuel.

Table 6. ESE results for second set with tree depth three.

source set		
	li	Bonaventura Cerretti
		Murder of Suzanne Jovin
		Elihan Tore
		Ugo Cerletti
		Mariano Rampolla
		Pio Laghi
		Giovanni Tacci Porcelli
		Francesco Ragonesi
		Enrico Gasparri
		Paolo Giobbe
Einstein	wup	Cardinal de Bouillon
Boris Podolsky		Death of Diane Whipple
Isaac Newton		Murder of Suzanne Jovin
Galileo		Isador Coriat
Stefan Banach		Charlotte Canda
		Kermit E. Krantz
		Luigi Oreglia di Santo Stefano
		Domenico Jacobini
		Camillo di Pietro
		John Jellicoe
		1st Earl Jellicoe
	path	Brighton Secondary College
		Antioch High School
		Popoviciu's inequality
		Hermite–Hadamard inequality
		Fatou's lemma
		Rochester High School (Michigan)
		Albert Einstein College of Medicine
		New York Law School
		Queensborough Community College
		Stella Maris College (Montevideo)

All the paths which we used are in the Tables 8 and 9. We can see that for example the data in the Table 2 are the results of Path (http://dbpedia.org/property/leaderTitle (normal), http://purl.org/dc/terms/subject (normal)) where both properties are traversed in their direction. Additionally as this path did not connect the elements of seed set we had to go back through those properties, which resulted in longer path. The result of "li" measure for the data about scientists are archived by traversing the path (http://dbpedia.org/ontology/wikiPageDisambiguates (reverse), http://dbpedia.org/onto

Table 7. ESE results for third set with tree depth three.

	li	Phenyl-2-nitropropene
		Oxime
		Methanation
		Oxidative coupling of methane
		DOTA-TATE
	wup	Deferiprone
		Dimercaprol
		2,3-Dimercapto-1-propanesulfonic acid
source set		Deferasirox
Methane		Dimercaptosuccinic acid
ethane		Isobutane
fluoroethane		Dimethyl ether
ethanol		Chloralose
		1,3,3,3-Tetrafluoropropene
		Coal
	path	Propellant
		Bioconversion of biomass to mixed alcohol fuels
		Oil shale gas
		Blau gas
		Kim reformer
		Valinol

Table 8. Paths used in Meta Path algorithm for depth 2.

source set	li	wup	path
Moscow Warsaw Washington Beijing London	(normal, http://dbpedia.org/property/leaderTitle) (normal, http://purl.org/dc/terms/subject)	(normal, http://dbpedia.org/property/leaderTitle) (normal, http://purl.org/dc/terms/subject)	(normal, http://dbpedia.org/property/leaderTitle), (normal, http://purl.org/dc/terms/subject)
Einstein Boris Podolsky Isaac Newton Galileo Stefan Banach	(reverse, http://dbpedia.org/ontology/wikiPage Disambiguates), (normal, http://purl.org/dc/terms/subject)	(reverse, http://dbpedia.org/ontology/wikiPage Disambiguates), (normal, http://purl.org/dc/terms/subject)	(normal, http://purl.org/dc/terms/subject), (reverse, http://www.w3.org/2004/02/skos/core# related)
Methane ethane fluoroethane ethanol	(normal, http://purl.org/dc/terms/subject), (normal, http://www.w3.org/2004/02/skos/core# related)	(normal, http://purl.org/dc/terms/subject), (normal, http://www.w3.org/2004/02/skos/core# related)	(normal, http://purl.org/dc/terms/subject), (reverse, http://www.w3.org/2004/02/skos/core# related)

Table 9. Paths used in Meta Path algorithm for depth 3.

source set	li	wup	path
Moscow Warsaw Washington Beijing London	(normal, http://dbpedia. org/property/leaderTitle), (normal, http://purl.org/ dc/terms/subject), (reverse, http://purl.org/ dc/terms/subject)	(normal, http://dbpedia. org/property/leaderTitle), (normal, http://purl.org/ dc/terms/subject), (reverse, http://purl.org/ dc/terms/subject)	(normal, http://dbpedia. org/property/leaderTitle), (normal, http://purl.org/ dc/terms/subject), (reverse, http://purl.org/ dc/terms/subject)
Einstein Boris Podolsky Isaac Newton Galileo Stefan Banach	(reverse, http://dbpedia. org/ontology/wikiPage Disambiguates), (normal, http://dbpedia. org/ontology/wikiPage Disambiguates), (normal, http://dbpedia. org/ontology/deathPlace)	(reverse, http://dbpedia. org/ontology/wikiPage Disambiguates), (normal, http://dbpedia. org/ontology/wikiPage Disambiguates), (normal, http://dbpedia. org/ontology/deathPlace)	(normal, http://purl.org/ dc/terms/subject), (reverse, http://purl.org/ dc/terms/subject), (normal, http://www.w3. org/2002/07/owl# differentFrom)
Methane ethane fluoroethane ethanol	(normal, http://purl.org/ dc/terms/subject), (reverse, http://purl.org/ dc/terms/subject), (reverse, http://dbpedia. org/property/caption)	(normal, http://purl.org/ dc/terms/subject), (reverse, http://purl.org/ dc/terms/subject)	(normal, http://purl.org/ dc/terms/subject), (reverse, http://purl.org/ dc/terms/subject)

logy/wikiPageDisambiguates (normal), http://dbpedia.org/ontology/deathPlace (normal) where first instance of `wikiPageDisambiguates` is traversed in reverse direction, second in normal and `deathPlace` is traversed also normally. Then, we return again through those properties and this gives us the final set from which we choose most similar entities. As we can see there is a possibility to explain step by step how we got the data. From those paths alone we can see also some further observations. For example, for the data set with chemical substances the paths for max tree depth equal 3 are shorter than three. From this, we can see that the Meta Path must have found the path linking entities from the seed set, as this is the stop condition for this algorithm.

The algorithm works on the large data set represented as a graph. This representation and the number of connection in such a large graph as DBpedia creates problems of resource consumption. In some cases we had even thousands of entities to process. Such large data increases the duration of the algorithm. Though large amount of data is processed the main issue which increased duration was not the offline resources such as processor or RAM, but the time needed to send queries to the online SPARQL endpoint, as for each element we had to create, send and process the query. In the data presented as the examples the time of the algorithm ranged from two hours forty minutes for the data set with cities in all of the instances, thirty minutes for chemical substances, in some cases even less than ten, to seven hours for scientists data set with tree depth of two and nine hours for the tree depth of three.

7 Summary

Capturing the essence of semantic similarity of words or concepts, in order to quantify and measure it, has been an inspiring challenge for the last decades. From the plethora of methods, it is not always clear which one to choose for a particular problem at hand. In this paper, we have reviewed various semantic similarity methods and to illustrate them in a practical context, we presented the Entity Set Expansion problem.

We proposed an algorithm for solving Entity Set Expansion problem using selected methods and tools. To do this, we decomposed the problem into three separate sub-problems. These sub-problems are then solved by implementing combination of existing solutions, as well as some adaptations, such as expanding the Meta Path algorithm by adding part which will return to the first class in case of not finding the path.

The problem was solved on the large data set - DBPedia, which forced some changes to the original Meta Path algorithm. From all the elements, we created a new method which can be parametrized by the metrics and the depth of the Meta Path tree. Different measurements are also more or less effective depending on the input data, which we could observe especially in data sets with chemical substances and people of science, where different measurements could make great difference.

The proposed algorithm and implementation are valid solution for the ESE problem. Depending on the parameters we are able to get new entities belonging to the same classes as the elements of the seed set, which is the goal of the ESE problem. With more computational power and by switching from external database accessed by sparql endpoint we could probably speed up the process and be able to efficiently use deeper trees, which will further improve results of the algorithm.

There are multiple ways in which we can develop and use the elements of this work. First of all, in the implementation we traversed nearly all of the properties existing in DBPedia. We could ascertain which of them are not viable to use in this algorithm, especially we could ignore those which are too common in DBPedia and could be found in most of the entities, because those properties usually do not add much, as they are generalising data. Second possible extension is to use other methods of solving each of the steps. As many possible solutions can be used interchangeably, we could check if other methods would give better results. While the sense disambiguation works in most cases pretty well, finding candidate entities have some problems, especially we could see that in cases of high difference between results with tree depth two and three, which showed that the final results could be improved by improving the candidate entities set.

References

1. Adrian, W.T., Skoczeń, S., Majkut, S., Kluza, K., Ligęza, A.: Tracing the evolution of approaches to semantic similarity analysis. In: Aveiro, D., Dietz, J.L.G., Filipe, J. (eds.) Proceedings of the 12th International Joint Conference on Knowledge Discovery, Knowledge Engineering and Knowledge Management, IC3K 2020, Volume 2: KEOD, 2–4 November 2020, pp. 157–164. SCITEPRESS (2020). https://doi.org/10.5220/0010108401570164. https://doi.org/10.5220/0010108401570164
2. Adrian, W.T., Manna, M.: Navigating online semantic resources for entity set expansion. In: Calimeri, F., Hamlen, K., Leone, N. (eds.) PADL 2018. LNCS, vol. 10702, pp. 170–185. Springer, Cham (2018). https://doi.org/10.1007/978-3-319-73305-0_12

3. Attneave, F.: Dimensions of similarity. Am. J. Psychol. **63**(4), 516–556 (1950)
4. Baader, F., Sertkaya, B., Turhan, A.Y.: Computing the least common subsumer wrt a background terminology. J. Appl. Log. **5**(3), 392–420 (2007)
5. Chen, J., Hu, P., Jimenez-Ruiz, E., Holter, O.M., Antonyrajah, D., Horrocks, I.: Owl2vec*: embedding of owl ontologies. Mach. Learn. **110**(7), 1813–1845 (2021). https://doi.org/10.1007/s10994-021-05997-6
6. Gabrilovich, E., Markovitch, S.: Computing semantic relatedness using Wikipedia-based explicit semantic analysis. In: IJcAI, vol. 6 (2007)
7. Gligorov, R., Kate, W., Aleksovski, Z., Harmelen, F.: Using google distance to weight approximate ontology matches, pp. 767–776 (2007). https://doi.org/10.1145/1242572.1242676
8. Grover, A., Leskovec, J.: node2vec: scalable feature learning for networks. In: Proceedings of the 22nd ACM SIGKDD International Conference on Knowledge Discovery and Data Mining, pp. 855–864 (2016)
9. Jiang, J.J., Conrath, D.W.: Semantic similarity based on corpus statistics and lexical taxonomy. arXiv preprint cmp-lg/9709008 (1997)
10. Leacock, C., Chodorow, M.: Combining local context and wordnet similarity for word sense identification. WordNet Electron. Lexical Database **49**(2), 265–283 (1998)
11. Lehmann, J., et al.: Dbpedia - a large-scale, multilingual knowledge base extracted from Wikipedia. Semantic Web **6**(2), 167–195 (2015). http://dblp.uni-trier.de/db/journals/semweb/semweb6.html#LehmannIJJKMHMK15
12. Li, Y., Bandar, Z.A., McLean, D.: An approach for measuring semantic similarity between words using multiple information sources. IEEE Trans. Knowl. Data Eng. **15**(4), 871–882 (2003)
13. Lin, D., et al.: An information-theoretic definition of similarity. In: ICML, vol. 98, pp. 296–304 (1998)
14. Mikolov, T., Chen, K., Corrado, G., Dean, J.: Efficient estimation of word representations in vector space. arXiv preprint arXiv:1301.3781 (2013)
15. Miller, G.A.: Wordnet: a lexical database for English. Commun. ACM **38**(11), 39–41 (1995)
16. Rada, R., Mili, H., Bicknell, E., Blettner, M.: Development and application of a metric on semantic nets. IEEE Trans. Syst. Man Cybern. **19**(1), 17–30 (1989)
17. Resnik, P.: Using information content to evaluate semantic similarity in a taxonomy. CoRR abs/cmp-lg/9511007 (1995). http://arxiv.org/abs/cmp-lg/9511007
18. Ristoski, P., Paulheim, H.: RDF2Vec: RDF graph embeddings for data mining. In: Groth, P., et al. (eds.) ISWC 2016. LNCS, vol. 9981, pp. 498–514. Springer, Cham (2016). https://doi.org/10.1007/978-3-319-46523-4_30
19. Seco, N., Veale, T., Hayes, J.: An intrinsic information content metric for semantic similarity in wordnet. In: ECAI, vol. 16, p. 1089 (2004)
20. Wu, Z., Palmer, M.: Proceedings of the 32nd annual meeting on association for computational linguistics. In: Las Cruces New Mexico. 981744: Association for Computational Linguistics Las Cruces (1994)
21. Zhang, X., Chen, Y., Chen, J., Du, X., Wang, K., Wen, J.R.: Entity set expansion via knowledge graphs. In: Proceedings of the 40th International ACM SIGIR Conference on Research and Development in Information Retrieval, pp. 1101–1104 (2017)
22. Zheng, Y., Shi, C., Cao, X., Li, X., Wu, B.: A meta path based method for entity set expansion in knowledge graph. IEEE Trans. Big Data **8**(3), 616–629 (2018). https://doi.org/10.1109/TBDATA.2018.2805366
23. Zhu, G., Iglesias, C.: Computing semantic similarity of concepts in knowledge graphs. IEEE Trans. Knowl. Data Eng. **29**(1), 72–85 (2016). https://doi.org/10.1109/TKDE.2016.2610428

Eliciting Semantic Types of Legal Norms in Korean Legislation with Deep Learning

Ho-Pun Lam[1]([⊠]), Thi Thuy Phan[2], Mustafa Hashmi[1,3], Kiet Hoang The[4], Sin Kit Lo[1,5], and Yongsun Choi[6]

[1] Data61, CSIRO, Sydney, Australia
{brian.lam,mustafa.hashmi,kit.lo}@csiro.au
[2] CMC Ciber, Hanoi, Vietnam
[3] La Trobe Law School, La Trobe University, Melbourne, Australia
[4] EM & AI JSC, Da Nang, Vietnam
[5] School of Computer Science and Engineering, UNSW, Sydney, Australia
[6] Inje University, Gimhae, Republic of Korea
yschoi@inje.edu

Abstract. Automating information extraction from legal documents and formalising them into a machine understandable format has long been an integral challenge to legal reasoning. Most approaches in the past consist of highly complex solutions that use annotated syntactic structures and grammar to distil rules. The current research trend is to utilise state-of-the-art natural language processing (NLP) approaches to automate these tasks, with minimum human interference. In this paper, based on its functional features, we propose a taxonomy of semantic type in korean legislation, such as obligations, rights, permissions, penalties, etc.. Based on this, we performed automatic classification of legal norms with a rule-based classifier using a manually labelled dataset formed by three korean acts, i.e., Insurance Business Act, Banking Act and Financial Holding Companies Act, of the Korean legislation ($n = 1237$) and a performance of $F_1 = 0.97$ was reached. In contrast, several supervised machine learning based classifiers were implemented and a performance of F-measure = 0.99 was achieved.

Keywords: Natural language processing · Korean legislation · Legal taxonomy · Legal norms classification · Semantic types

1 Introduction

The legislation that we have nowadays is not simply a corpus of legal documents. It contains lots of information that needs to be interpreted, explained, and processed in order to determine whether an organisation complies with legislative requirements. However, working with legal documents can be both costly, time-consuming and error-prone, as it requires domain experts to understand what to be expected from the legislations with respect to its interpretation and intents.

Over the years, much research has been focused on representing information captured inside legal documents into machine understandable formalisms so that we can

A. Fred et al. (Eds.): IC3K 2020, CCIS 1608, pp. 70–93, 2022.
https://doi.org/10.1007/978-3-031-14602-2_4

reason on and make sense of it using a computer, and various promising results have been obtained [4,33]. Recently, the research focus has been shifted to the task of applying natural language processing (NLP) techniques to generate legal norms from legal documents with some success [9,10,64,73]. However, most of these approaches consist of highly complex solutions that utilise annotated syntactic structures and grammar to automatically distil rules, which hinder the developments in this area.

Nevertheless, at the core of these technologies is an ontology that defines the underlying *principles*, *concepts*, *assumptions*, and *legal effects* of terms, i.e., the taxonomy that are commonly used in the legal domain. It classifies the terms into different categories and defines their interrelations, such as whether a term is *subsumed*, *equivalent*, or in *conflict* with another term. It is a foundation stone that can facilitate the development of automated *legal analysis* and automatic *machine translation*.

The Language for Legal Discourse (LLD [40]) is a first attempt to define legal knowledge in the context of legal reasoning. Since then, many different projects, such as LYNX[1], SPIRIT[2], MARCELL[3], have dedicated efforts for creating legal knowledge graphs and multilingual legal ontologies to automate the linking and translation from heterogeneous legal sources, such as laws, decrees, regulations, which helps enterprises to remove their legal and language barriers in trade and to localise their products and services.

However, as can be seen above, the research efforts in this area target mostly Indo-European languages. In South Korea, works related to this area is still in its incubation stage. Regulation technologies (RegTech) and their related products have started gaining attention from the government only until 2018[4]. Several word embedding representations [39,67] and NLP tools in Korean language have been proposed [24,27,28], but not much useful and efficient systems have been reported.

Extracting normative information from legal documents is a process that is far from being trivial and intuitive. Legal documents are typically so complex that even human lawyers are having difficulties in understanding and applying them [71]. Thus, works on the automated transformation of Korean legislations into a machine understandable formalism are in high demand.

The primary challenge to the classification of legal norms lies in the underlying legal theory with empirical observations, which is under-represented in korean legal sciences. In this regard, the purpose of this paper is to fill the gap in this area by creating a taxonomy of semantic types that can be applied to the statutory text of korean legislation, which is the foundation of many legal analysis and interpretation tasks.

In this paper, we extend our previous publication [52] by investigating the application of several deep learning architectures to classify the korean legislation and compare their performance with a rule-based classifier.

The rest of this paper is organised as follows. An informal introduction and problems related to the Korean language is described in Sect. 2. Sections 3 and 4 present

---

[1] LYNX: http://lynx-project.eu/.

[2] SPIRIT: https://www.spirit-tools.com/.

[3] MARCELL: http://marcell-project.eu/.

[4] Fintech In South Korea: Regulators Step In To Boost Innovation: https://fintechnews.hk/4823/fintechkorea/fintech-south-korea-fintech-regulators-step-boost-innovation/.

the taxonomy of semantic types that we have developed on korean legislation and the evaluation results of the taxonomy based on different types of classifier, respectively. Section 5 presents the related works, followed by conclusions and pointers to future research.

2 Background

Technically, a taxonomy typically refers to a hierarchical arrangement of terminologies that describes a particular branch of science or field of knowledge [41]. A legal taxonomy, in addition to this, reflects also the culture and history of a given legal system. As commented by Mattei [37], it is the product of interactions of the legal tradition and that of the new sensibilities. It provides a means where people working in the legal sector can communicate with each other, to discuss problems and exchange ideas of mutual concern among themselves.

However, creating a legal taxonomy that accurately reflects the legislations and to avoid misattribution errors is not an easy task. It requires the terms selected and arranged to be mutually exclusive, thus a unique ordered structure for different terms can be created [41].

2.1 Problems with Korean Language

There are a few phenomena that make NLP in Korean language a challenging task to accomplish.

Firstly, Korean has traditionally posed challenges for word segmentation and morphological analysis [39]. This is because Korean is a phonetic language with a subjectobject-verb (SOV) syntax while permitting a high degree of freedom in word order [25]. In fact, Korean is a left-branching language such that the head that determines the correct phrasal category comes at the end of a phrase [45]. For a noun phrase that is compatible with a higher phrase type, it could be the left-branching daughter of a higher phrase, noun phrase, or verb phrase, which imposes substantial demand for the model being developed [45].

Secondly, it also allows multiple concepts to be synthesised into a single *eojeol*, i.e., a Korean spacing unit similar to a word in English. As a result, depending on the context, the same *eojeol* can be analysed into different morpheme which yields different part of speech (POS) tags of morpheme combinations [65].

Thirdly, Korean is an agglutinative language such that words may contain different morphemes to determine their meanings. For example, the word "*mountain*" in English can only be derived from itself; whereas in Korean, "산을" (san-eul (mount)), "산은" (san-eun (saneun)), "산도" (san-do (acidity)), "산이" (san-yi (sanyi)), "산이나" (san-ina (sanna)), etc., can all be derived from the root "산" san (mountain) [34]. To make things even more complex, there are also some special rules in Korean language that can apply across character boundaries, implying that morphological transformation may also occur among adjacent graphemes.

Over the years, several lexical databases have been developed. For instance, Kor-Lex [75] was developed by translating and mapping the English terms into Korean.

Following the idea of lexical concept network (LCN)—a lexical database that provides various information of a word in terms of its relation to other lexical units, Choi *et al.* [7] developed ETRI LCN for the Korean language, but for verbs and nouns only. Later, the same group of researchers also established (and maintained) another LCN called UWordMap [46], which consists of 514,314 words, including nouns, adjectives, and adverbs, and is currently the largest lexical database of its kind. However, all these works are for general purposes only, they do not cater to the needs of the legal domain that requires a more rigid understanding of the legal text.

2.2 Semantic Types

Generally, legal rules govern the behavior of citizens, prescribing the code of actions that citizens must follow. These codes provide applicability conditions, capturing various intuitions in different situations and prescribe on how to act. Several research efforts have been reported providing classifications of legal rules, defining the semantic meanings to facilitate properly interpreting of and reasoning about the legal rules, For instance, von Wright [72] classifies legal rules as (i) *determinative rules* (a.k.a. *constitutive rules*) which define the concepts or activities that cannot exist without legal rules; (ii) *technical rule* that prescribe what needs to be done in order to attain some legal effects, and (iii) *prescriptive rules* that prescribe the actions and making obligatory, prohibited, or permitted regulating thus the behavior of the subject.

Gordon *et al.* [15] give an extended catalog of requirements for a formal language necessary for reasoning on legal rules which includes jurisdiction [44], authority, rules validity [36], deonticity and defeasibility of rules, normative effects [56], contra-position [54], conflicting [57] and exclusionary rules [54,57], and temporal properties.

Hilty *et al.* [21] provides a charaterisation of legal norms along temporal bounds and invariants properties capturing the application of norms in the time space; whereas Hashmi *et al.* [20] classify deontic effects of legal norms on the temporal validity aspects. The former provides the mapping of the norms from requirements to the enforcement while the latter studies when a norm enters into force, terminated after a deadline, what constitutes the violations of a legal norm and under what circumstances a violated norm can be compensated. Besides, they also study the persistent effects of legal norms such that even after being violated, a norm may still remain valid until it is performed or terminated.

More recently, Hashmi *et al.* [19] discuss a taxonomy of legal terms and concepts aiming at creating a legal ontology and a socio-legal graph for sharing the Australian legal knowledge on the web. Their taxonomy is based on the notion of legal quadrant for the rule of law [3], which includes themes such as binding power, social dialog, privacy, trust, security, sanctions, etc., and *sources* for legal validity [60] emerging from regulatory dimensions, such as hard law, soft law, policies, and ethics covering a range of requirements from various social, political and legal aspects.

3 The Legal Taxonomy

Failure to properly understand the real meanings of a legal term may result in the misunderstanding of legislation provisions. In practice, the way that we interpret legislations may also affect the outcome of a case.

Technically, legislation can be characterised as a combination of a set of (normative) provisions and the totality of norms that follow from executing that finite set of provisions. In the past, legislations were interpreted mainly based on the plain meanings of the text as derived from the ordinary definitions of an individual word and the overall structure of the statement [29]. Contemporary approaches to legislation interpretations focus on determining the original intent of the legislation, i.e., the goals that the legislation intended to achieve. Interpretations will be made in the context of the legislation as a whole where the interpretation of a specific provision should be determined consistently with respect to other provisions. Hence, to meet the needs of both the legal practitioners and design requirements of the automated machine translation and interpretations process, having a clear definition of terminologies is crucial to avoid any ambiguity and eliminate potential misinterpretations in the legislations.

3.1 The Basic Concepts

In this subsection, we present a basic set of definitions that will be used throughout the entire discussion of the taxonomy of the Korean legislation. These concepts could optionally appear in some semantic types but mandatory to the others.

Applicability Condition. The applicability conditions (a.k.a. preconditions) specify when and under what circumstances a norm becomes applicable (or activated). In Korean language, this can be detected as a phrase or clause that ends with the following words.

- 면 (where), except the case (없으면) (unless, if not): <situation>
- 경우, 경우에는, 경우에도 (where/in case): <situation>
- 할 때 (in dealing with/when) except the case of 때부터 (from the time) and 때까지 (by the time): <situation>
- 자는, 자가 (a person who...): <a qualification for individual, or legal entities>.

Legal Effects. Legal effects are the normative effects that follow from applying a norm, such as *obligation*, *permission*, *prohibition*, and also other articulated effects introduced for the law (see [56,58] for details). While applicability conditions can be optional, legal effects are mandatory components of every legal norm.

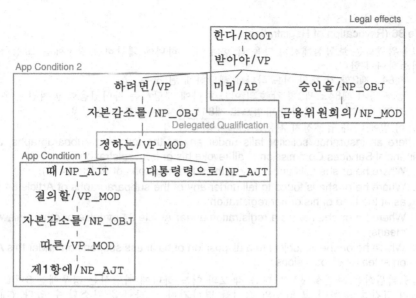

Fig. 1. Parse tree of the statement: "제1항에 따른 자본감소를 결의할 때 대통령령으로 정하는 자본감소를 하려면 미리 금융위원회의 승인을 받아야 한다" (adopted from [52]).

Figure 1 shows the parse tree of the statement[5,6]: "제1항에 따른 자본감소를 결의할 때 대통령령으로 정하는 자본감소를 하려면 미리 금융위원회의 승인을 받아야 한다 " which means "Where a stock company intends to reduce its capital (정하는 자본감소를), as prescribed by Presidential Decree (대통령령으로), in resolving the reduction of its capital under paragraph (1) (제1항에 따른 자본감소를), it shall obtain approval (승인을 받아야 한다) from the Financial Services Commission (금융위원회의) in advance (미리).". It illustrates how the applicability conditions and the legal effects that it inferred (in this case, an *obligation* to obtain an approval beforehand) are written in Korean language as well as how applicability conditions can be nested together.

From the parse tree, it can also be observed that, as Korean is a left-branching language, the legal effects typically appear as the *rightmost* component of the tree, which is the feature that we utilised in the NLP classifiers that we implemented. We leave the details to Sect. 4 and focus here on the semantics of Korean language.

Cross-Referencing. Similar to other jurisdictions, legislation in Korean is divided into parts that promotes clarity for presentation, structure and expression. As described

---

[5] This statement is extracted from the 2nd paragraph of Article 18 in Insurance Business Act. The English translation available from: https://elaw.klri.re.kr/kor_service/lawView.do?hseq=43318&lang=ENG.

[6] The parse tree in Fig. 1 was generated using syntaxnet tree generator [38], i.e., a Korean language parse tree generator that combine komoran3 [63] with google syntaxnet dependency parser [50], available at: http://andrewmatteson.name/psg_tree.htm (last accessed: 7 Oct 2021).

제86조 (등록의 취소 등)
Article 86 (Revocation of Registration)

① 금융위원회는 보험설계사가 다음 각 호의 어느 하나에 해당하는 경우에는 그 등록을
취소하여야 한다.
1. 제84조제2항 각 호의 어느 하나에 해당하게 된 경우
2. 등록 당시 제84조제2항 각 호의 어느 하나에 해당하는 자이었음이 밝혀진 경우
3. 거짓이나 그 밖의 부정한 방법으로 제84조에 따른 등록을 한 경우
4. 이 법에 따라 업무정지 처분을 2회 이상 받은 경우

Where an insurance solicitor falls under any of the following subparagraphs, the
Financial Services Commission shall revoke his or her registration:
1. Where he or she falls under any of the subparagraphs of Article 84 (2);
2. Where he or she is found to fall under any of the subparagraphs of Article 84 (2)
   as at the time of his or her registration;
3. Where he or she makes a registration under Article 84 by false or other unlawful
   means;
4. Where he or she is subject to a disposition of business suspension under this Act
   on at least two occasions.

② 금융위원회는 보험설계사가 다음 각 호의 어느 하나에 해당하는 경우에는 6개월 이
내의 기간을 정하여 그 업무의 정지를 명하거나 그 등록을 취소할 수 있다. 〈개정
2014.1.14〉.
1. 모집에 관한 이 법의 규정을 위반한 경우
2. 보험계약자, 피보험자 또는 보험금을 취득할 자로서 제102조의2를 위반한 경우
3. 제102조의3을 위반한 경우

Where an insurance solicitor falls under any of the following subparagraphs, the
Financial Services Commission may order him or her to suspend his or her work for
the specified period of up to six months, or revoke his or her registration: 〈Amended
by Act No. 12262, Jan. 14, 2014〉
1. Where he or she violates the provisions of this Act governing insurance
   solicitation;
2. Where he or she, as an insurance policyholder, an insured person or a person
   that is to receive insurance money, violates Article 102-2;
3. Where he or she violates Article 102-3;

⋮

[전문개정 2010.7.23]
[This Article Wholly Amended by Act No. 10394, Jul. 23, 2010]

Fig. 2. Insurance Business Act: Article 86 (Revocation of Registration) (adopted from [52], original legal text available at: http://www.law.go.kr/법령/보험업법 , English translation available at:
https://elaw.klri.re.kr/kor_service/lawView.do?hseq=43318&lang=ENG.

in [74], drafting legislation like this allows legal drafters to demonstrate the intuition
behind the legislation, maintain the coherence of the legislative text, and can stress the
interrelation between different provisions.

Figure 2 illustrates a typical structure of Korean legislation, which is compara-
tively less complex than legislations of other jurisdictions. In general, a legislation may
consist of different chapters, which can then be further divided into different articles,
(sub)paragraphs, items and points. Table 1 shows the section names, and useful terms
that are commonly used in korean legislation, and some cross-referencing examples.

Table 1. Section names, useful terms and cross-referencing examples (adopted from [52]).

		(a) Section names and useful terms †	(b) cross-referencing Examples ‡	
	Korean	English	Example	Example (in English)
Section label	편	Part	이 장	This Chapter
	장	Chapter	제1조	Article 1
	조	Article	제32조제2항	Article 32 (2)
	항	Paragraph	제2조제8호나목	Article 2 (8) point 2
	목	Item / Point	제1항과 제2항	Paragraph 1 and Paragraph 2
Useful term	제	in the current legislation or section	제410조부터 제412조까지	From Article 420 to Article 412
	부터	starts from	제193조、제252조 및 제531조제2항	Article 193, Article 252 and Article 532 (2)
	까지	ends with		
	과, 및	and		

† Note that the word "제" can have multiple meanings in the Korean language. When used in cross-referencing, it means to "in the current legislation".

‡ Instead of writing "*paragraph #*", in some cases, for simplicity, the paragraph number will be put inside curly brackets next to the article number in cross-referencing.

It should be noted that, when referring to other legislations, the name of the referred legislations should be enclosed in square brackets. For instance, "「상법」" should be used when referring to the "Commercial Act"[7]; while "「상법」제255조제2항" should be used when referring to "Article 255 (2) of the Commercial Act".

3.2 Semantic Types in Korean Legislations

When determining the semantic type of a legal statement, it is the legal effects part that plays a pivotal role. It specifies the normative effects and the order of validity a legal statement has. Typically, such provisions have been made transparent by the use of *modal verbs* [22] that appear at the end of the statements [51]. Its usage is similar to the words *shall* and *must* in English legislations which show the natural dispose of a connection to the normative value contained in the provisions, as well as the normative functions of these provisions.

Following a functional classification approach, we have analysed the modal verbs that have been used in the legal statements and identified *eleven* different categories, i.e., semantic types, that appear in Korean legislation: *Definitional provision, Application provision, Deeming provision, Continuation clause, Delegation provision, Penalty provision*, and different types of *Deontic provisions*, such as *Obligation, Liability, Rights, Permission*, and *Prohibition*. Table 2 shows examples of different types of statements extracted from the Insurance Business Act (IBA). In what follows, we are going to elicit on each of these categories.

Definitional Provision. Definitional provisions define commonly used concepts or relevant terms that appear in (and in some cases, specific to) the legislation.

In korean legislation, it uses "X 란/이란...Y 을/를 말한다" to denote the pattern "X means Y", where X is called a *definiendum* which can be a word, a phrase, or a symbol, and is normally enclosed inside double quotes, Y is called a *definien* and is used to describe/define the definiendum X. Note that definitional provisions, in general, do not contain any applicability condition as the terms was defined in a general sense (within the context of the legislation). Unless otherwise specified, it should be used without any restriction.

Application Provision. Application provisions set out situations or timeframes in which the law, or section(s) of law, applies (적용한다 (shall apply), or 에 따른다 (shall be governed by)), applies with some changes (준용한다 (shall apply *mutatis muntandis*)), or does not apply (적용하지/그러하지 아니한다) .

In some cases, an application provision may also be used to specify the statuses (and/or timeframes)) of other legislations.

Deeming Provision. A deeming provision indicates something to be deemed or construed ((으)로 본다) as if something else (through cross-referencing) if the two can be construed as the same thing, or the latter inherits some qualities that the former does not have.

On the contrary, latest research also found that deeming provisions can also be used to indicate something cannot be deemed or construed ((으)로 보지 아니한다) as something else [2]. Hence, it is suggested that deeming provision should always be construed on its own terms under the context concerned and purposes of the legislations.

---

[7] The word "'상법" means "Commercial Act" in Korean language.

Table 2. Examples of semantic types of norms from the Insurance Business Act (the full act is available at: http://www.law.go.kr/법령/보험업법, English translation available at: https://elaw.klri.re.kr/eng_service/lawView.do?hseq=43318&lang=ENG) (adopted from [52]).

Semantic type	Example (Korean)	Example (translation in English)
Definitional provision	"생명보험업"이란 생명보험상품의 취급과 관련하여 발생하는 보험의 인수, 보험료 수수 및 보험금 지급 등을 영업으로 하는 것을 말한다.	The term "life insurance business" means the business of underwriting insurance, receiving premiums, paying insurance proceeds, etc. which arise in selling life insurance products.
Application provision	상호회사의 임사·청약자나 사원에 대한 통지 및 최고(催告)에 관하여는 「상법」 제353조를 준용한다.	Article 353 of the Act on Corporate Governance of Financial Companies shall apply *mutatis mutandis* to mutual companies.
Deeming provision	이 경우 "보험회사"는 "자회사"로 본다.	In such cases, "insurance company" shall be construed as "subsidiary".
Continuation clause	보험계약을 이전하지 아니하게 된 경우에도 또한 같다.	This shall also apply where it decides not to transfer its insurance contracts.
Delegation provision	제1항과 제2항에 따른 출연금의 납부방법 및 절차에 관하여 필요한 사항은 대통령령으로 정한다.	Necessary matters concerning procedures for and methods of paying contributions under paragraphs (1) and (2) shall be prescribed by Presidential Decree.
Penalty provision	제91조제1항에 따른 금융기관보험대리점등 또는 금융기관보험대리점등이 되려는 자가 제83조제2항 또는 제100조를 위반한 경우에는 1억원 이하의 과태료를 부과한다.	Where an insurance agency, etc. of a financial institution prescribed in Article 91 (1) or a person that intends to become an insurance agency, etc. of a financial institution violates Article 83 (2) or 100, he/she or it shall be punished by an administrative fine not exceeding 100 million won.
Deontic provision		
Obligation	보험협회는 정관으로 정하는 바에 따라 다음 각 호의 업무를 한다. …	The insurance association shall perform any of the following affairs, as prescribed by the articles of association: …
Liability	상호회사의 채무에 관한 사원의 책임은 보험료를 한도로 한다.	The liability of the members of every mutual company for the debts of their company shall be limited to their insurance premiums.
Right	보험계약자나 보험금을 취득할 자는 피보험자를 위하여 적립한 금액을 주식회사가 이 법에 따라 금융위원회의 명령에 따라 예탁한 자산에서 다른 채권자보다 우선하여 변제를 받을 권리를 가진다.	A policyholder or a person who is to receive insurance proceeds is entitled to be paid the amount accumulated for the insured in preference to any other creditors from assets deposited by the relevant stock company pursuant to orders issued by the Financial Services Commission under this Act.
Permission	주식회사는 그 조직을 변경하여 상호회사로 할 수 있다.	A stock company may convert its organization into a mutual company.
Prohibition	보험대리점 또는 보험중개사는 자기 또는 자기를 고용하고 있는 자를 보험계약자 또는 피보험자로 하는 보험을 모집하는 것을 주된 목적으로 하지 못한다.	An insurance agency or insurance broker shall not be mainly engaged in soliciting any insurance contract which is to make himself/herself or a person who employs himself/herself as the policyholder or the insured.

Continuation Clause. A continuation clause is a provision that is used to extend or limit the scope of application of a precedent legal statement. It is expected that, unless otherwise specified, the legal effects inferred by the continuation clause should be the same as (또한 같다) , or applies to the same objects (과 같다) , as the original statement.

Delegation Provision. Under normal situations, a person who is vested with a particular statutory power, duty or function may exercise it himself/herself. However, for the sake of convenience in practice, the power, duty or function may be delegated pursuant to an instrument of delegation through a delegation provision and exercise the power in the name of the delegated [68].

A delegation provision is used to state clearly the nature of powers, duties, or functions being delegated, as well as the entitlements, conditions, and restrictions that it may have on the delegate. In Korean legislation, it can be distinguished by the phrases: (으)로/가 정한다 (shall be prescribed by), or 로/가 정하여 고시한다 (shall be determined and announced).

Penalty Provision. The primary function of a penalty provision is to stipulate potential consequences (legal effects) when a breach of legislation, i.e., a violation of a prescribed requirement, or non-performance of an obligation has occurred, and it can be identified with the phrases: 벌금에 처한다, 처벌한다, 부과한다 , or 부과할 수 있다 (shall be punished).

Besides, a penalty provision may also stipulate the conditions under which a government agency may/shall revoke, suspend, or cancel the penalties stipulated by the legislation (취소할 수 있다 (may revoke/suspend/cancel) or 취소하여야 한다 (shall revoke/suspend/cancel)).

Deontic Provision. Deontic concepts of *obligations*, *dispensations* (exception from obligations), *liabilities*, *rights*, *permissions*, and *prohibitions* are important concepts in legalisms and legal reasonings, and are used to *manipulate* or *restrict* the behaviour of an entity.

For one, the use of 야 한다 (shall do) in korean legislation makes it clear that an entity has an obligations (i.e., a duty to comply), or committing herself, to such action. Whilst the provision indicates a specific state a legal entity should be into, the phrase 법인으로 한다 (shall be a juristic person) is used. If the provision, however, requires an entity to carry out some specific actions, then the phrase 책임을 진다 (shall perform tasks) will be used instead.

Liabilities, on the other hand, determine what an entity responsible or answerable for, and is indicated using the terms: 책임을... 못한다 (shall take responsibility), 책임은... 한도로 한다 (may not be released from responsibility), 의무를 지지 아니한다 (the liability shall be limited to), and 권리를/을 가진다 (may not take any responsibility).

Rights dictate the principle of entitlement, or a valid claim, that one may have under some specific conditions and are expressed with the phrases: 권리와 의무는... 승계한다 (is entitled/have the right to), 권리와 의무는... 승계한다 (rights and duties shall be succeeded); while *permissions* refer to a licence to do something, or an act that an entity is authorised to do, which in principle, such actions would have been unlawful[8], and are identified by the terms ㄹ or 을 수 있다 (may do).

---

[8] Notice however that, in the literature, there are some discussions in the legal reasoning domain that explicitly permitting an action makes little sense when such action has not (generally)

From a legal reasoning perspective, permissions and rights are similar in nature as they can both be considered as a dual of obligations, i.e., if an entity has the obligation to perform a task, then she should have the permission or right to carry out such task.[9] The main difference between the two is that the entitlement enjoyed by an entity under rights cannot be infringed or retracted by other person, government, or authorities; whereas the case for permissions may still be subject to other conditions as prescribed in the legislation.

Lastly, *prohibitions* prescribe the states or actions that should *not* be undertaken by a legal entity or a violation will appear. It can be identified by the phrases: 아니 된다 no... shall do, 못한다 (shall be prohibited), and 수 없다 (not permitted).

As a summary to this section, Table 3 presents a summary of semantic types and their corresponding terminologies in Korean legislations.

4   Classification of Legal Norms with Natural Language Processing

Advances in NLP research are now focused on formalising normative information from legal documents so that normative information can be extracted and formalised in a formalism that can be interpreted and reasoned about by machines. However, due to the high-level semantics and abstract nature of natural languages, it presents many challenges and difficulties.

Text classification defines as the automatic assignment of text to one or more predefined classes. Formally, given a set of text and a set of categories, we are going to construct a model that can map the text into one of the category (or, in some cases, multiple categories).

A number of approaches have been proposed in the literature and with certain success. These include the Naïve Bayes classifier, support vector machine (SVM), decision trees, logistic regression and neural networks (NNs). In this section, we explore the use of two approaches, namely: (i) rule-based approach, and (ii) supervised machine learning approach (or deep learning approach), to categorize statements written in Korean language into the semantic types discussed in the previous section.

4.1   Dataset

To evaluate the taxonomy discussed in the previous section, an empirical analysis has been undertaken. The used dataset comprises 1,237 sentences which constitute the statements from three different Korean legislations, namely: Insurance Business Act (IBA), Banking Act (BA), and Financial Holding Companies Act (FHCA).

In the pre-processing phase, the raw text of these legislations was segmented into sentences. As sentences in the Korean language are ended with a *period*, punctuation marks e.g. comma, colons, semi-colons, etc., will be ignored. In the case of enumerations or lists, the same rule is applied. That is, all items in an enumeration or a list will be considered as a single sentence unless one of them ended with a period.

---

been prohibited before. Besides, such permission may limit the effects of an obligation (or a prohibition). As the discussion of this topic is outside the scope of this paper, we refer the interested reader to [18] for details.

[9] Note that the reverse might not be true as an entity having the rights or permission to do an act does not necessarily mean that the entity is obliged to perform the act.

Table 3. Semantic types and their corresponding terminology used in Korean legislations (adopted from [52]).

	Term	Description
Definitional provision		
1.1	을/를 말한다	means
Application provision		
2.1	준용한다	shall apply *mutatis muntandis*
2.2	적용한다	shall apply
2.3	적용하지 그러하지 아니한다	shall / does not apply
2.4	에 따른다	shall be governed by
Deeming provision		
3.1	(으)로 본다	shall be deemed
		shall be construed
3.2	(으)로 보지 아니한다	shall not be deemed
		shall not be construed
Continuation clause		
4.1	또한 같다	the same as
4.2	과 같다	shall also apply
Delegation provision		
5.1	(으)로/가 정한다	shall be prescribed by
5.2	위탁한다	shall be entrusted
Penalty provision		
6.1	벌금에 처한다	shall be punished
	처벌한다	
	과태료를 부과한다	
	벌금형을 과(科)한다	
6.2	벌금을 병과할 수 있다	a fine may be imposed
	병과(倂科)할 수 있다	
6.3	과징금을 부과할 수있다	may impose a penalty surcharge
Deontic provision		
Obligation		
7.1	야 한다	shall do
7.2	책임을 진다	shall take responsibility
Permission		
8.1	ㄹ/을 수 있다	may do
Prohibition		
9.1	아니 된다	No ... shall do
9.2	아니한다	shall not do
9.3	수 없다	No... may do, may not do
9.4	못한다	shall be prohibited
Right		
10.1	권리를/을 가진다	is entitled, have the right
Liability		
11.1	책임은... 한도로 한다	the Liability shall be limited to
11.2	의무를 지지 아니한다	may not take any responsibility for
11.3	책임을 진다	shall take responsibility

In the next step, all sentences were manually classified by the domain experts according to the taxonomy discussed in Sect. 3. Table 4 shows the semantic types distributions in each of the legislations and their total occurrences in the dataset. As can be seen, some types appear regularly, e.g., definitional provisions, application provisions and most types of deontic provisions, whereas some have very low support, e.g., deeming provisions, continuation clauses, rights, and liabilities. Besides, as are common in other legislations, the three types of deontic provisions, namely: obligations (31.69%), permissions (21.34%), and prohibitions (10.75%), together constitute to more than half (63.78%) of the total number of statements found in the three legislations.

4.2 Experiment: Rule-Based Approach

To evaluate the taxonomy of automated legal norms classification, a rule-based classifier has been implemented. In each iteration, a statement from the dataset is selected and passed to the syntax tree generator, *syntaxNet*, mentioned before. The resulting parse tree is then analysed and the semantic type of the statement is determined through applying the regular expression rules generated based on the taxonomy and the sentence patterns identified in [51] to the legal effect component of the tree, which typically appear at the rightmost part of the tree [51].

The results are shown on the right-hand side of Table 4. Thereby, different semantic types are differentiated, and the precision and recall are determined for every type individually. Out of the 1,237 statements tested, 1,190 statements (96.20%) has been correctly classified, with an overall precision and recall rate of 0.99 and 0.96, respectively. As evidenced by these results, the taxonomy presented in the previous section can help in effectively classifying the semantic types of statements in the korean legislation with only limited issues appeared, which is due to the fact that legal statements are often written in boilerplate expressions where a fixed set of terminologies was used.

Those misclassification that were not caused by missing terms were instead caused by either the statements were so complex that the rule are not capable to handle, or the

Table 4. Semantic types distribution of statements and evaluation results with rule-based classifier (adopted from [52]).

Semantic type	IBA	BA	FHCA	Total occurrences	Relative occurrences (%)	Precision	Recall	F_1
Definitional provisions	20	11	10	41	3.31	1.00	1.00	1.00
Application provisions	101	35	47	183	14.79	0.98	0.98	0.98
Deeming provisions	22	5	8	35	2.83	0.95	1.00	0.97
Continuation clauses	6	0	1	7	0.57	1.00	1.00	1.00
Delegation provisions	42	23	22	87	7.03	1.00	0.99	0.99
Penalty provisions	34	27	23	84	6.79	0.99	0.89	0.94
Deontic provisions								
Obligations	192	113	87	392	31.69	0.99	0.93	0.96
Permissions	114	79	71	264	21.34	0.97	0.99	0.98
Prohibitions	59	32	42	133	10.75	1.00	1.00	1.00
Rights	6	0	0	6	0.49	1.00	1.00	1.00
Liabilities	4	0	1	5	0.40	1.00	1.00	1.00
Total	600	325	312	1237	100.00	0.99	0.96	0.97

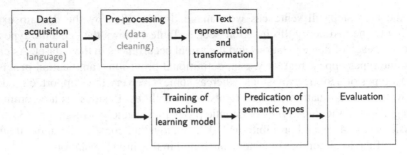

Fig. 3. Process steps for the classification of legal norms.

taxonomy terms have appeared at some places other than the main paragraph, which negatively impacted the performance of the classifier.

4.3 Experiment: Supervised Machine Learning Approach

As an alternative to rule-based approach for classification, we have attempted a deep learning approach, as literature on general text classification, such as [26,30,70], suggests that it is superior to knowledge-based approach.

The KDD Process. The implementation of the classification of legal norms using supervised machine learning followed a basic workflow consists of six interrelated steps, namely: (i) Data acquisition, (ii) Pre-processing, (iii) Text representation and transformation, (iv) Training of machine learning model, (v) Prediction of semantic types, and (vi) Evaluation, as depicted in Fig. 3.

Data Acquisition and Pre-processing. As train and test dataset we used the same 1,237 sentences and following the same pre-processing step described in Sect. 4.1.

Text Representation and Transformation. Text transformation is the process of representing text corpus so that they form a suitable input to a classification algorithm [31]. A common approach is to divide a statement into segments with a window size w, disregarding the order in which they appear. This approach is commonly known as Bag-of-Words (BOW) model, which includes the widely used word embedding approaches such as Word2vec [43] and GloVe [49].
Apparently, for a classifier to obtain good performance, the expected word distribution should have a clear classification boundary such that words in the same category are close to each other and far away from words in other categories. However, as commented by Liu *et al.* [35], the actual distribution obtained from such approaches is normally not satisfactory as they mainly focused on contextual similarities and ignored functional features, such as word order, in the training process, making them inefficient to the text classification task. Hence, to reconcile the issue, Kor2Vec [34], a word embedding model that was designed to convert legal statements in Korean language into a sequence of morpheme tokens based on the morphological meanings, was used.

Sentence 1: Article 6 (Requirements, etc. for Licenses) of Insurance Business Act

보험종목을 추가하여 허가를 받으려는 보험회사는 다음 각 호의 요건을 갖추어야 한다.
An insurance company which intends to obtain a license by adding the types of insurance shall meet the following requirements.

Tokenized sentence	보험종목을[1] 추가하여[2] 허가를[3] 받으려는[4] 보험회사는[5] 다음[6] 각[7] 호의[8] 요건을[9] 갖추어야[10] 한다[11].
Kor2Vec embedded tensor	$(v_1, v_2, v_3, v_4, v_5, v_6, v_7, v_8, v_9, v_{10}, v_{11})$
Normalized tensor	$(v_2, v_3, v_4, v_5, v_6, v_7, v_8, v_9, v_{10}, v_{11})$

Sentence 2: Article 4 (License for Insurance Business) of Insurance Business Act

금융위원회는 제1항에 따른 허가에 조건을 붙일 수 있다.
The Financial Services Commission may impose terms and conditions on the license referred to in paragraph (1).

Tokenized sentence	금융위원회는[1] 제1항에[2] 따른[3] 허가에[4] 조건을[5] 붙일[6] 수[7] 있다[8].
Kor2Vec embedded tensor	$(w_1, w_2, w_3, w_4, w_5, w_6, w_7, w_8)$
Normalized tensor	$(<BLANK>, <BLANK>, w_1, w_2, w_3, w_4, w_5, w_6, w_7, w_8)$

Fig. 4. Examples of tokenized embedded tensor and normalized tensor with sequence length $s = 10$.

Besides, as mentioned in previous section, owing to the semantics of Korean language, the semantic types of the statements largely depends on the prescribed terms that appear at the end of the statements. Hence, to reduce the dimensions of feature space in the trained models, we normalised the size of input space by retaining only the last s tokens as input (denoted as *sequence length*); while statements with token lengths less than s will be padded by special token "<BLANK>" that do not carry meaning, as illustrated in Fig. 4.

Training of Text Classifiers. We have split the dataset into 3 parts, of which 100 sentences has been reserved for evaluation. For the rest of the statements, we randomly split them into training and validation set of 80:20 ratio using a fivefold cross-validation. For each split we train the designed models with different sequence lengths by the training set, and then score their performance by the validation set. These results will be used to fine-tune the hyperparameters of the models for better performance.

Prediction of Semantic Types. We have chosen to evaluate three deep learning models that have been proven for their high performance in text classification problem, namely: (i) recurrent neural network (RNN), (i) RNN with long-short-term-memory (LSTM), and (iii) convolutional neural network (CNN). The training, validation and evaluation of the models were implemented in python using the pytorch library [48]. In the experiments, both the RNN and RNN+LSTM models were trained using the same set of features with the number of hidden layer states set with respect to the values of the sequence lengths; while cnn was trained with number of channels equals to 5 times the value of sequence lengths and with a dropout rate of 0.5. All models were trained with pre-trained word embeddings and without features as one advantage of this type of model is its ability to learn feature representation automatically [11].

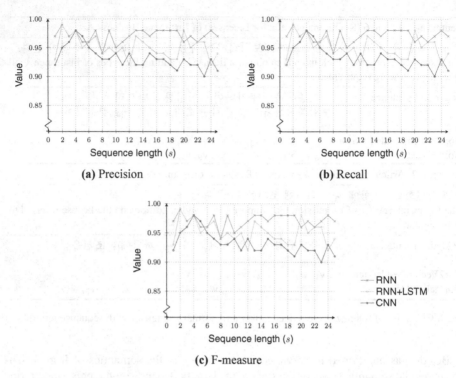

(a) Precision   **(b)** Recall

(c) F-measure

Fig. 5. Prediction result of deep learning models with different sequence lengths.

Evaluation. As can be seen from Table 4, the number of statements in each semantic type did not distribute evenly, which may affect the performance of the classifiers to correctly classify statements in the minority classes. To alleviate this problem, following Kobayashi *et al.* [31], we used the weighted variant of precision, recall and F-measure to evaluate the classifiers [53]. Besides, we also evaluate the effect of sequence length used under different models.

Comparison of Classifier Performance. Figure 5 shows the evaluation results of the trained classifiers with varied sequence lengths between 1 and 25. As can be seen from the charts, most of the classifiers tested performed quite well and have achieved a F-measure values between 0.90 and 0.99.

As can be seen from Fig. 5, all classifiers have achieved its best F-measure values when n is small (≤ 4) with 0.99 for RNN and RNN+LSTM, and 0.98 for CNN. However, the performances of all classifiers started to became unstable or even deteriorated as the value of n increase. In an attempt to explain this difference, a possible source is due to the semantics of Korean language. As mentioned in the previous sections, most of the prescribed terms used to determine the semantic types of the statements typically appeared at the last part of the statements. Increasing the value of n will, for sure, add more irrelevant information to sort through, which thus affected the performances of the classifiers.

Compared to the rule-based classification, most of the classifiers performed better in terms of F-measure values (when n is small). However, as deep learning model are

Table 5. Inspection of the performance differentiated by semantic types of different classifiers with sequence length $s = 3$.

Semantic type	RNN			RNN+LSTM			CNN			Support
	Precision	Recall	F-measure	Precision	Recall	F-measure	Precision	Recall	F-measure	
Definitional provisions	1.00	1.00	1.00	1.00	1.00	1.00	1.00	1.00	1.00	37
Application provisions	1.00	1.00	1.00	1.00	1.00	1.00	1.00	1.00	1.00	169
Deeming provisions	1.00	1.00	1.00	1.00	1.00	1.00	1.00	1.00	1.00	32
Continuation clauses	1.00	1.00	1.00	1.00	1.00	1.00	1.00	1.00	1.00	5
Delegation provisions	1.00	1.00	1.00	1.00	1.00	1.00	1.00	1.00	1.00	80
Penalty provisions	0.88	1.00	0.93	0.88	1.00	0.93	1.00	1.00	1.00	77
Deontic provisions										
Obligations	1.00	1.00	1.00	1.00	1.00	1.00	0.94	1.00	0.97	363
Permissions	0.90	0.95	0.93	0.90	0.95	0.93	0.91	1.00	0.95	244
Prohibitions	1.00	1.00	1.00	1.00	1.00	1.00	1.00	1.00	1.00	123
Rights	1.00	1.00	1.00	1.00	1.00	1.00	0.00	0.00	0.00	4
Liabilities	0.00	0.00	0.00	0.00	0.00	0.00	0.00	0.00	0.00	3
Average (weighted)	0.95	0.97	0.96	0.95	0.97	0.96	0.92	0.96	0.94	1137

notoriously data-hungry, the classifiers might not be sufficiently trained to classes with only a few samples in the dataset.

This can be confirmed by examining the result of the deep learning models in greater details, as shown in Table 5. As can be seen from the table, all classifiers perform very well for classes with high support. In fact, except penalty provisions and permissions, the majority of classifiers had performed better than the rule-based approach and have achieved F-measure values of 1 or close to 1.

On the contrary, if the prescribed terms used by certain classes varies and with low support, such as penalty provisions and liabilities, the performance of the deep learning classifiers will drop significantly; whereas rule-based approach did not have such restriction and can perform well once the prescribed terms have been identified correctly.

5 Related Works

The development of legal taxonomies and ontologies have received unprecedented attention, and various dedicated works has been proposed in the past two decades. For instance, PRONTO [47], a legal ontology on General Data Protection Regulation (GDPR)[10], provides the legal knowledge modelling of the privacy agents, data types, types of processing operations, rights and obligations. Contrary to HL7 Security and Privacy Ontology (HL7)[11] which was designed to manage health data for electronic health records, the goal of PRONTO is to support legal reasoning with defeasible reasoning. Rubino et al. [56] presented an OWL-DL based ontology of basic legal concepts [59] such as obligations, permissions, rights, erga-omnes rights, liabilities, legal power. While these studies are relevant to our work, their goal is different from ours. In particular, the focus of PRONTO ontology is limited to privacy and data rights in the context of GDPR, while Rubino's work is focused on basic legal concepts.

---

[10] General Data Protection Regulation (GDPR): https://gdpr-info.eu/.

[11] HL7 Security and Privacy Ontology (HL7): https://wiki.hl7.org/index.php?title=Security_and_Privacy_Ontology.

The computer assisted legal norms analysis is highly relevant and has attracted researchers from different areas ever since. For instance, Hachey and Grover [17] presented an early attempt to address the legal norm classification problem with different machine learning (ML) algorithms, such as naïve bayes, Winnow, maximum entropy model and SVM, to classify UK House of Lords judgements according to their rhetorical role and found that SVM and maximum entropy sequence tagger yield the best results. Similarly, Merchant and Pande [42] proposed an approach to summarize legal judgements based on *latent semantic analysis* [14], and was able to achieve an average ROGUE-1 score of 0.58.

Zeni *et al.* [77], on the other hand, proposed a framework, GaiusT 2.0, to semi-automate the legal concepts extraction and annotation process. Boella *et al.* [1] presented a rather similar approach which automatically extract semantic knowledge from legal texts based on the syntactic dependencies between different lexical terms. However, the downside of these studies is that they still need substantial manual efforts and time to prepare, model training and development.

Recently, the use of NLP techniques to automate the legal norms classifications process has been advocated. Rule-based, or pattern-based, approach has been traditionally the most commonly used approach due to its simplicity nature and traceability in determining whether a particular rule apply or not to certain patterns [16,23,32,61].

Modern approaches focuses on the use of heuristic, machine learning based approaches. For instance, Sleimi *et al.* [64] used NLP techniques to extract the legal provisions information such as modalities, actors, conditions, exceptions and violations. Wei *et al.* [70] compared the results of CNN and SVM in legal text classification and found that cnn performed better with large volume of training dataset. Besides, their results also showed that their self-trained word imbedding outperforms the pre-trained GloVe word embedding as GloVe is too general with respect to legal domain. However, only limited information on the dataset used has been provided.

The work of Waltl *et al.* [69] is closely related to us. In the paper, the authors have applied both rule-based and machine learning approach and classified German Civil Law into 9 different semantic types, such as duties, prohibitions, permission, etc. We share the common objective with their works in the context of constructing the legal knowledge ontological graph from the Korean legal sources; however, their work is limited in scope as we consider more granular functional aspects of the Korean legislation, which results in 12 different semantic types.

Nevertheless, it should be noted that machine learning based approaches are much slower and require more memory as compared to rule-based approaches [5]. Besides, the behavior of machine learning classifiers can only be observed like a black box and could easily be affected by many factors, such as the word embedding model and tokenization approaches used [6,8]. Recent work in explainable AI (XAI) attempts to improve the transparency of these models and with some success [55,66,76].

As a side note, Ferrato *et al.* [12,13] have evaluated several state-of-the-art NLP approaches to automate the normative mining process and identified several issues, such as different types of lexical ambiguities, inconsistent use of terminologies, sentential complexities, cross-referencing between different provisions, etc., when acquiring knowledge from legal documents, indicating that there is still a gap to fill in this area.

6   Conclusions

In conclusion, extracting normative information captured in a legal document is a time-consuming and error-prone task. The taxonomy presented in this paper has filled a gap to legislation written in the korean language, which to the best of our knowledge is the first of its kind.

We conducted two experiments to exploit the potential of the automated classification: (i) a rule-based approach using hand-crafted regular expression pattern classification, and (ii) a supervised machine learning based approach comparing the performance of different deep learnings classification methods (RNN, RNN+LSTM, and CNN), and the effect of sequence lengths used. We have achieved a F_1 scores of 0.97 and 0.99 for the classification task, respectively.

Our research so far indicates that the majority of semantic types in korean legislation can be easily identified automatically due to the use of clear keywords; while, at the same time, our results also showed that the deep learning approaches may possess some difficulties in classifying statements with limited support, such as liabilities. However, it seems that this problem does not appear in the rule-based approach as the classification is done via keywords matching.

We will continue the development of the prototype in two directions, which will make it a more comprehensive tool for the linguistic analysis of legal documents. Firstly, we plan to extend the taxonomy to cater the wider need of the korean legislation, analysis and investigate different NLP approaches to automate the legal norms classification process. Secondly, through the use of different sentence patterns identified in [51], on system level, we plan to a develop sentence components analyzer, to divide a legal statement into different components and formalize them into legal norms that can be understand and reason on by machine from the korean statutory texts directly.

References

1. Boella, G., Di Caro, L., Robaldo, L.: Semantic relation extraction from legislative text using generalized syntactic dependencies and support vector machines. In: Morgenstern, L., Stefaneas, P., Lévy, F., Wyner, A., Paschke, A. (eds.) RuleML 2013. LNCS, vol. 8035, pp. 218–225. Springer, Heidelberg (2013). https://doi.org/10.1007/978-3-642-39617-5_20
2. Bracher, P.: Interpretation: the nature of a deeming provision, April 2018. https://www.financialinstitutionslegalsnapshot.com/2018/04/interpretation-the-nature-of-a-deeming-provision/. Accessed 27 Aug 2021
3. Poblet, M., Casanovas, P., Rodríguez-Doncel, V.: Legal linked data ecosystems and the rule of law. In: Linked Democracy. SL, pp. 87–126. Springer, Cham (2019). https://doi.org/10.1007/978-3-030-13363-4_5
4. Ceci, M., Khalil, F.A., O'Brien, L.: Making sense of regulations with SBVR. In: Proceedings of the RuleML 2016 Challenge, Doctoral Consortium and Industry Track, July 2016
5. Chiticariu, L., Krishnamurthy, R., Li, Y., Raghavan, S., Reiss, F., Vaithyanathan, S.: SystemT: an algebraic approach to declarative information extraction. In: Hajič, J., Carberry, S., Clark, S., Nivre, J. (eds.) Proceedings of the 48th Annual Meeting of the Association for Computational Linguistics, ACL 2010, pp. 128–137, July 2010
6. Cho, D., Lee, H., Kang, S.: An empirical study of Korean sentence representation with various tokenizations. Electronics 10(7), 845 (2021)

7. Choi, M., Hur, J., Jang, M.G.: Constructing Korean lexical concept network for encyclopedia question-answering system. In: Proceedings of the 30th Annual Conference of IEEE Industrial Electronics Society, vol. 3, pp. 3115–3119. IEEE, November 2004

8. Chung, T., Post, M., Gildea, D.: Factors affecting the accuracy of Korean parsing. In: Seddah, D., Koebler, S., Tsarfaty, R. (eds.) Proceedings of the NAACL HLT 2010 First Workshop on Statistical Parsing of Morphologically-Rich Languages, pp. 49–57, June 2010

9. Dragoni, M., Villata, S., Rizzi, W., Governatori, G.: Combining natural language processing approaches for rule extraction from legal documents. In: Pagallo, U., Palmirani, M., Casanovas, P., Sartor, G., Villata, S. (eds.) AICOL 2015-2017. LNCS (LNAI), vol. 10791, pp. 287–300. Springer, Cham (2018). https://doi.org/10.1007/978-3-030-00178-0_19

10. van Engers, T.M., van Gog, R., Sayah, K.: A case study on automated norm extraction. In: Gordon, T. (ed.) The 17th International Conference on Legal Knowledge and Information Systems, JURIX 2004, pp. 49–58 (2004)

11. Ferraro, G., Loo Gee, B., Ji, S., Salvador-Carulla, L.: Lightme: analysing language in internet support groups for mental health. Health Inf. Sci. Syst. **8**(1), 1–10 (2020). https://doi.org/10.1007/s13755-020-00115-7

12. Ferraro, G., Lam, H.P.: NLP techniques for normative mining. J. Appl. Log. **8**(4), 941–974 (2021)

13. Ferraro, G., et al.: Automatic extraction of legal norms: evaluation of natural language processing tools. In: Sakamoto, M., Okazaki, N., Mineshima, K., Satoh, K. (eds.) JSAI-isAI 2019. LNCS (LNAI), vol. 12331, pp. 64–81. Springer, Cham (2020). https://doi.org/10.1007/978-3-030-58790-1_5

14. Foltz, P.: Semantic processing: statistical approaches. In: Smelser, N.J., Baltes, P.B. (eds.) International Encyclopedia of the Social and Behavioral Sciences, pp. 13873–13878. Pergamon, Oxford (2001)

15. Gordon, T.F., Governatori, G., Rotolo, A.: Rules and norms: requirements for rule interchange languages in the legal domain. In: Governatori, G., Hall, J., Paschke, A. (eds.) RuleML 2009. LNCS, vol. 5858, pp. 282–296. Springer, Heidelberg (2009). https://doi.org/10.1007/978-3-642-04985-9_26

16. Gruzitis, N., Gosko, D., Barzdins, G.: RIGOTRIO at SemEval-2017 Task 9: combining machine learning and grammar engineering for AMR parsing and generation. In: Proceedings of the 11th International Workshop on Semantic Evaluation, SemEval 2017, pp. 924–928, August 2017

17. Hachey, B., Grover, C.: Sentence classification experiments for legal text summarisation. In: Gordon, T. (ed.) The 17th Annual Conference on Legal Knowledge and Information Systems, JURIX 2004, pp. 29–38 (2004)

18. Hansen, J.: Reasoning about permission and obligation. In: Hansson, S.O. (ed.) David Makinson on Classical Methods for Non-Classical Problems. OCL, vol. 3, pp. 287–333. Springer, Dordrecht (2014). https://doi.org/10.1007/978-94-007-7759-0_14

19. Hashmi, M., Casanovas, P., de Koker, L.: Legal compliance through design: preliminary results of a literature survey. In: Proceedings of the 2nd Workshop on Technologies for Regulatory Compliance, TERECOM 2018, Groningen, The Netherlands, pp. 59–72, December 2018

20. Hashmi, M., Governatori, G., Wynn, M.T.: Normative requirements for business process compliance. In: Davis, J.G., Demirkan, H., Motahari-Nezhad, H.R. (eds.) ASSRI 2013. LNBIP, vol. 177, pp. 100–116. Springer, Cham (2014). https://doi.org/10.1007/978-3-319-07950-9_8

21. Hilty, M., Basin, D., Pretschner, A.: On obligations. In: di Vimercati, S.C., Syverson, P., Gollmann, D. (eds.) ESORICS 2005. LNCS, vol. 3679, pp. 98–117. Springer, Heidelberg (2005). https://doi.org/10.1007/11555827_7

22. Höfler, S.: Making the law more transparent: text linguistics for legislative drafting. In: Vogel, F. (ed.) Legal Linguistics Beyond Borders: Language and Law in a World of Media, Globalisation and Social Conflicts, pp. 229–252. Duncker & Humblot, Berlin (2019)
23. Hwang, R.H., Hsueh, Y.L., Chang, Y.T.: Building a Taiwan law ontology based on automatic legal definition extraction. Appl. Syst. Innov. **1**(3), 22 (2018)
24. Hwang, S., Jung, Y., Yoon, A., Kwon, H.-C.: Building Korean classifier ontology based on Korean WordNet. In: Sojka, P., Kopeček, I., Pala, K. (eds.) TSD 2006. LNCS (LNAI), vol. 4188, pp. 261–268. Springer, Heidelberg (2006). https://doi.org/10.1007/11846406_33
25. Jeong, H., et al.: Effect of syntactic similarity on cortical activation during second language processing: a comparison of English and Japanese among native Korean trilinguals. Hum. Brain Mapp. **28**(3), 194–204 (2007)
26. Jindal, R., Malhotra, R., Jain, A.: Techniques for text classification: literature review and current trends. Webology **12**(2) (2015)
27. Jung, S., Lee, C., Hwang, H.: End-to-end Korean part-of-speech tagging using copying mechanism. ACM Trans. Asian Low-Resour. Lang. Inf. Process. **17**(3), 19:1–19:8 (2018)
28. Junho, J.P., Jo, Y., Shin, H.: The KOLON system: tools for ontological natural language processing in Korean. In: Proceedings of the 24th Pacific Asia Conference on Language, Information and Computation, JUCLIC 2010, pp. 425–432. Tohoku University, Sendai, November 2010
29. Karkkainen, B.C.: Plain meaning: Justice Scalia's jurisprudence of strict statutory construction. Harv. J. Law Public Policy **17**(2), 401–477 (1994)
30. Kim, Y.: Convolutional neural networks for sentence classification. In: Proceedings of the 2014 Conference on Empirical Methods in Natural Language Processing, EMNLP 2014, pp. 1746–1751, October 2014
31. Kobayashi, V.B., Mol, S.T., Berkers, H.A., Kismihók, G., Hartog, D.N.D.: Text classification for organizational researchers: a tutorial. Organ. Res. Methods **21**(3), 766–799 (2018)
32. Kwiatkowski, T., Zettlemoyer, L., Goldwater, S., Steedman, M.: Lexical generalization in CCG grammar induction for semantic parsing. In: Proceedings of the 2011 Conference on Empirical Methods in Natural Language Processing, EMNLP 2011, pp. 1512–1523, July 2011
33. Lam, H.P., Hashmi, M.: Enabling reasoning with LegalRuleML. Theory Pract. Log. Program. **19**(1), 1–26 (2019)
34. Lee, D.: Morpheme-based efficient Korean word embedding. M.Sc. thesis, Seoul National University, Seoul, South Korea, February 2018
35. Liu, Q., Huang, H., Gao, Y., Wei, X., Tian, Y., Liu, L.: Task-oriented word embedding for text classification. In: Bender, E.M., Derczynski, L., Isabella, P. (eds.) Proceedings of the 27th International Conference on Computational Linguistics, COLING 2018, pp. 2023–2032, August 2018
36. Marín, R.H., Sartor, G.: Time and norms: a formalisation in the event-calculus. In: Proceedings of the 7th International Conference on Artificial Intelligence and Law, ICAIL 1999, pp. 90–99, June 1999
37. Mattei, U.: Three patterns of law: taxonomy and change in the world's legal systems. Am. J. Comp. Law **45**(1), 5–44 (1997)
38. Matteson, A.: SyntaxNet Tree Generator (Korean/Komoran3) (2018). http://andrewmatteson.name/psg_tree.htm. Accessed 18 Aug 2021
39. Matteson, A., Lee, C., Kim, Y., Lim, H.: Rich character-level information for Korean morphological analysis and part-of-speech tagging. In: Proceedings of the 27th International Conference on Computational Linguistics, COLING 2018, pp. 2482–2492, August 2018
40. McCarty, L.T.: A language for legal discourse: I. Basic features. In: Proceedings of the 2nd International Conference on Artificial Intelligence and Law, ICAIL 1989, pp. 180–189 (1989)

41. McGregor, B.: Constructing a concise medical taxonomy. J. Med. Libr. Assoc. **93**(1), 121–123 (2005)
42. Merchant, K., Pande, Y.: NLP based latent semantic analysis for legal text summarization. In: 2018 International Conference on Advances in Computing, Communications and Informatics, ICACCI 2018, pp. 1803–1807 (2018)
43. Mikolov, T., Sutskever, I., Chen, K., Corrado, G., Dean, J.: Distributed representations of words and phrases and their compositionality. In: Proceedings of the 26th International Conference on Neural Information Processing Systems, NIPS 2013, Lake Tahoe, NV, USA, vol. 2, pp. 3111–3119 (2013)
44. Mills, A.: Rethinking jurisdiction in international law. Br. Yearbook Int. Law **84**(1), 187–239 (2014)
45. Müller-Gotama, F.: The cross-linguistic survey. In: Grammatical Relations: A Cross-Linguistic Perspective on Their Syntax and Semantics, pp. 78–140. De Gruyter Mouton (1994)
46. Ock, C.: UWordMap. University of Ulsan, Ulsan, South Korea, July 2013. http://nlplab.ulsan.ac.kr/. Accessed 27 Aug 2021
47. Palmirani, M., Martoni, M., Rossi, A., Bartolini, C., Robaldo, L.: PrOnto: privacy ontology for legal reasoning. In: Kő, A., Francesconi, E. (eds.) EGOVIS 2018. LNCS, vol. 11032, pp. 139–152. Springer, Cham (2018). https://doi.org/10.1007/978-3-319-98349-3_11
48. Paszke, A., et al.: PyTorch: an imperative style, high-performance deep learning library. In: Proceedings of the 33rd Conference on Neural Information Processing Systems, NeurIPS 2021, pp. 8024–8035 (2019)
49. Pennington, J., Socher, R., Manning, C.: GloVe: global vectors for word representation. In: Moschitti, A., Pang, B., Daelemans, W. (eds.) Proceedings of the 2014 Conference on Empirical Methods in Natural Language Processing, EMNLP 2014, Doha, Qatar, pp. 1532–1543, October 2014
50. Petrov, S.: Announcing SyntaxNet: The World's Most Accurate Parser Goes Open Source, May 2016. https://ai.googleblog.com/2016/05/announcing-syntaxnet-worlds-most.html. Accessed 18 Aug 2021
51. Phan, T.T.: Types and semantic components of Korean financial regulation statements: insurance law case. Master of Engineering thesis, Inje University, Gimhae, South Korea, February 2020
52. Phan, T.T., Lam, H.P., Hashmi, M., Choi, Y.: Towards construction of legal ontology for Korean legislation. In: Proceedings of the 12th International Conference on Knowledge Discovery, Knowledge Engineering and Knowledge Management, IC3K 2020, vol. 2: KEOD, pp. 86–97, November 2020
53. Powers, D.M.W.: Evaluation: from precision, recall and F-measure to ROC, informedness, markedness and correlation. J. Mach. Learn. Technol. **2**(1), 37–63 (2011)
54. Prakken, H., Sartor, G.: A dialectical model of assessing conflicting arguments in legal reasoning. Artif. Intell. Law **4**(3), 331–368 (1996)
55. Ribeiro, M.T., Singh, S., Guestrin, C.: "Why should i trust you?" Explaining the prediction of any classifier. In: Proceedings of the 22nd ACM SIGKDD International Conference on Knowledge Discovery and Data Mining, KDD 2016, pp. 1135–1144, August 2016
56. Rubino, R., Rotolo, A., Sartor, G.: An OWL ontology of fundamental legal concepts. In: van Engers, T.M. (ed.) Proceedings of the 19th Annual Conference on Legal Knowledge and Information Systems, JURIX 2006, Paris, France, pp. 101–110. IOS Press, December 2006
57. Sartor, G.: Normative conflicts in legal reasoning. Artif. Intell. Law **1**(2–3), 209–235 (1992). https://doi.org/10.1007/BF00114921
58. Sartor, G.: A Treatise of Legal Philosophy and General Jurisprudence. Volume 5: Legal Reasoning, A Cognitive Approach to the Law, Springer, Dordrecht (2005). https://doi.org/10.1007/1-4020-3505-5

59. Sartor, G.: Fundamental legal concepts: a formal and teleological characterisation. Artif. Intell. Law **14**(1), 101–142 (2006). https://doi.org/10.1007/s10506-006-9009-x
60. Sartor, G.: Legal validity: an inferential analysis. Ratio Juris **21**(2), 212–247 (2008)
61. Selway, M., Grossmann, G., Mayer, W., Stumptner, M.: Formalising natural language specifications using a cognitive linguistic/configuration based approach. Inf. Syst. **54**, 191–208 (2015)
62. Shibatani, M.: The Languages of Japan. Cambridge Language Surveys, Cambridge University Press, Cambridge (1990)
63. Shineware: Komoran 3.0 (2019). http://www.shineware.co.kr/. Accessed 18 Aug 2021
64. Sleimi, A., Sannier, N., Sabetzadeh, M., Briand, L.C., Dann, J.: Automated extraction of semantic legal metadata using natural language processing. In: Proceedings of the 26th IEEE International Requirements Engineering Conference, RE 2018, Banff, AB, Canada, pp. 124–135, August 2018
65. Song, H.J., Park, S.B.: Korean morphological analysis with tied sequence-to-sequence multitask model. In: Inui, K., Jiang, J., Ng, V., Wan, X. (eds.) Proceedings of the 2019 Conference on Empirical Methods in Natural Language Processing and the 9th International Joint Conference on Natural Language Processing, EMNLP-IJCNLP 2019, pp. 1436–1441, November 2019
66. Sridharan, M., Meadows, B.: Towards a theory of explanations for human-robot collaboration. KI - Künstliche Intelligenz **33**, 331–342 (2019). https://doi.org/10.1007/s13218-019-00616-y
67. Stratos, K.: A sub-character architecture for Korean language processing. In: Proceedings of the 2017 Conference on Empirical Methods in Natural Language Processing, EMNLP 2017, pp. 721–726, September 2017
68. Victorian Government Solicitor's Office: Current issues in delegations. In: Client Newsletter. Administrative Law, Victorian Government, May 2008. http://vgltp.vgso.vic.gov.au/sites/default/files/Adminlaw.pdf. Accessed 27 Aug 2021
69. Waltl, B., Bonczek, G., Scepankova, E., Matthes, F.: Semantic types of legal norms in German laws: classification and analysis using local linear explanations. Artif. Intell. Law **27**(1), 43–71 (2018). https://doi.org/10.1007/s10506-018-9228-y
70. Wei, F., Qin, H., Ye, S., Zhao, H.: Empirical study of deep learning for text classification in legal document review. In: 2018 IEEE International Conference on Big Data, Big Data 2018, pp. 3317–3320, December 2018
71. Wieringa, R.J., Meyer, J.J.C.: Applications of deontic logic in computer science: a concise overview. In: International Workshop on Deontic Logic in Computer Science, pp. 17–40, December 1993
72. von Wright, G.H.: Norm and Action: A Logical Enquiry. Routledge and Kegan Paul, London (1963)
73. Wyner, A., Peters, W.: On rule extraction from regulations. In: Atkinson, K.M. (ed.) Proceedings of the 24th International Conference on Legal Knowledge and Information Systems, JURIX 2011, pp. 113–122, December 2011
74. Xanthaki, H.: Structure of a bill. In: Drafting Legislation: Art and Technology of Rules for Regulation. Hart Publishing (2014)
75. Yoon, A.S., Hwang, S.H., Lee, E.R., Kwon, H.C.: Construction of Korean WordNet "KorLex 1.5". J. KIISE Softw. Appl. **36**(1), 92–108 (2009)
76. Zahavy, T., Ben-Zrihem, N., Mannor, S.: Graying the black box: understanding DQNs. CoRR abs/1602.02658 (2016)
77. Zeni, N., Kiyavitskaya, N., Mich, L., Cordy, J.R., Mylopoulos, J.: GaiusT: supporting the extraction of rights and obligations for regulatory compliance. Requirements Eng. **20**(1), 1–22 (2013). https://doi.org/10.1007/s00766-013-0181-8

Context-Aware Knowledge Management as an Enabler for Human-Machine Collective Intelligence

Alexander Smirnov$^{(\boxtimes)}$![ORCID], Nikolay Shilov ![ORCID], and Andrew Ponomarev ![ORCID]

St. Petersburg Federal Research Center of the Russian Academy of Sciences,
14th Line 39, St. Petersburg 199178, Russia
{smir,nick,ponomarev}@iias.spb.su

Abstract. The effectiveness of maintaining and accessing decentralized organization's information and knowledge is crucial for the competitiveness of the company and its ability to adapt to ever-changing business environment. Most of this knowledge is typically scattered across various socio-cyber-physical systems inside the company. The concept of socio-cyber-physical system and the related reseach aims on providing a holistic view on heterogeneous systems, including physical, software and human components and their real-time interactions via multilevel connections. Context-aware knowledge management is becoming de facto one of the essential business strategies to support such systems. Its purpose is to facilitate the transfer and exchange of knowledge in the context of business structures and activities related to cultural norms. This paper discussess emerging trends (including role organization, dynamic motivation mechanisms, and multidimensional ontology) in knowledge management for socio-cyber-physical systems. These trends can contribute to the creation of an innovative IT and HR environment based on the collective intelligence of humans and machines, where information and knowledge is shared among participants and among collectives of participants who can be either humans (collective intelligence as methods used by humans to take collective action to solve problems) or software services (based on artificial intelligence models). The paper discusses examples of trends and experiences of their implementation in a global manufacturing company and also proposes a concept human-machine collective intelligence environment utilizing the discussed technologies to support human-computer collaboration in decision support scenarios.

Keywords: Socio-cyber-physical systems · Collective intelligence · Hybrid systems · Context-aware knowledge management · Ontology-based systems · Multi-aspect ontology · Role-based organization · Dynamic motivation

1 Introduction

Modern IT landscape is represented with physical systems (e.g., physical production equipment, vehicles, devices), software components (e.g., enterprise resource planning,

A. Fred et al. (Eds.): IC3K 2020, CCIS 1608, pp. 94–116, 2022.
https://doi.org/10.1007/978-3-031-14602-2_5

manufacturing execution systems or other information systems), and human actors (organizational roles and stakeholders) with variety of multilevel interconnections between them, that may be interpreted as communication and social networks. The concept of Socio-Cyber Physical System (SCPS), providing a holistic view on this heterogeneous systems, and their real-time interactions is becoming more and more important in understanding the IT landscape as well as for managing it.

Nowadays, increasingly large number of systems (including "system of systems") in many areas are recognized as socio-cyber-physical, and this fact is stimulating research in the field of SCPSs, aimed at creating a set of tools and methodologies for the development of SCPSs, their optimization and evolution. Many indicative examples of SCPSs can be found in modern production environments, especially those that follow the Industry 4.0 concept guidelines.

Knowledge management (KM), which allows finding knowledge and/or skills to solve a given problem, is critical for successful collaboration, especially in systems with heterogeneous entities (as in SCPS). Distributed work in product design, manufacturing and supply management projects requires decision support by each of the the parties involved, adapted to the actual context of those parties (depending on their nature). From a network point of view, modern SCPS are based on the integration of a number of networks supported by the following information technologies [1]:

- Social networks: who knows whom = > Virtual Communities;
- Knowledge networks: who knows what => Human & Knowledge Management;
- Information networks: who informs what => Internet/Intranet/Extranet/Cloud;
- Work networks: who works where => Decision Support based on Crowdsourcing and Recommendation Systems;
- Competency networks: what is where => Knowledge Map;
- Inter-organizational network: organizational linkages => Semantic-Driven Interoperability.

In general, SCPSs are reconfigurable dynamic systems; their elements may have variety of possible states and arrange in dynamically arrange in problem-centric compositions. This provides an additional requirement for successful KM in SCPSs. Namely context-awareness. The context is usually defined as any information that can be used to characterize the situation of an entity, where an entity is a person, place, or object that is considered relevant to the interaction between a user and an application, including the user and applications themselves [2].

This paper describes some trends in implementing context-aware KM in human-machine collaborative systems and also proposes a human-machine collective intelligence environment providing a set of knowledge-based mechanisms to support human-AI teaming and partnership. This paper is an extended and revised version of an earlier paper of the same authors [3]. In particular, in this version we provide deeper analysis of the presented trends and discuss the proposed human-machine collective intelligence environment in more detail. Besides, we map the possibilities offered by the proposed environment to the major modes of human-AI collaboration [26].

The rest of the paper is organized as follows. Section 2 describes some important trends in KM in SCPSs. Section 3 discusses practical application of these trends in solving KM problems in a production company. Finally, Sect. 4 presents a design of a human-machine collective intelligent environment, which follows these trends and can be used in a variety of problem domains to effectively solve KM problems at decision support by human-machine collectives.

2   Modern Trends in CAKM for SCPS

This section describes some modern trends in the context-aware knowledge management (CAKM) for socio-cyber-physical systems and shows how the respective emerging technologies can facilitate the creation of innovative IT&HR environments.

Ontology-based knowledge representation is in the core of these trends; it is their enabler. The purpose of ontologies is to represent knowledge about a certain domain in a machine-readable way. Ontologies allow to describe, share and process knowledge considering its syntax along with its semantics. They are formal conceptualizations of certain domain of interest that are shared between different applications [4, 5]. The ontology describes concepts, their relationships and axioms thought to exist in the given domain. They are considered an efficient mean to solve the interoperability problem. In particular, ontologies turn out to be effective in encoding context.

Context model serves to represent the knowledge about a current situation (the environment properties, the current problem, as well as states of the stakeholders).

These models, for instance, are used to reveal user preferences based on the analysis of the context representations in conjunction with the implemented decisions.

2.1   Role-Based Organization

Personalized support is important for modern business applications. As a rule, it is based on the application of profiling technology. Each user (a human or an information system) works on a particular problem or scenario represented via a context that may be characterized by a particular customer order, its time, requirements, etc.

Research efforts in the area of information logistics show information and knowledge needs of a particular employee depend on his/her tasks and responsibilities [6]. Therefore, in business applications the idea of personalization (identification of implicit context of the request) can be extended with the knowledge of the user's role. Besides, it is also the case that representatives of adjacent (in terms of business process) roles can have slightly different goals and use different terminology (even referring to the same concepts).

The idea of the role-based approach is to consider the workflows and information models from perspectives of different roles that deal with them.

Role-based organization for ontology-based KM assumes the following steps:

1. Structural information about workflows and the problem domain is collected and described in the common ontology.
2. User roles are identified and their relevant parts of the common ontology are defined.
3. Tasks assigned to the identified roles are defined.
4. Knowledge required for performing identified tasks is defined.

5. Based on the identified roles, tasks, and knowledge new knowledge-based workflows are defined.
6. Corresponding role-based knowledge support of the workflows is provided based on the usage of the common ontology and knowledge/information storages.

This process repeats for each particular role, with some knowledge being reused by several roles.

The implementation of the approach is described in Sect. 3.

2.2 Dynamic Motivation Mechanisms

In a broad sense, a motive (motivation) is understood as the desire of the subject to achieve a particular goal. The concept of the stimulus (or stimulation) is inextricably linked with the concept of motive, which is understood as the process of influencing the subject, pushing him to one or another action. A stimulus is effective if it corresponds to one or another motive present in the subject. The development and application of adequate incentives are an essential part of research devoted to the management of systems that include active elements (with their own, individual, motives) ranging from humans to autonomous artificial agents. The need to adapt to a changing environment necessitates the variability of the agent's behaviors, which cannot always be programmed directly (and is achieved indirectly via offering proper incentivization schemes).

The analysis of motivational models in systems of various natures (based on human participation and on the participation of autonomous software agents) showed that, regardless of the type of agents, there are two types of motivational models – external and internal. Following the definition of intrinsic motivation (which arises as a desire inherent in subjects for a certain action, regardless of the perceived consequences of this action in the form of obtaining certain benefits), such motivation can (and has) a significant impact on the quality of the results obtained by an agent, but cannot be directly involved by incentive mechanisms. Nevertheless, to a certain extent (indirect) use of intrinsic motivation is possible in the sense that placing an agent in a situation that corresponds to his intrinsic goals leads to the activation of the corresponding motivational components and, consequently, to the more effective functioning of the agent. Thus, the use of intrinsic motivation is possible through a certain design of the team formation mechanism that takes into account this aspect.

Extrinsic motivation can be activated through the incentive mechanism. Accordingly, the organization (or an environment dealing with active elements) should support the main set of incentive methods: first of all, monetary and social recognition (in the form of reputation, status). It should be noted that the concept of reputation has a complex effect, which involves both the motive of striving for social recognition (provided that the value of reputation is demonstrated to other participants) and often affecting the financial motive in a long-term (via wider possibilities offered to agents with higher reputation).

The use of motivational mechanisms turns out to be useful in adoption of KM. Often the KM mechanisms add responsibilities and activities that have to be done by employees and that are not seen as important as the primary (productive) activities. Therefore, employees may evade using the organized KM solutions or even feel threatened by organizing their knowledge in an accessible manner as it might make them 'replaceable'. An important task of management is to establish an open and fair corporate culture that values KM. One of the most important aspects that have to be considered is aligning organization and employees goals via employee motivation [7]. Especially, dynamic motivation (the type of motivation that changes within a short period of time). Particular examples of dynamic motivation used by the retailer companies are the best sellers boards, scores in the corporate systems, etc.

The empirical study has proven that dynamic motivation seems to yield high levels of engagement, learning, and also of performance and effectiveness in organizational implementation processes. Besides, dynamic motivation also seems to positively contribute to collaborative work and team performance [8].

The use of dynamic motivation in some SCPS relies on answering two questions:

1. How should the participants be motivated (what rewards are effective)?
2. What software solutions can be used to define dynamic motivation mechanisms?

The first question is extensively studied in the human resources management area.

The second one is more relevant to IT. There are two classes of solutions: specialized solutions (tailored for the particular problem) and generic solutions.

An example of using a specialized solution for implementing the dynamic motivation approach to increase project management efficiency based on the competency management system is described in [9]. The solution includes reference and mathematical models of language expert network, which are used for the automated assignment of the organization's personnel to projects. They allow formalizing not only the skills of individual employees but also their achievements and strengths.

A prominent example of a generic solution is PRINGL language [10] allowing to define motivation policies in an application-independent way and connect to some information system via an application programming interface.

2.3 Multi-aspect Ontology

Ontologies are aimed at representing knowledge about a certain domain in a machine-readable way. However, in complex domains, like Product Lifecycle Management (PLM), the application of ontologies is complicated since it has to deal with interdisciplinary information and knowledge related to different processes [11]. The terminology and notations used in these processes are different since they are aimed at solving tasks of different nature that require different techniques [12, 13]. To a certain extent, this problem can be compared to that of role-based information representation, where the information and knowledge have to be presented to different roles using different views and terminologies.

There have been undertaking research efforts aiming to solve this problem. One of the driving domains is product lifecycle information and knowledge management since the processes of product engineering, production, sales, and others often require very different information representation, but have certain of information in common. The authors of [14] propose a model-driven framework for interoperability support aimed at maintaining relationships between manufacturing equipment and products. The paper suggests creating a "connection framework" that describes relationships between different ontologies describing manufacturing capabilities of the Manufacturing Process Management system and product ontologies of the PLM system. However, having multiple ontologies for different tasks cannot be considered as an efficient solution to the problem identified since the translation of information from one specific ontology to another is in fact a translation between the source ontology and the common ontology and then between the common ontology and the target ontology, what eventually might cause information losses due to differences in formalisms.

Some research efforts were aimed at enriching ontologies with supplementary information that could represent additional facts originally described in a different notation (e.g., semantic annotations [15], DAML + OIL extensions for configuration problem descriptions [16], and others). However, this is not an efficient solution for the considered problem of integrating information and knowledge from multiple different notations and terminologies, which is the case for systems based on human-machine collective intelligence.

Another possible solution for organizing knowledge in multi-domain systems is to have a common ontology at the top and to extend it for specific subdomains (e.g., configuration problem solving, routing, competence management). This solution is not efficient for dynamic domains with a large number of sub-domains, since it would require continuous ontology matching and modifications of the common ontology.

Ontology matching can be considered as one of the means to facilitate the usage of the above-mentioned approaches for establishing links between multiple domain-specific ontologies and the common ontology. However, manual ontology matching would require too much time and effort in dynamically changing domains and automatic ontology matching is still not a reliable instrument since the existing methods deliver sufficient precision only in narrow domains.

A promising group of approaches is centered around preserving the original domain ontologies and building an additional layer above them. The authors of [17] propose to use a Basic Formal Ontology (BFO) as a top-level ontology for describing various engineering domains and to re-engineer the existing ontologies so that they would be compliant with it.

Another approach from this group is based on viewing the problem domain from several viewpoints supported by the Multi-Viewpoints Ontology (MVpOnt). In MVpOnt each viewpoint is a knowledge representation model useful for a particular task, process, or a group of people co-existing in a common information environment and sharing some information and knowledge. The viewpoints are described in a specialized language for the multi-viewpoint ontologies called MVP-OWL [18]. MVP-OWL extends OWL-DL as follows: (1) it introduces viewpoints that describe information and knowledge related to a certain task or process; (2) classes and properties are divided into two groups: local (observed only from one viewpoint), and global (observed from two or more viewpoints); (3) it also introduces "bridge rules" of four types, which enable relating concepts from different viewpoints. In 2018 this approach was extended with probabilistic reasoning support [19].

This approach is the most suitable for the problem at hand since it supports resolving terminological issues, and also makes it possible to preserve original formalisms used in existing ontologies. However, it is mainly aimed at describing knowledge of one domain, and the viewpoints are very tightly related. The considered problem assumes dealing with loosely connected processes and aspects of a complex domain, which only share some of the concepts. As a result, the approach had to be adapted resulting in the idea of multi-aspect ontology.

3 CAKM Implementation

This section describes several particular organizational KM problems and how they are successfully approached by modern solutions described in Sect. 2.

The problem at hand is product and knowledge management in a large automation manufacturing company. This section integrates results of several projects carried out by the research team, the paper authors belong to, together with representatives of the company.

3.1 Role-Based Organization

This approach was implemented in the frame of the project reported in [20]. The first step of the approach implementation was the ontology creation. The resulting ontology consists of over 1000 classes organized into a four level taxonomy based on the VDMA (Verband Deutscher Maschinen – und Anlagenbau, German Engineering Federation) classification [21]. Later it was extended with descriptions of complex products, their components and compatibility rules.

At the second step, the major roles, whose workflows were addressed by KM implementation, have been identified. They included product manager, product engineer, production manager, and production engineer.

Then, at steps 3 and 4, their tasks and knowledge/information needs were analysed. For example, the product manager works with customers and their needs. Since the terminology used by customers differs from that used by product engineers, a mapping between the customer needs and internal product requirements had to be established.

At steps 5 and 6 the knowledge-based workflows were defined, and corresponding supporting tools were built.

The project showed that such approach enabled implementing KM incrementally, with initiative coming from employees. E.g., an experimental knowledge-based support of one workflow could be implemented for one user role letting the users estimate its efficiency and convenience. Then, workflows reusing some knowledge of the experimental workflow can be added, etc. Representatives of other roles seeing the improvements of the implemented knowledge-based workflows also wish to join and actively participate in the identification of the knowledge needed for their workflows and further turning their workflows into the knowledge-based ones.

3.2 Dynamic Motivation

An example of successfully leveraging dynamic motivation is automating and facilitating a translation process involving company employees from different countries [9]. The translation process was implemented as a distributed network of language experts, and dynamic motivation was leveraged to incentivize experts (found by maximization of the global fitness function) to take part in the translation.

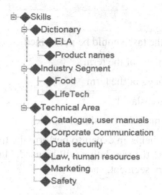

Fig. 1. Example of skill tree (from [3]).

An example of the generated skill tree that is used to describe expert's competence profile as well as task requirements is presented in Fig. 1. The skill tree for the developed language experts network consists of three main parts: dictionary, industry segment, and technical area that describes the mentioned problem domains.

Every expert is described by a competence profile. The expert profile contains: information about the expert, list of competencies, and professional assessment (global skill level, GSL). Global skill level is calculated based on a number of successfully completed tasks this expert performed, his/her availability estimation for task performing, estimation of how long the expert works in the company, qualification of the expert, and rewards the expert received from the manager.

For the definition of the proofreading task it is proposed to use the following structure (see Table 1). The task form accessible to the expert includes the task structure presented in the table as well as the task discussion interface that allows proofreaders to exchange their knowledge about it.

The list of possible motivations used in the system includes two main groups of motivations: material and non-material. Every motivation is specified by budget, value, and monetary benefit as well as it can be supported globally or only by one or several local companies.

For example, an expert can be motivated by a shopping voucher (20 EUR). In this case spent budget will be 20 EUR as well as monetary benefit that determines the value of this present for the expert. At the same time the value of a positive recommendation to the expert's boss could be evaluated as 10 (maximum value) but budget and monetary benefit is 0, since the company does not spend money on it.

Table 1. Proofreading task description (from [3]).

Name	Description
Due Date	Date when the task should be performed
Source Language	Source language of the term
Target Language	Target language of the term
Term	Term to be translated
Translation	Translation made by translation agency
Task Context	Context that helps an expert to perform the translation. It includes the project where the translation will be used, "in sentence context", technical area, industry segment, and etc.

The system also provides a number of forms for managing rewards. First, a form to display the list of rewards assigned to each expert (including date/time of the assignment) and define new rewards (Fig. 2). Using this form, a manager can select an expert(s) and reward. The system shows the left monetary benefit for each expert in the current year.

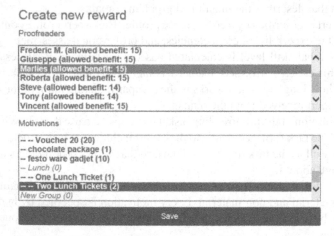

Fig. 2. Example of the new reward definition (from [3]).

3.3 Multi-aspect Ontology

As it was mentioned above, providing for interoperability in complex dynamic domains such as product lifecycle management requires new approaches. A number of projects that have been carried out for a production company have led to a necessity to share information and knowledge between several workflows and departments that do not share the same terminology. This was complicated by the fact that different workflows required the application of different formalisms. The suggested approach is based on developing a multi-aspect ontology [22] as a formalized instrument supporting various sub-domains and their processes. It assumes considering sub-domains of a complex domain as aspects integrated with a specific layer built on top of them to synchronize and match these.

The developed notation of multi-aspect ontologies divides all classes and properties of the ontology into global (visible from at least two aspects) and local (visible from one aspect), and is described as

$$O = (C^G, P^G, A, R),$$

where
  C^G – global classes,
  P^G – global properties,
  A – aspects,
  R – bridging rules.
  Each aspect is described as:

$$A_i = \left(C_{A_i}^A, P_{A_i}^A, E_{A_i}^L, R_{A_i} V_{A_i} \right)$$

where
  $C_{A_i}^A$ – aspect classes,
  $P_{A_i}^A$ – aspect properties,
  $E_{A_i}^L$ – local elements (the local elements are specific for the aspect's formalism),
  R_{A_i} – relationships between aspect elements (aspect classes and aspect properties) and local elements: $e_j^A \xrightarrow{\equiv} e_k^L$, where $e_j^A \in C_{A_i}^A \cup P_{A_i}^A$, $e_k^L \in E_{A_i}^L$ (only the equivalence relationship is considered);
  V_{A_i} – individuals.
  The following three types of bridging rules have been introduced corresponding to the rules defined in distributed description logic:
  $G{:}c \xrightarrow{\sqsubseteq} A_i{:}d$ – "inclusion in" rule: an instance of the global element c is an instance of the aspect element d;
  $G{:}c \xrightarrow{\sqsupseteq} A_i{:}d$ – "inclusion of" rule: an instance of the aspect element d is an instance of the global element c;
  $G{:}c \xleftrightarrow{\equiv} A_i{:}d$ – bidirectional "equivalence" rule: the sets of individuals of the global element c and the aspect element d are equal.
  The notation supports independence from (local) aspect notations and is OWL compatible. However, unlike distributed description logic or Context OWL (C-OWL) focused on the coordination and matching of various ontologies, and MVP-OWL focused on integrating closely related viewpoints on a problem domain, the suggested notation is focused on independent aspects sharing only relatively small amount of knowledge.

For the reason of solving the interoperability problem in the considered company, the ontology had to cover processes addressed during the development of the information and knowledge management systems. For illustrative purposes, the aspects of "Product Engineering", "Sales", and "Strategic Planning and Production" that correspond to different PLM phases and have different formalisms have been selected for this paper.

Since the multi-aspect ontology does not restrict usage of a certain formalism for its aspects, aspect ontologies can be developed on the basis of any existing methodology of ontology development, e.g., METHONTOLOGY [23]. They can also be based on the reuse of existing ontologies since typical subproblems usually already have established ontologies.

The resulting multi-aspect ontology is shown in Fig. 3. Earlier developed ontologies for different tasks have been used as the aspects on the "one task – one aspect" principle. Below, each of the aspects them is described in detail.

The *Product Engineering* aspect describes the task of defining new products and their features [24] by a product engineer and is defined in OWL. During this process, the product engineer has to make sure that the defined products and characteristics are consistent (the Pellet reasoner is used for this purpose). The sample classes presented in the figure include *"Product Family"* (a high level generalization of products), *"Product Group"* (a lower level generalization of products, a subclass of *Product Family*), *"Product"* (simple or modular product, a subclass of *Product Group*), and *"Feature"* (product characteristics, associated with the class *Product*).

The *Sales* aspect describes the task of defining and using constraints between product characteristics and product combinations in an assembly. Definition of the constraints is done using a special tool by a product manager, and they are used in the configuration tool by customers or product/solution managers [25]. To support the constraint satisfaction technology, the formalism of object-oriented constraint networks was used. The example classes from this aspect are *"Product"* (can be a product or a product combination), *"Parameter"* (parameter of a product, e.g., *"mass"*, *"power"*, that can match product characteristic but it is not always the case), and *"Constraint"* (mathematical constraints limiting or calculating values of product characteristics depending on other characteristics).

The *Strategic Planning and Production* aspect supports the task of the defining strategies related to production classes. Three classes are considered: *"ETO"* (engineered to order, this production class has the longest lead time), *"ATO"* (assemble to order, this production class has medium lead time), and *"PTO"* (pick to order, this production class has the shortest lead time) [25]. Solving this task is based on pre-defined rules, and, hence it is defined as a set of classes and production ("if … then …") rules. These rules are used for defining lead times and production plants for products. Example classes of this aspect are *"Production Class"* (the superclass for the above mentioned *"ETO"*, *"ATO"*, and *"PTO"* classes), *"Product"*, and *"Plant"*.

To sum up the following elements of the multi-aspect PLM ontology have been defined:

Aspects: Product Engineering, Sales, Strategic Planning and Production.

Local Classes (by aspect):

Product Engineering aspect: Product Family, Product Group, Product, Feature.

Sales aspect: Product, Parameter, Constraint.

Strategic Planning and Production aspect: Product, Production Class, Plant, Rule.

Global level has the following classes: Thing, Attribute, Product, Dependency, Group, Resource.

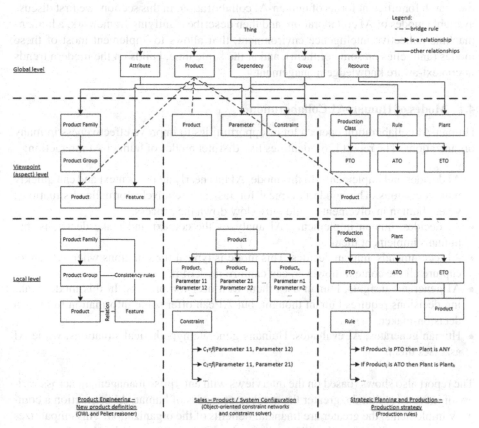

Fig. 3. Multi-aspect ontology for three aspects (from [3]).

Below, the **bridge rules** (in this particular example only the bidirectional equivalence rules are shown) for the class *Product* are demonstrated:

Product $\equiv$ Product$_{ProductEngineering}$;
Product $\equiv$ Product$_{Sales}$;
Product $\equiv$ Product$_{StrategicPlanningAndProduction}$

i.e., the concept product in different aspects has the same meaning.

The resulting ontology made it possible to establish links between heterogeneous information models, and, for example, changes made in the *Product Engineering* task can be easily reflected in the *Sales*.

4 Human-Machine Collective Intelligence

Currently, with the digitalization of businesses and the development of AI more and more organization processes include both actions performed by people and actions performed by AI tools. In general, the near future of many organization systems is connected to the search for efficient forms of human-AI collaboration. In this section, we first discuss available modes of AI collaboration, and then describe a unifying framework, a human-machine collective intelligence environment, that allows to implement most of these modes (and relies on some of them), and at the same time, builds on the modern trends in context-aware knowledge management.

4.1 Modes of Human-AI Collaboration

Human-AI collaboration opens a lot of opportunities to improve effectiveness in many organizations. The report [26] identifies five distinct modes of human-AI interaction:

- AI decides and implements. In this mode, AI has nearly all the context and can quickly make decisions. This mode is typical for fast and relatively formalized situations, where human involvement would only slow down the process.
- AI decides, human implements. AI analyzes the context and make decisions, but humans implement them.
- AI recommends, human decides. This mode is typical for situations when AI cannot capture all the context, however, can capture most of it.
- AI generates insights, human uses them in a decision process. In this mode, making decisions requires human thought, but AI can offer some information to inform decision-maker.
- Human generates, AI evaluates. Humans generate hypothetical situations, while AI assesses them.

The report also shows (based on the interviews with enterprise management across variety of industries) that the greater the number of modes of human-AI interaction a company implements, the greater are financial benefits of the organization. This empathizes the importance of human-AI collaboration and potential outcomes of such collaboration.

No doubt, that integration of AI into organization processes is a complex endeavor, requiring managerial effort, technological solutions (including the solutions in the area of human-machine interface). This paper considers the technological part of this problem. Moreover, we argue, that cornerstone problems limiting the effectiveness of human-AI collaboration are interoperability as well as knowledge representation and management. Therefore, we propose a human-machine collective intelligence environment that utilizes the discussed trends in knowledge management and helps to implement each of the five modes of human-AI interaction during the decision support, potentially allowing companies to fully use the potiential of hybrid human-AI processes.

4.2 Concept of Human-Machine Collective Intelligence Environment

The experience of implementing the above novel techniques for CAKM in a production environment and benefits they brought have led to an idea that they could be applied in a more general way to create an environment supporting human-machine collective intelligence.

The problem of human-machine collaboration and collective intelligence in particular have attracted attention of researchers in several perspectives and have posed a number of important questions [27].

The proposed human-machine collective intelligence environment is based on the following foundations:

- One of the established facts about collaborative work on complex problems is that it requires certain agent autonomy and self-organization [28].
- To achieve interoperability between human and software participants, the environment should support some structured representation of the discourse contents and/or task distribution. A good example is the Dicode project implemented within the framework of the European FP7-ICT program [29], proposing an ontological presentation of the argumentation process and a number of visual tools for working with a formalized set of interrelated arguments.

In this research, however, an environment is built where heterogeneous agents (human and software) would be able to collectively decide on the details of the workflow. Its distinguishing features are:

- The support for self-organization (in contrast to pre-defined workflows);
- Flexible role-based distribution of responsibilities;
- The use of ontologies (and, in particular, multi-aspect ontologies) to support human-machine interoperability and knowledge management.

The purpose of this environment is to implement basic discovery, information exchange and organization routines to allow agents of different nature (human and software) to collectively tackle organizational decision-making problems. In particular, the goal is to support cooperation of relatively short-lived (hours to several days) *ad hoc* teams. The primary application area of the environment is complex decision-making, therefore, the design is influenced by decision-making methodologies and the workflow implemented by a team mostly corresponds to a typical decision-making process.

Environment Ontology. The following types of actors are differentiated by the environment design: end-user (decision-maker), participant, and service provider. End-user (decision-maker) uses the environment to get help in making a decision. He/she describes the problem and posts it so that the problem description is visible to a specified community. Participant is an active entity (human or a software service) working on a problem given by the end-user. Finally, a service provider develops, integrates to the environment, and supports software services that can act as participants working on some problem given by the end user.

Main entities of the proposed environment and relationships between them are shown in Fig. 4, illustrating the high-level ontological model of the environment. Core entities, involved in most of the processes taking place in the environment and in some sense organizing and connecting other entities are the *problem* and the *team*. The problem is formulated by an end-user and then is addressed by the participants' team.

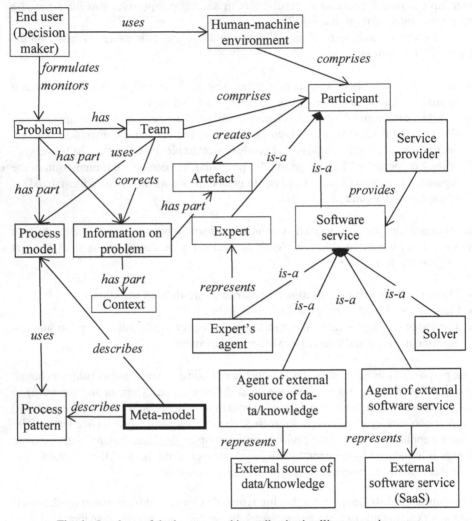

Fig. 4. Ontology of the human-machine collective intelligence environment.

The concept of a problem is also used to structure all the activities, related to the particular problem situation described by the user. On the one hand, it includes particular information on the problem (specified by the end-user, and further produced by the team), on the other hand, it includes process model (specification of what activities and in what sequence are planned by the team in order to satisfy the request of the end-user). A team is created from HMCI participants in order to address some problem, so each problem has a team dedicated to it. The team follows (and clarifies) the process and enriches the information on the problem, so that during team's activity the problem is becoming more and more detailed. Enriching the information on the problem is done via creation of various artefacts by the team participants. The role and contents of these artefacts depend on the particular stage of the decision support process.

Interoperability. An important in supporting human-machine collective intelligence is to provide interoperability between human participants and software team members. In particular, both problem information and current process definition have to be both human-readable and machine-readable. To enable an effective interpretation of this information by software participants, it is represented in a semi-structured way: in the form of ontological structure and at the same time in the natural text, corresponding to the ontological structure. Ontological knowledge representation provide a well-studied and effective way of reaching semantic interoperability, however, they turn out to be relatively hard to use by non-expert users. To facilitate the use of ontologies for people the environment makes it as implicit as possible by relying on three techniques:

- Implicit ontological representation of the structure of problem information.
- Natural language processing. Using advances in this area it is possible to infer the role of some information pieces, its relationship with the goal and/or some line of argumentation and so on.
- GUI-based nudging participants to encode problem structure in an ontology-compatible way. I.e., the environment tries to map the artefacts provided by the participants to an ontological representation, and in case of ambiguity 'nudges' paticipants to resolve it by proposing possible solutions.

The environment defines several basic ontologies, representing different aspects of the collaborative decision support (Fig. 4):

- Decision-making ontology. This ontology defines main concepts that are used during decision-making (criterion, alternative, evaluation etc.) and interaction between them. The ontology is based on the analysis of existing decision-making methodologies and has been built to support majority of them.
- Collaboration and coordination ontology. It defines the concepts used in distributing work among team members (role, responsibility, dependency etc.).
- HMCI environment ontology. This ontology defines entities of the proposed environment, most important of them are discussed above (Fig. 4).

The use of above ontologies allows artificial agents to interpret the processes taking place in the team and contribute to them. However, these ontologies do not take into account domain of the problem defined by the end-user. A team may reuse any existing domain ontology. Several ontologies used to describe the current problem state are connected by the multi-aspect ontology approach (Fig. 5). For example, if the environment is used in a smart tourism scenario to select a tourist itinerary, then possible alternatives to consider and evaluate are tourist itineraries. Therefore, class Alternative of the decision-making aspect in this problem setting is connected with the Itinerary concept of the domain aspect. Further, evaluation of the itineraries done by the team can be interpreted as evaluations of the alternatives which is an essential step in making a decision. It should be noted, that mutual mapping of the aspects is realized in the context of the problem (in location problems Alternative is mapped to geographic point, etc.).

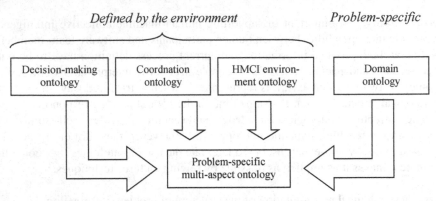

Fig. 5. Multi-aspect ontology composition.

Team Structure. The team in the context of the environment is defined as a heterogeneous group (consisting of human participants and software services) working towards solution of a particular problem. A participant may be a member of several teams, or not a member of any team.

Initial team formation is based on the same principles used in most of the crowdsourcing platforms and knowledge networks [30]: each participant has a profile describing key specializations, problem-solving history, as well as the history of previous collaborations (with mutual evaluations). There is a massive list of publications why each of this components of the profile is necessary and how it affects the efficiency of teaming. The initiative in this process is mixed in the sense that a contributor should send a proposal to the end-user, consisting of one or more team members (proposal may include several participants that already have some positive experience of working together), and end-user has to collect the initial team. However, decisions of the both parties – participants and end-users – are assisted by environment. The participants may choose to receive recommendations if some problem touching his/her area of competences is posted. On the other hand end-users may explore the description and history of all the participants mentioned in the proposals.

Due to much uncertainty typically associated with decision-making, it is often the case that during the work on the problem, the team understands that it lacks some competencies or resources. Therefore, the team may create a new resource requirements, that are registered in the environment and resolved in a manner, similar to the initial team formation process (participants have to actively apply for the positions in the team, however, both sides are assisted by the environment mechanisms).

It should be noted, that it does not fully apply to the software participants (services). As the throughput of software services is not as limited as the throughput of humans, and the execution is relatively cheap, software services are passively connected to any team and by the mechanisms of the environment (ontology-based publish-subscribe) are watching the processes taking place with the problem. There are two states a software service can be in w.r.t. the team: dormant and active. Initially, all services are in the dormant state and are waiting for specific conditions during the problem-solving. If these conditions defined by a particular service are met, the service tries to activate, describing its purpose and terms of use. If the team agrees that the service is useful for the problem, the service is allowed to activate (change state to active) and become a member of the team. Otherwise, the service remains dormant. Active service may also be transferred to the dormant state by a decision of the team. Besides, the services can be accessed via a service catalogue and activated manually by team members (Fig. 6).

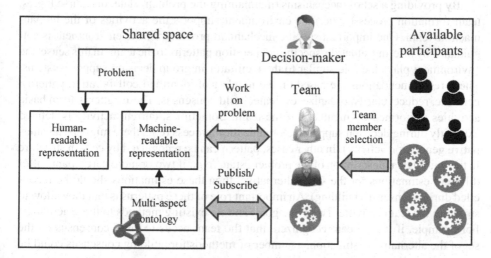

Fig. 6. Conceptual model of the environment

Active services can be used by the team members. The mechanics of their usage depends on the service's kind. There are two main types of services:

- Problem-solving service;
- External tool and database access service.

Problem-solving service accesses the problem information described in the form of ontology and natural text, and can actively add information pieces to it. An example of such service is a statistics-based question answering service – if it detects a question about some facts (e.g., "How many people die from tuberculosis in the World in one year?") and can answer it in some form, it adds an answer to the question. Another example is a service that derives from the problem information a current set of alternatives and their evaluations, builds a Pareto optimal set and adds it to the problem information.

External tool and database access services in their activated form only provide an access to a specified resource. For example, if the team needs an epidemic database, it can activate the service that grants access to this database and use it for queries.

Processes. Simultaneously two processes take place when team works on a problem: *solution preparation* and *decision support (re)organization*. Both of these processes are supported by mechanisms provided by the environment. Solution preparation is main productive process, during which problem is enriched with new information and artefacts created by team members. The result of this process is fully detailed description of a problem situation, weighted alternatives and their estimated consequences – accepted by the end-user. Decision support (re)organization process represents all the activities aimed at planning and organization of team work (e.g., deciding whether additional resources are required, assigning team member responsibilities, setting task deadlines and identifying new tasks to be solved in order to reach the goals of the whole process).

By providing a set of mechanisms (maintaining the problem state, discourse logics, team formation processes etc.) the environment supports the activities of the human-machine team. One important specific mechanism provided by the environment is soft guidance by offering situation-specific cooperation patterns to the team. In this sense, the environment plays the role similar to the facilitator in group decision support systems. These recommendations are based on the number of identified collaboration patterns: generate, reduce, clarify, organize, evaluate, build consensus. These patterns form basic activities performed by members of the team. Sometimes, current activity is defined explicitly during decision support (re)organization process (e.g., there might be an alternative generation activity). In other cases, pattern can be recognized by certain structure in the ontological description of the problem state (e.g., if two or more participants offer different estimations for the same alternative, then these estimations should be reconciled during consensus building). An important role of these patterns is that they allow to structure the team activities (w.r.t. the goal) and tie existing methods to these activities. For example, if it has been recognized, that the team needs to build consensus on the set of the alternatives estimation, a number of methods for building consensus could be recommended.

It can be seen, that the design of the environment is heavily affected by the discussed trends. First of all, ontology-based context modeling and specialization are at the core of the problem representation. The problem situation and all the artefacts are represented in the form of ontology, which allows to achieve interoperability between human and software participants. Role-based organization and multi-aspect ontologies are used to help to reconcile different aspects of the decision support (e.g., domain structure vs. process structure), besides, role-based organization is used also in the foundational layer, because every decision-making process in a coarse decomposition can be viewed as an interaction of different roles (project leader, data analyst, domain expert, etc.), and the environment supports the definition of the team via set of roles. Finally, dynamic motivation mechanisms play a role in process planning and team recruiting, because reward sharing is an important aspect of process definition.

4.3 Implementation of the Human-AI Collaboration Modes

This section explains how the proposed environment is related to the Human-AI Collaboration modes listed in Sect. 4.1. In general, the proposed HMCI is used mostly as a tool to help in making complex decisions, providing an amalgamation of collective intelligence and artificial intelligence, that is why the process of implementing a decision (or, sometimes even making it) is mostly out of scope for the HMCI, as it is used mostly to collect the required information and develop a reasonable set of alternatives. However, the environment itself extensively uses AI methods, so some of the collaboration modes are implemented not with respect to the decision of a business problem (developed with a help of HMCI), but with respect to smaller decisions that take place during management of the human-machine team activities.

AI Decides and Implements. In this mode, AI agents has the most influence. It is possible mostly when decisions are made very fast (seconds, or faster) and all the context needed for a decision can be formalized. The HMCI is developed for more complex situations, where decisions require human expertise (of even a collaborative effort of several people), so this mode in general is not relevant for the HMCI. However, there might be some smaller decisions during the course of common human-machine activity that could be taken solely by the AI components.

AI Decides, Human Implements. This mode is used by the environment only for some small decisions that are usually related to the integrity of the problem description information. For example, the environment may check the consistency, and if there are some problems with it, it can decide to make a task (or a number of tasks) to human participants of the team to fix these problems. There may also be software team members implementing a hybrid information processing cycle – issuing subtasks that should be assigned to human members of the team.

AI Recommends, Human Decides. This is the most typical mode for the environment. This mode can be exemplified by the behavior of built-in environment components. For example, during the complex collaborative activity a team may need some additional member with some expertise. The participant search service looks for candidates and recommends them to join the particular group (based on their profile). When there is some non-productive situation (e.g., conflicting alternatives) the environment proposes possible resolutions (protocols) that may be accepted or rejected by the team. On a larger scope, the whole result obtained by a team is usually a recommendation presented to a responsible decision-maker.

AI Generates Insights, Human Uses Them in a Decision Process. This is a basic scenario for software participants of a team. They may offer various services, but typically they react of current context change by offering some context-related information that can be used by the team.

Human Generates, AI Evaluates. This mode is also implemented, mostly by AI-powered software team participants. For example, in mobility support problem (e.g., tourist route development) there may be an agent evaluating candidate routes based on transport availability and typical target audience preference profiles.

5 Conclusions

In the modern world, efficient knowledge management is crucial in adaptation to ever-changing environments, allowing a business entity to identify available resources and reorganize them to better match new challenges. The paper discusses three modern trends in context-aware knowledge management for socio-cyber-physical systems:

- role-based organization,
- dynamic motivation mechanisms, and
- multi-aspect ontology.

The paper also discusses practical experience in implementing each of these trends in industrial organizations, which allowed to improve the effectiveness of knowledge eliciting, storing, and utilization, and had a major positive impact on the effectiveness of the whole system (organization).

Further, the paper describes a novel concept of a human-machine collective intelligence environment for decision support, based on the amalgamation of these trends. The environment implements basic discovery, information exchange and organization routines to allow agents of different nature (human and software) to collectively tackle complex organizational decision-making problems.

Acknowledgements. The research is partially funded by the Russian State Research, project 0073-2019-0005. The research on the human-machine collective intelligence for decision support is funded by the Russian Science Foundation, project 19-11-00126.

References

1. Smirnov, A., Sandkuhl, K.: Context-oriented knowledge management for decision support in business networks: modern requirements and challenges. In: BIR 2015 Workshops, vol. 1420 (2015)
2. Dey, A.K., Abowd, G.D., Salber, D.: A conceptual framework and a toolkit for supporting the rapid prototyping of context-aware applications. Hum. Comput. Interact. **16**, 97–166 (2001). https://doi.org/10.1207/S15327051HCI16234_02
3. Smirnov, A., Shilov, N., Ponomarev, A.: Context-aware knowledge management for socio-cyber-physical systems: new trends towards human-machine collective intelligence. In: Proceedings of the 12th International Joint Conference on Knowledge Discovery, Knowledge Engineering and Knowledge Management, pp. 5–17. SCITEPRESS - Science and Technology Publications (2020). https://doi.org/10.5220/0010171800050017
4. Gruber, T.R.: A translation approach to portable ontology specifications. Knowl. Acquis. **5**, 199–220 (1993). https://doi.org/10.1006/knac.1993.1008
5. Staab, S., Studer, R. (eds.): Handbook on Ontologies. IHIS, Springer, Heidelberg (2009). https://doi.org/10.1007/978-3-540-92673-3
6. Lundqvist, M.: Information Demand and Use: Improving Information Flow within Small-scale Business Contexts (2007)
7. Friedrich, J., Becker, M., Kramer, F., Wirth, M., Schneider, M.: Incentive design and gamification for knowledge management. J. Bus. Res. **106**, 341–352 (2020). https://doi.org/10.1016/j.jbusres.2019.02.009

8. Ferreira, A.T., Araújo, A.M., Fernandes, S., Miguel, I.: Gamification in the workplace: a systematic literature review. In: Rocha, Á., Correia, A.M., Adeli, H., Reis, L.P., Costanzo, S. (eds.) WorldCIST 2017. AISC, vol. 571, pp. 283–292. Springer, Cham (2017). https://doi. org/10.1007/978-3-319-56541-5_29

9. Smirnov, A., Kashevnik, A., Petrov, M., Shilov, N., Schafer, T., Jung, T.: Competence-based language expert network for translation business process management. In: 2019 25th Conference of Open Innovations Association (FRUCT), pp. 279–284. IEEE (2019). https://doi.org/ 10.23919/FRUCT48121.2019.8981515

10. Scekic, O., Truong, H.-L., Dustdar, S.: PRINGL – a domain-specific language for incentive management in crowdsourcing. Comput. Netw. **90**, 14–33 (2015). https://doi.org/10.1016/j. comnet.2015.05.019

11. Shilov, N., Smirnov, A., Ansari, F.: Ontologies in smart manufacturing: approaches and research framework. In: 2020 26th Conference of Open Innovations Association (FRUCT), pp. 408–414. IEEE (2020). https://doi.org/10.23919/FRUCT48808.2020.9087396

12. Asmae, A., Souhail, S., Moukhtar, Z. El, Hussein, B.: Using ontologies for the integration of information systems dedicated to product (CFAO, PLM…) and those of systems monitoring (ERP, MES..). In: 2017 International Colloquium on Logistics and Supply Chain Management (LOGISTIQUA), pp. 59–64. IEEE (2017). https://doi.org/10.1109/LOGISTIQUA.2017.796 2874

13. Palmer, C., Urwin, E.N., Young, R.I.M., Marilungo, E.: A reference ontology approach to support global product-service production. Int. J. Prod. Lifecycle Manage. **10**, 86 (2017). https://doi.org/10.1504/IJPLM.2017.083003

14. Lafleur, M., Terkaj, W., Belkadi, F., Urgo, M., Bernard, A., Colledani, M.: An onto-based interoperability framework for the connection of PLM and production capability tools. In: Harik, R., Rivest, L., Bernard, A., Eynard, B., Bouras, A. (eds.) PLM 2016. IAICT, vol. 492, pp. 134–145. Springer, Cham (2016). https://doi.org/10.1007/978-3-319-54660-5_13

15. Liao, Y., Lezoche, M., Panetto, H., Boudjlida, N.: Semantic annotations for semantic interoperability in a product lifecycle management context. Int. J. Prod. Res. **54**, 5534–5553 (2016). https://doi.org/10.1080/00207543.2016.1165875

16. Felfernig, A., Friedrich, G., Jannach, D., Stumptner, M., Zanker, M.: Configuration knowledge representations for Semantic Web applications. Artif. Intell. Eng. Des. Anal. Manuf. **17**, 31–50 (2003). https://doi.org/10.1017/S0890060403171041

17. Hagedorn, T.J., Smith, B., Krishnamurty, S., Grosse, I.: Interoperability of disparate engineering domain ontologies using basic formal ontology. J. Eng. Des. 1–30 (2019). https://doi. org/10.1080/09544828.2019.1630805

18. Hemam, M., Boufaïda, Z.: MVP-OWL: a multi-viewpoints ontology language for the Semantic Web. Int. J. Reason. Based Intell. Syst. **3**, 147 (2011). https://doi.org/10.1504/IJRIS.2011. 043539

19. Hemam, M.: An extension of the ontology web language with multi-viewpoints and probabilistic reasoning. Int. J. Adv. Intell. Parad. **10**, 1 (2018). https://doi.org/10.1504/IJAIP.2018. 10003857

20. Smirnov, A., Levashova, T., Shilov, N.: Role-driven context-based decision support: approach, implementation and lessons learned. In: Fred, A., Dietz, J.L.G., Aveiro, D., Liu, K., Filipe, J. (eds.) IC3K 2014. CCIS, vol. 553, pp. 525–540. Springer, Cham (2015). https://doi.org/10. 1007/978-3-319-25840-9_32

21. VDMA: German Engineering Federation (2018). www.vdma.org/en_GB/

22. Smirnov, A., Shilov, N., Parfenov, V.: Building a multi-aspect ontology for semantic interoperability in PLM. In: Fortin, C., Rivest, L., Bernard, A., Bouras, A. (eds.) PLM 2019. IAICT, vol. 565, pp. 107–115. Springer, Cham (2019). https://doi.org/10.1007/978-3-030-42250-9_10

23. Fernández-López, M., Gómez-Pérez, A.: Overview and analysis of methodologies for building ontologies. Knowl. Eng. Rev. **17**, 129–156 (2002). https://doi.org/10.1017/S02698889020 00462
24. Oroszi, A., Jung, T., Smirnov, A., Shilov, N., Kashevnik, A.: Ontology-driven codification for discrete and modular products. Int. J. Prod. Dev. **8**, 162–177 (2009). https://doi.org/10. 1504/IJPD.2009.024186
25. Smirnov, A.V., Shilov, N., Oroszi, A., Sinko, M., Krebs, T.: Changing information management for product-service system engineering: customer-oriented strategies and lessons learned. Int. J. Prod. Lifecycle Manage. **11**, 1–18 (2018). https://doi.org/10.1504/IJPLM. 2018.091647
26. Ransbotham, S.: Expanding AI's impact with organizational learning. Findings from the 2020 Artificial Intelligence Global Executive Study and Research Project (2020)
27. Jennings, N.R., et al.: Human-agent collectives. Commun. ACM **57**, 80–88 (2014). https:// doi.org/10.1145/2629559
28. Retelny, D., Bernstein, M.S., Valentine, M.A.: No workflow can ever be enough: how crowdsourcing workflows constrain complex work. In: Proceedings of the ACM on Human-Computer Interaction, vol. 1, Article 89 (2017). https://doi.org/10.1145/3134724
29. Karacapilidis, N., Tampakas, V.: On the exploitation of collaborative argumentation structures for inducing reasoning behavior. In: Proceedings of the 18th International Conference on IEEE/Internet (2019)
30. Ahmad, S., Battle, A., Malkani, Z., Kamvar, S.: The jabberwocky programming environment for structured social computing. In: Proceedings of the 24th annual ACM symposium on User interface software and technology - UIST 2011, pp. 53–64 (2011). https://doi.org/10.1145/ 2047196.2047203

Knowledge Sharing and Innovative Work Behavior: The Mediating Role of Task Knowledge

Valmira Osmanaj(✉) ⓘ, Shahnawaz Muhammed ⓘ, Atik Kulakli ⓘ, and Syed Faizan Hussain Zaidi

College of Business Administration, American University of the Middle East, Egaila, Kuwait
{valmira.osmanaj,shahnawaz.muhammed,atik.kulakli,
syed.zaidi}@aum.edu.kw

Abstract. Given the highly dynamic and competitive business environment, attaining sustainable competitive advantage and organizational innovativeness in long run is considered a challenging endeavor. From the perspective the social exchange theory and social capital theory, knowledge sharing is considered a primary driver to the organization innovativeness and employees' innovation at individual level. The aim of this study is to examine how knowledge sharing affects the employees' innovative work behaviors. Moreover, we focus on the mediating role of task knowledge in the relationship between knowledge sharing and innovative work behavior. For this purpose, the three dimensions of task knowledge, comprising conceptual, contextual, and operational knowledge, were analyzed using confirmatory factor analysis. Survey tool was utilized to collect the data from knowledge employees in diverse manufacturing and service-based enterprises. The empirical result of our research confirms that knowledge sharing plays a significant positive impact on helping individuals to become more innovative in their workplace. Furthermore, it indicates a partial mediation of task knowledge in the relationship between knowledge sharing and innovative work behavior. These findings serve as a solid theoretical background for future research work related to the current topic. While managers in organizations may use these research outcomes to introduce supporting mechanisms and incentives which promote knowledge sharing and encourage employees to share their expertise among peers.

Keywords: Task knowledge · Knowledge sharing · Innovative work behavior · Mediator · Survey methodology

1 Introduction

Nowadays, the focus of the organizations on fostering innovation within their workforce has increased considerably, urged by the need to introduce new products faster, rising

An earlier version of the paper was presented at the 12th International Joint Conference on Knowledge Discovery, Knowledge Engineering and Knowledge Management.

© Springer Nature Switzerland AG 2022
A. Fred et al. (Eds.): IC3K 2020, CCIS 1608, pp. 117–136, 2022.
https://doi.org/10.1007/978-3-031-14602-2_6

competition, changing global environment, and merely to maximize the use of available resources. In the interest of achieving sustainable competitive organizational innovation in the long term, organizations need to combine innovative ideas with good organizational innovation management practices [1, 3, 4, 112]. As Kahn [52, p. 453] noted "innovation is everywhere today", achieving increased presence not only in organizational mission and vision statements but also in business school curricula [52].

Despite the vast research in the area of organizational innovativeness, the debate on what innovation really means in an organizational context is still an ongoing concern [31]. In his research, Normann [82] argued that organizational innovativeness is a very complex process that needs to be considered from a broader perspective of the organization-environment relationship. As such, the phases, and types of innovations in the organization are influenced by the characteristics of the organizational subsystems-the task system, the cognitive system, and the political system [82]. Kahn [52] suggests that it could be understood from an outcome, process, and mindset perspective. From each of these perspectives, as organizations focus on producing innovative outputs related to their products, process, and other organizational outcomes, focus on the innovation process itself, and develop an innovation supportive culture in their organizations, they must do this firstly by enabling their workforce to be innovative [110].

In addition to innovations occurring in dedicated business functions, such as in R&D and new product development, researchers have emphasized the importance of innovations arising from all functions of the organization due to their potential to come up with creative ideas and the impact that it might have on organizations [9, 15, 44, 56, 85, 99]. We adopt such a broad perspective of innovation and focus on innovative work behavior (IWB) of employees across the spectrum in this study.

Several authors have suggested that knowledge sharing is an important element facilitating such innovations in the workplace [7, 21, 53, 57, 93, 109]. While how knowledge sharing facilitates the development of intellectual capital that eventually leads to organizational innovation is well documented in the literature, a clear understanding of how knowledge sharing may contribute to innovation at the individual level is still inconclusive.

This research aims to contribute to a better understanding of how such a contribution is possible at the individual level. While contemporary studies have shown that knowledge sharing impacts innovation at the individual level [7, 57, 93], the tacit assumptions in most of these studies have been that sharing knowledge (both knowledge giving and knowledge taking) bestows certain qualities in the individuals that make them more innovative. However, very few studies have empirically examined what these qualities are in relation to knowledge sharing that makes employees more innovative. Similarly, to how knowledge sharing at an organizational level contributes to the organizational knowledge [81, 111, 113], we present individual's task-related knowledge as a key mediator in the relationship between knowledge sharing and their innovative work behavior using the framework of social capital theory and social exchange theory. In substance, through this research, we aspire to explore the contention that for knowledge sharing to have an impact on workers' innovation, it does so by primarily enhancing their task-related knowledge.

2   Theoretical Background

2.1   Knowledge Sharing

Knowledge sharing in organizations has been widely discussed in the management literature and particularly in the literature related to knowledge management. It is considered one of the most important processes in an organization, no matter the size of the organization. Knowledge sharing is viewed as a behavior, process or operation, through which information essential to the organizational functioning becomes available to the organizational entities. The employees engage in exchanging their knowledge, in the form of information, skills, and expertise [71, 106]. The shared knowledge may generate new knowledge, contribute to the organizational knowledge, and enhance the organizational innovativeness and performance [65, 70, 89].

Though contributions to society at individual level are important in various ways, organizations amplify such impact. An essential aspect of these organizations and its success is their ability to communicate and coordinate the actions of its sub-units, and more fundamentally, the individual entities in it, for a larger common purpose [38, 104]. Knowledge sharing is a form of communication where provider and recipient are engaged in transferring one's understanding to the recipient of that knowledge [73, 106]. As such, providing a constructive communication climate (intensity, quality, and the use of various instruments for communication) contributes positively to the knowledge sharing process (both knowledge donating and knowledge collecting) and effective commitment of the organizational members to its organization [106]. On the other side, the more knowledge the organizational member collects, the more he or she is willing to also donate knowledge to others, generating a norm of reciprocity from the recipient, and creating stronger relationships with his/her colleagues [76, 106].

Ipe [48, p. 341] indicates that knowledge sharing is "the act of making knowledge available to others within the organization. Knowledge sharing between individuals is the process by which knowledge held by an individual is converted into a form that can be understood, absorbed, and used by other individuals.". In an organizational context, Bartol & Srivastava [17, p. 65] define knowledge sharing as "individuals sharing organizationally relevant information, ideas, suggestions, and expertise with one another". Similarly, building up into the outcomes of previous studies [26, 91, 108] individual knowledge sharing in an organizational context involves "provision of task information and know-how to help others and to collaborate with others to solve problems, develop new ideas, or implement policies or procedures" [108, p. 117].

However, knowledge sharing is a broad concept that can be viewed from many perspectives. In understanding knowledge sharing, one may focus on what is being shared [48] or on the direction of the knowledge flow [64]. Further, knowledge sharing may be viewed at an inter-organizational level or at the intra-organizational level. Intra-organizational knowledge sharing that occurs within organizations can further be focused on various organizational levels such as at the level of business units, at team level or at the individual level. Intra-organizational knowledge sharing can also be viewed based on the direction of knowledge flow within the organization as horizontal knowledge flow or vertical knowledge flow with further focus on if the vertical knowledge flow is bottom-up, top-down [97]. From the process perspective, Van Den Hooff, & De Ridder [106, p. 118] outline the knowledge sharing process consisting of "two central processes as follow: (1) knowledge donating, communicating to others what one's personal intellectual capital is; and (2) knowledge collecting, consulting colleagues in order to get them to share their intellectual capital".

Individual knowledge sharing, being the fundamental aspect of knowledge sharing that takes place at higher levels of abstraction. In this paper, we focus on the knowledge outflow of individual level knowledge (knowledge giving) and define knowledge sharing as an act of making individual knowledge available to others, similar to the definition adopted by Ipe [48]. We adopted this perspective of knowledge sharing in this research, to evaluate the extent to which individual knowledge sharing contributes to their innovative work behavior through their task related knowledge.

2.2 Task Knowledge

Knowledge is an abstract concept, thus defining and explaining its nature is elusive [20, 79, 95]. Instead, knowledge has been categorized from various perspectives, based on the knowledge objectives. One such perspective is to view individual knowledge that is relevant to their work as task knowledge. A task may be simply defined as an application problem to be solved [77], where implicitly it requires "the existence of one or more procedures that can generate a set of meaningful output data from a set of input data-in accordance with a set of essential relationships among the inputs and the outputs" (p. 446). From the service innovation perspective, task knowledge is the accumulation of facts, comprehension, skills, and lessons learned from previous and emergent service development activities and originating from different functions within the company [102].

Task knowledge structures are functionally equivalent to the knowledge structures that people have and use when they carry out any task at their work [51]. The foundation of the task approach relies on influential work which divides workplace's activities into tasks. Tasks are constructed on the activities accomplished by organizations' employees related to their specific occupations [14].

Helfat and Peteraf [42, p. 999] describe organizational capability as "the ability of an organization to perform a coordinated set of tasks, utilizing organizational resources, for the purpose of achieving a particular end result" In his study, Normann [82] has seen the organization as "consisting of various subsystems representing types of specialized knowledge or competence-the task system" (p. 203).

Therefore, organizational knowledge plays a vital role in the successful completion of these set of tasks. Organizations are sustained by acquiring knowledge relevant to its various tasks and allocating them to the right positions for accomplishing the task. From this point, optimal level of knowledge acquisition and talent is required to determine the complexity of task knowledge. Communication plays an important role in shaping the relationship between individual talents and administers the organizational process and structure that integrates detached knowledge to perform tasks more proficiently. The task-based approach identifies the organization process that optimizes the relations between tasks and talents as the core of organizational capital [35].

In a study conducted by Fonseca et al. [32], the organization innovation process was explained from a task-based perspective, and viewing the human capital as based on the tasks that organizations' workers accomplish. Authors proposed a measure of cognitive analytical and interpersonal tasks as the degree of abstractum. They contend that "the level of abstractum of a firm not only has an effect on a firm's propensity to innovate, but also on its product innovation performance" (p. 616). Further, authors proposed measures of task which allow the assessment of the optimal organizational task structure to maximize the inclination of an organization to innovate and subsequently enhance its product innovation performance. Thus, innovation performance is exploited at transitional value of the degree of abstractionism in organizations. Innovation management literature emphasizes the relationship between human capital characteristics and innovation performance [30].

While task knowledge can be viewed from many perspectives in organizations, measuring it at the right level of abstraction that it is usable for substantive analysis is very challenging. For the purpose of maintaining a generic abstraction, required to capture the full breadth of individual's task knowledge in differing contexts while keeping the construct at a manageable level for such research, we have adopted the conceptualization proposed by Muhammed et al. [74] and view task knowledge as consisting of conceptual, contextual, and operational knowledge.

Conceptual knowledge represents the "deeper understanding of why a person is engaged in a particular task" [74, p. 4] and it provides the rationale for individuals for their actions and addresses the 'know-why' aspect of a given task [36, 47]. It becomes easier to assimilate other types of information when such knowledge related to one's organizational task is present [58]. Operational knowledge comprises the knowledge individuals immediately need to accomplish their task (such as know-what and know-how) [36, 47]. This is often referred to as the declarative and procedural knowledge that individuals possess [96, 114]. In the absence of a satisfactory level of operational knowledge, individuals may not be able to even accomplish their routine tasks let alone to be innovative in their work. Contextual knowledge denotes what individuals know in addition to the immediate knowledge required to accomplish the task (operational knowledge) and may enrich the existing knowledge with what may not be obvious (such as know-who, know-where, and know-when) [13, 43]. These three knowledge components capture the breadth of knowledge that employees bear in accomplishing their organizational tasks.

2.3 Innovative Work Behavior

Knowledge sharing as an efficient way to enrich the employee's knowledge leading to new ideas generation, is considered vital for the organizations which aspire to innovate their products and services, achieve competitive advantages, and attain a strong market position [69, 86]. Henceforth, the innovation performance is an essential indicator of the success or failure of organizations [33]. The creativity and innovation at work, may be seen as "the process, outcomes, and products of attempts to develop and introduce new and improved ways of doing things" [10].

Che et al. [22] defined innovation as a combination of idea generation (generation of domain-specific, novel, and useful new ideas) and idea implementation (implementing new ideas to practice). Similarly, in the view of new product development, Normann [82] analyzed the innovation process in two stages: the initiation stage "which begins with the process of idea formation and ends when the basic properties of the new product are conceptually outlined, and some decision is made to take up the idea and continue the project" and the realization, that comprises "the rest of the process, until the product has been put on the market, and it is possible to judge the success of the project".

While substantial research has investigated the innovation process at organizational level [94, 100], there is a growing interest on studying innovation at an individual level and how it affects organizations [39, 66, 84]. The innovation capability of the organizations emanates from their employees' innovation capabilities; hence the employees' innovative work behavior (IWB) is crucial to the organization success and innovation [11, 84, 98]. IWB comprises the intentional creation, introduction and application of new ideas, processes, products or services within their work-role, group, or organizational performance [50, 84, 92, 95]. Further, Janssen [50] defined IWB as a process that encompasses three main stages: idea generation (developing novel ideas), idea promotion (obtaining external support), and idea application (producing a model or prototype of the idea).

There are a few process-oriented studies that elaborate innovation process [15]. In a study conducted by Odetunde [84], a three-phase employee innovation process was introduced, encompassing: employee creativity (idea generation phase), employee innovation (idea implementation phase) and employee innovation adoption (innovation acceptance and use phase). Whereas another study identifies five phases of innovation, specifically: project formation, idea generation, service design, testing and implementation [55].

Many researchers have analyzed the relationship between the knowledge sharing behavior and the innovative work behavior [11, 15, 41, 92]. Based on the literature review, it is widely accepted that employees who share knowledge engage more in creating, promoting, and implementing innovations [11, 15, 37, 41, 69, 92]. Moreover, according to Hassan et al. [41], knowledge sharing not only positively impacts the innovative employee behavior, but it has a positive impact on their living standard as well. Sharing knowledge ignites transformation and exploitation capabilities that help those who share information to innovate their own work practices [92].

It is believed that the employee's ideas are promoted through communication and exchange of expertise that are indispensable for stimulating innovative ideas [69]. Furthermore, knowledge sharing enables them to quickly broaden their individual knowledge range, improve their problem-solving ability and increase the work output [46]. Both the knowledge donating and knowledge collecting significantly affect employee's innovative behavior [8, 41]. When an employee participates in a knowledge donation process, they do not merely provide information to their colleagues, but they also combine, elaborate, and translate into a clear and relevant form [40]. Likewise, when the employee collects knowledge from others, his/her own capability to innovate will improve [92]. Even though the ability to elaborate, re-combine and disseminate knowledge is considered a skill set required both for knowledge sharing and innovation [92], the way how such innovations take place has not been sufficiently explored. Therefore, the focus of the current study is to analyze the impact knowledge sharing has on employee's ability to be creative, by generating domain-specific, novel and useful new ideas and implementing these new ideas into their work, and the role of task knowledge in this relationship.

3 Theories and Hypotheses

The focus of this research is understanding if and how knowledge sharing contributes to employees' innovative work behavior. A central theme in this argument is that individuals become more innovative when knowledge sharing helps them build knowledge relevant to their work which we address in this paper as 'task knowledge'. We base this on two widely accepted and used theories in this field: social exchange theory [18, 25] and social capital theory [78]. While there are several reasons for sharing knowledge within the organizational context, ranging from managerial directive to altruism [108], it is widely noted that knowledge sharing leads to gaining reciprocal benefits [54]. Social exchange theory describes knowledge sharing as a rational behavior of individuals engaged in exchange of their knowledge with the perceived possibility of rewards that they would gain from such exchange. Irrespective of the organizational rewards that they may reap in engaging in the sharing of their knowledge, what they gain is the social connections and the potential knowledge that other participants in such social settings possess. Individuals often depend on such knowledge as they navigate evolving requirements within their organizations and engage in innovation [59, 105].

Further, based on social capital theory, individuals, and social connections they have, are seen as an integral part of organizational knowledge and intellectual capital. Based on this theory, Wang & Noe [108] denote that "employees do not work, learn, or share knowledge in isolation but are embedded in social networks" (p. 122). While individuals' knowledge becomes part of an organization's intellectual capital through their social networks, they gain from the increased exposure such networks provide [111]. The broader knowledge base that they may be able to access depending on the structural, relational, and cognitive elements of such a network can be helpful in the level of innovation they may be able to exhibit in their work [72]. In the light of these two theories, we present the substantive hypotheses of this research in the subsequent subsections.

3.1 Knowledge Sharing and Innovative Work Behavior

Radaelli et al. [92] argued in their study that employees who share knowledge engage more in creating, promoting, and implementing innovations in their work. Similarly, Githii [37] concurred that those exchanging ideas and information through communication fosters innovation. Employees who share knowledge can improve self-quality by taking positive values in the form of capability, competence, skill, and trust [11]. Further, knowledge sharing enlivens knowledge recombination and re-elaboration that stimulates the generation, promotion, and application of new ideas [92].

In another study conducted by [6], the authors found out that knowledge sharing is positively related to individual performance. Moreover, they argued that successful knowledge transfer requires a high level of individual motivation so that knowledge seeker and knowledge provider openly share and accept it [6]. There is overwhelming evidence showing that knowledge management practices play a substantial role in innovation and scholars suggest that employee innovation should be supported by organizational systems and structures that stimulate their efforts to learn and acquire new knowledge [37]. Also, Masih et al. [69] contend that knowledge sharing promotes employees' innovation capabilities, and the employees should be given incentives by the management in order to increase both their knowledge sharing and innovative capabilities.

Phung et al. [87] studied the impact of knowledge-sharing behavior on the innovative work behavior at a university setting in developing countries, focusing on the moderating role of transformational leadership. The authors asserted that knowledge sharing behavior positively affects innovative work behavior and recommended that leaders should focus on promoting innovative behaviors of employees during their daily work, which encourages knowledge sharing. There are additional studies that point to the positive and significant impact of knowledge sharing on innovation [21, 49, 53, 60, 63, 92].

Based on the above literature and arguments, the following hypothesis is formulated:

H1: Knowledge sharing has a significant positive effect on innovative work behavior.

3.2 Task Knowledge as a Mediator

Organizations that address knowledge management, mostly concentrate on the macro elements, such as organizational level innovation, improved performance, and competitive advantage. This approach may be considered crucial from a strategic perspective, nevertheless it neglects the fact that such innovations are driven by a combination of innovations by individual employees in their day-to-day work. Further, organizations innovation is materialized as a result of employees sharing their knowledge and innovations across the organization. Knowledge sharing thus is considered a fundamental area in organizational knowledge management initiatives. Knowledge sharing consists of delivering task information in a collaborative environment to resolve problems. Elaborating new ideas to fulfil the task and employ policies and procedures are crucial aspects of knowledge sharing [26]. Based on the literature, some of the main implications of the knowledge sharing process include factors such as creativity, learning, and performance [3]. Hence, knowledge sharing is considered one of the main contributors to developing the social capital in organizations that can boost innovation [111].

According to Storey & Kahn [102], there is a positive relationship between task knowledge and innovation, since task knowledge increases the organization knowledge base that is further utilized to increase proficiency and drive innovation through new service development. Similarly, it was found that team knowledge contributes positively to the new product development [5]. Studies convey that both declarative and procedural knowledge of the team positively affects the team's knowledge base, which further leads to a positive impact in the new products' creativity and success. Moreover, the task complexity has a significant effect on motivation to learn and develop their work-related knowledge, which improves the innovative work behavior of the employees [2].

Another streamline of research suggests that knowledge could sometimes impede innovation, when employees become too comfortable with the knowledge that they have in doing their work, resulting in change resistance, and seeking new knowledge. For example, Subramaniam & Youndt [103] discovered in their study that human capital negatively affects the radical innovative capability, which consists of generating innovations that radically transform existing products and services). The authors also argue that having viciously independent experts, who hesitate to share their ideas with their colleagues, may be counterproductive for organizations. Despite that, in a knowledge sharing context, employees search for new knowledge and are inclined to share what they know. While it is relevant to understand what triggers the employee's willingness to share knowledge and a substantial work has been done in this regard [19, 64], our research focus lies in exploring how knowledge sharing impacts their own innovative capability by constructing their task related knowledge.

As previously discussed, knowledge at an organizational context could be conceived as comprising three elements: conceptual, contextual, and operational knowledge [74]. As employees share their knowledge among their colleagues or other communities related to their work, they establish a network of connections on which they could rely on when they face certain obstructions in their work, thus directly contributing to their operational knowledge. Such networks and communities also act as a platform where they may discover a broad range of information contributing to their contextual knowledge. Engaging in sharing knowledge requires employees to think about what they may tacitly know and consciously convert it into a form that is understandable and receivable by the audience [73]. This process can enhance the conceptual understanding of what they may already know and acquire from this endeavor. As a result, sharing knowledge can contribute to acquiring knowledge. Such an approach may be considered a more effective way to promptly gain and broaden one's task knowledge subsequently leading to new ideas and further innovations.

For example, Engestrom et al. [29], indicate that to produce hybrid and novel solutions leading to innovation, it is essential that individuals gain multi-domain contextual information that may not be directly related to task, sharing knowledge can facilitate individuals to gain such contextual knowledge. Further, successful innovations are created at workplaces when individuals can combine use knowledge with technological knowledge [68, 107]. Use knowledge they describe is the operational knowledge directly related to their work, and the technological knowledge may be part of the operational knowledge with a substantial part of it being contextual in nature due to the evolving characteristic of technology. In the context of sustainable innovation, Stoffers et al. [101] denote the importance of such knowledge as "skill development" for the development of workplace innovation.

It is widely acknowledged that innovation consists of more than creating new ideas, and may comprise selection, development, and implementation of those ideas [15, 28]. On one hand, contextual knowledge enables employees to consolidate disparate ideas, resulting in novel outcomes in their work [43]. On the other hand, conceptual knowledge helps them to develop a broader and more critical perspective of such creation and would facilitate in evaluating which of those creative ideas may be best implemented. Since operational task knowledge is the knowledge related to the concrete skill and know-how of one's task, a higher level of such operational task knowledge would contribute to the implementation of their novel ideas as well leading to a successful innovation. Taken together, we can firmly suggest that employees' task knowledge, consisting of conceptual, contextual, and operational knowledge contribute to all the phases of innovation [83]. Hence, in line with the hypothesis proposed in the previous section, while knowledge sharing may directly impact employees' innovative work behavior, there is a compelling rationale suggesting that a large portion of this impact may be attributed to the enhanced task knowledge that knowledge sharing may contribute to achieve. Based on the above analysis, we hypothesize the following:

H2: Task knowledge mediates the relationship between knowledge sharing and innovative work behavior.

4 Research Methodology

4.1 Survey Design

The current research employs a cross-sectional survey design to gather the data used to test the proposed model. Measures used in this study were developed upon generally accepted psychometric principles [24]. Face validity of the measures were assessed in the pre-test stage by having five experts and five target respondents examine the items against the construct definition [80].

Moreover, measures were refined based on a pilot survey, which was conducted prior to using it in the large-scale data collection. After receiving the responses, the data was assessed for any potential problems and missing values. Further, it was evaluated for any potential biases, such as non-response bias and common method bias. Next, validity and reliability of the measures were appraised, before assessing the substantive relationships. Once the measures were validated to be sound, substantive relationships and the related hypotheses were tested using structural equation modelling (SEM) approach in LISREL adopting maximum likelihood estimation.

4.2 Measurement

The majority of the responses to the assessed measures were anchored on a five-point Likert type scale, except for the outcome variable innovative work behavior, which was measured on a seven-point Likert type scale. Participants were requested to reflect over the past six months at their workplace, in order to answer the questionnaire. Regarding the final measure for knowledge sharing, three items were included in the questionnaire, comprising "I have shared my insights with others", "I have shared my knowledge with others" and "I have shared my work-related knowledge with others". In order to assess task knowledge, a three-dimensional measure consisting of conceptual, contextual, and operational knowledge, as proposed by Muhammed et al. [74] was utilized. The knowledge sharing and tasks knowledge items were both anchored using labels ranging from "(1) none or to a very little extent" to "(5) to a very great extent".

For the purpose of measuring the innovative work behavior, a three-item measure similar to the one applied by [2, 27] were used. It included items such as "my work was creative", "my work was original and practical", and "I was the first to use certain ideas in my kind of work". In addition, the respondents were requested to indicate the level of their innovative output in comparison to the one of other individuals in similar positions, and the items were anchored from "(1) Not at all" to "(7) To an exceptionally high degree". The other controls used in the measurement, consists of the respondent's position in the organization, level of education, age and gender.

4.3 Data Collection

A web-based survey, targeting knowledge workers in various manufacturing and related industries, was utilized to collect the data. The majority of the responses were obtained from US firms. In total, 154 usable responses were received for a response rate of 24% based on the click-through. Responses were received from knowledge workers employed in a wide spectrum of industries, where 42% of them worked in various manufacturing and related firms, 39% from computer, information technology or software firms and the remaining 19% indicated that they were from firms other than these two sectors. The respondents also represented firms of various sizes with the greatest number of responses from individuals working in large organizations that employed more than 500 individuals (40%), 25% of the responses were from individuals in small firms that employed fewer than 50 and the rest were from medium sized organizations.

Out of all the respondents, 36.4% held upper-level management positions, 22.7% held supervisory or middle level managerial positions, 31.2% were identified as professionals, and the remaining were employed at the operational level or in other than the above categories. In terms of the respondent's education level, 43.5% of them had a master's degree or above, 33.8% held bachelor's degree, 14.3% held an associate degree and the remainder had an educational level of high school. From the gender perspective, 81.2% of the respondents identified themselves as men. Also, 39% of the respondents were in the age group of 46 to 55, 23.4% between 36 and 45, 18.8% were between 56 and 65 with the remaining either younger than 36 or older than 65 years.

5 Results

5.1 Measurement Assessment

Initially, a confirmatory factor analysis was undertaken in order to assess the overall measurement model. Before proceeding with the substantive analysis tests, assessing the convergent validity and the discriminant validity of the measures is an imperative. For this purpose, the three-dimensional task knowledge, consisting of conceptual, contextual and operational knowledge was analyzed using confirmatory factor analysis in LISREL. Initially, each of those dimensions had three items except for contextual knowledge which comprised four items. However, one of the items had low loadings and was dropped from further analysis. Factor loading for these items ranged from 0.69 to 0.92. The resultant model with three items for each dimension of task knowledge had an excellent fit ($\chi 2$ = 31.6, df = 23, p-value = 0.1086, RMSEA = 0.039, GFI = 0.97, NNFI = 0.99, CFI = 1.0) based on commonly used fit indices for model-data fit [67]. Since the hypotheses in this study are based on the task knowledge as a second order construct, a second order factor with summated scales for each of its dimensions was constructed for task knowledge.

Next, it was conducted a confirmatory factor analysis with the remaining items and summated scales of the task knowledge. Factor loading for all items in this measurement model were significantly loaded on their respective constructs. The loadings ranged from 0.73 to 0.94, exceeding the minimum requirement. The resultant measurement model showed excellent fit ($\chi 2$ = 36.8, df = 24, p-value = 0.045, RMSEA = 0.046, GFI = 0.97, NNFI = 0.99, CFI = 0.99). The composite reliabilities were 0.92 for knowledge sharing, 0.80 for task knowledge, and 0.89 for innovative work behavior. Similarly, AVE ranged from 0.58 (task knowledge) to 0.79 (knowledge sharing), demonstrating a good convergent validity of the measurement instruments.

Discriminant validity measures the ability of the constructs to differentiate from other unrelated constructs and is assessed by evaluating the AVE for each construct [34, 61]. The squared correlations for each construct were less than its AVE, indicating sufficient discriminant validity [23, 34]. Highest correlation was 0.45 (between knowledge sharing and task knowledge) and was below the recommended 0.70 serving as additional evidence of discrimination confirmation [88]. The scales also showed good reliability, after being assessed using Cronbach's alpha and resulting in a range from 0.79 (Task knowledge) to 0.91 (knowledge sharing).

5.2 Mediating Effect of Task Knowledge

The mediating effect of task knowledge in the relationship between knowledge sharing and innovative work behavior, was tested employing a three-step regression approach [16]. This procedure consists of testing first the direct effect of independent variable (knowledge sharing) on dependent variable (innovative work behavior) as hypothesized in H1. In the case of a significant relationship, then two other models are evaluated. The second one with the independent variable and the moderator, and in the third model, the outcome variable - innovative work behavior is regressed on both knowledge sharing and task knowledge. Aiming to further test the mediation hypothesis, hierarchical regression analysis was used, which summated scales of the measures.

Table 1. Results of regression analysis for testing mediation [75].

	Innovative Work Behavior				Innovative Work Behavior				Task Knowledge			
	Unstandardized coefficients				Unstandardized coefficients				Unstandardized coefficients			
	Model 1				Model 2				Model 3			
	β	Std. Error	t	Sig.	β	Std. Error	t	Sig.	β	Std. Error	t	Sig.
(Constant)	4.953	0.602	8.230	0.000	3.247	0.700	4.639	0.000	2.702	0.312	8.651	0.000
Control variables												
Poisition	-0.060	0.061	-0.993	0.322	-0.077	0.058	-1.340	0.182	0.027	0.032	0.858	0.392
Education	-0.265	0.083	-3.201	0.002	-0.224	0.079	-2.831	0.005	-0.065	0.043	-1.515	0.132
Age	0.084	0.085	0.988	0.325	0.032	0.082	0.387	0.699	0.083	0.044	1.880	0.062
Gender	-0.182	0.230	-0.789	0.431	-0.250	0.219	-1.144	0.255	0.109	0.119	0.910	0.364
Main effect												
Knowledge Sharing	0.387	0.101	3.825	0.000	0.240	0.102	2.356	0.020	0.232	0.052	4.422	0.000
Mediating effect												
Task Knolwedge					0.631	0.150	4.204	0.000				
N	154				154				154			
F-Value	4.834				7.427				6.214			
R-sq	0.140				0.233				0.174			
Δ R-sq					0.092							

Table 1 shows the results of the three regression models. The first model is represented as Model 1 and indicates that, after considering the effect of the control variables, knowledge sharing had a significant impact on innovative work behavior ($\beta = .39$, p < .001), supporting hypotheses H1.

Surprisingly, level of education had a negative impact on innovative work behavior as evident in Model 1 & Model 2 (p < .01). A plausible explanation for this is that individuals with higher levels of education may have a higher bar for what is considered as innovation, possibly, due to the broader knowledge base they may have. They may feel that the ideas that they come up with and implement in their work are normally expected from them as part of their education and work, and hence, not as innovative from their perspective. Those very outcomes; however, may be perceived to be more innovative by individuals with lower levels of education. Education, however, did not have a significant impact on the respondents' self-reported task related knowledge, but had a weak positive impact on their knowledge sharing ($\beta = 0.13$, p < .1), suggesting that individuals with higher levels of education shared their knowledge slightly more than individuals with lower levels of education. Age had a weak positive relationship to only task knowledge ($\beta = .08$, p < .1), suggesting that older respondents perceived themselves to have greater task knowledge supporting the widely held belief between age and wisdom. Apart from these findings, other control variables did not have any significant impact on innovative work behavior or task knowledge.

Model 2 illustrates the regression result of knowledge sharing and task knowledge on innovative work behavior. In this model, both knowledge sharing (p < .05) and task knowledge (p < .001) had a significant positive impact on innovative work behavior and showed a significant increase in the variance explained (9.2%) compared to Model 1. In an effort to fully establish mediation, it is also indispensable that we test task knowledge as the criterion variable with knowledge sharing as the predictor (Model 3). This model showed a strong significant relationship between knowledge sharing and task knowledge ($\beta = .23$, p < .001). The above findings combined support the hypotheses related to task knowledge as the mediator (Hypotheses H2). As additional evidence for supporting the mediation, we conducted Sobel's test, as suggested by many researchers, and performed in similar contexts [45, 90]. The results show a significant indirect effect of knowledge sharing on innovative work behavior via employee's task knowledge ($z = 3.046$, p < .01). Support for both hypothesis H1 and H2, demonstrates a partial mediation of task knowledge in the relationship between knowledge sharing and innovative work behavior.

6 Discussion, Implications and Limitations

Knowledge sharing has been linked to innovation in a variety of circumstances. However, the ways it contributes to innovation at the individual level have not been adequately examined in the literature. The goal of this study was to fill that gap. It was hypothesized that one of the fundamental processes by which people can be more innovative by sharing knowledge is when such knowledge sharing contributes to their task-related knowledge. This study confirms the role knowledge sharing can play in assisting individuals in becoming more creative and innovative at work, as indicated in hypothesis H1 and validated by results. Managers who want their employees to be more innovative should take note of this and encourage knowledge sharing inside their organizations. They should consider encouraging people to share their expertise and provide structural support mechanisms such as technology platforms and incentives built into corporate reward systems to promote knowledge sharing [17, 62].

The findings also validated our second hypothesis; task knowledge plays a mediating role in the relationship between knowledge sharing and employees' innovative work behavior. This provides crucial insights into how people can become more creative by way of sharing their knowledge. They should consider how knowledge sharing might increase their expertise, allowing them to be more innovative at work. This study finds that knowledge sharing adds to employees' innovative work behavior when such knowledge sharing leads to more task-relevant knowledge, which is in line with social exchange theory and social capital theory. While social exchange theory explains how sharing knowledge enhances an individual's task knowledge, the social cognitive theory emphasizes the value of such expertise within the more extensive organizational web of knowledge that allows people to be more innovative at work. These findings open up the possibility of digging deeper into these connections from these theoretical viewpoints to better understand the function of knowledge sharing in innovation. Because there is currently no unified theory of knowledge sharing, the findings offer a chance to understand better the micro-level mechanisms of knowledge sharing in companies, bringing us closer to an approach. Given that knowledge sharing is one of the essential aspects of many knowledge management initiatives. Therefore, managers would benefit from a better understanding of what motivates employees to participate in knowledge sharing and its impact on their work and how that impact manifests itself. Other studies have found that knowledge sharing in firms positively influences performance only when employees use the knowledge, they receive through knowledge sharing [115].

Despite the research implications for and contributions to knowledge sharing and innovative work behavior, several limitations exist in this study. First, while task knowledge is an essential mediator of the impact of information sharing on innovations, the findings of this study reveal that it only partially mediates this link. Second, the study concentrates innovative knowledge behavior as mediating role of task knowledge, and it would be extended to cover more sub-fields. Third, this research does not focus on any specific industry or sector to explore the functions and benefits of empirical evidence. Further, it would be extended with the different sectoral initiatives and practices for better comparisons with relevant insights. In other words, those studies will be able to assess other facets of information sharing's impact on innovation due to this discovery. Fourth, papers published rather than English are not included; therefore, cross-cultural differences would not be considered.

Future research could use a comparable measure of task knowledge to evaluate different meaningful relationships, specifically those inside the knowledge management field, considering that understanding how the various elements improve the knowledge repository of individuals and corporates could be of interest to researchers and professionals in this discipline. In a recent study conducted by Asurakkody & Hee [12], self-leadership was revealed to be a mediator in this relationship. While acknowledging the limitations of measuring personal knowledge in an organizational context at such a broad scale and the various complexities that such an approach may obscure, this study demonstrates the utility of measuring task knowledge at such a scale and the critical substantive relationships that can be influenced by it.

References

1. Adams, R., Bessant, J., Phelps, R.: Innovation management measurement: a review. Int. J. Manag. Rev. **8**(10), 21–47 (2006)
2. Afsar, B., Umrani, W.A.: Transformational leadership and innovative work behavior: the role of motivation to learn, task complexity and innovation climate. Eur. J. Innov. Manag. **23**(3), 402–428 (2019)
3. Ahmad, F., Karim, M.: Impacts of knowledge sharing: a review and directions for future research. J. Work. Learn. **31**(3), 207–230 (2019)
4. Ahmed, P.K.: Benchmarking innovation best practice. Benchmarking Qual. Manag. Technol. **5**(1), 45–58 (1998)
5. Akgün, A.E., Dayan, M., Di Benedetto, A.: New product development team intelligence: antecedents and consequences. Inf. Manag. **45**(4), 221–226 (2008)
6. Akram, F., Bokhari, R.: The role of knowledge sharing on individual performance, considering the factor of motivation-the conceptual framework. Int. J. Multidiscip. Sci. Eng. **2**(9), 44–48 (2011)
7. Akram, T., Lei, S., Haider, M.J., Hussain, S.T.: The impact of organizational justice on employee innovative work behavior: mediating role of knowledge sharing. J. Innov. Knowl. **5**(2), 117–129 (2019)
8. Akram, T., Lei, S., Haider, M.J., Hussain, S.T.: Exploring the impact of knowledge sharing on the innovative work behavior of employees: a study in China. Int. Bus. Res. **11**(3), 186–194 (2018)
9. Amabile, T.M.: Creativity and Innovation in Organizations. Harvard Business School Background Note, Harvard Business Publishing Education, Boston, pp. 396–239 (1996)
10. Anderson, N., Potocnik, K., Zhou, J.: Innovation and creativity in organizations: a state-of-the-science review, prospective commentary, and guiding framework. J. Manag. **40**(5), 1297–1333 (2014)
11. Arsawan, I.W.E., Kariati, N.M., Prayustika, P.A., Wirga, I.W.: Elucidating knowledge sharing on innovative work behavior: multiperspective analysis. ICORE **5**(1), 670–686 (2019)
12. Asurakkody, T.A., Hee, S.: Effects of knowledge sharing behavior on innovative work behavior among nursing students: mediating role of self-leadership. Int. J. Africa Nurs. Sci. **12**, 1–6 (2020)
13. Atherton, A.: Organisational 'know-where' and 'know-when': re-framing configurations and distributions of knowledge in organisations. Knowl. Manag. Res. Pract. **11**(4), 410–421 (2013)
14. Autor, D.H., Levy, F., Murnane, R.J.: The skill content of recent technological change: an empirical exploration. Q. J. Econ. **118**(4), 1279–1333 (2003)
15. Backstrom, I., Bengtsson, L.: A mapping study of employee innovation: proposing a research agenda. Eur. J. Innov. Manag. **22**(3), 468–492 (2019)
16. Baron, R.M., Kenny, D.A.: The moderator–mediator variable distinction in social psychological research: conceptual, strategic, and statistical considerations. J. Pers. Soc. Psychol. **51**(6), 1173 (1986)
17. Bartol, K.M., Srivastava, A.: Encouraging knowledge sharing: the role of organizational reward systems. J. Leadersh. Organ. Stud. **9**(1), 64–76 (2002)
18. Blau, P.: Exchange and Power in Social Life. Wiley, New York (1964)
19. Bock, G.W., Zmud, R.W., Kim, Y.G., Lee, J.N.: Behavioral intention formation in knowledge sharing: examining the roles of extrinsic motivators, social-psychological forces, and organizational climate. MIS Q. **29**(1), 87–111 (2005)

20. Bolisani, E., Bratianu, C.: The elusive definition of knowledge. In: Bolisani, E., Bratianu, C. (eds.) Emergent Knowledge Strategies: Strategic Thinking in Knowledge Management, vol. 4, pp. 1–22. Springer, Cham (2018). https://doi.org/10.1007/978-3-319-60656_1

21. Bontis, N., Bart, C., Sáenz, J., Aramburu, N., Rivera, O.: Knowledge sharing and innovation performance. J. Intellect. Cap. **10**(1), 22–36 (2009)

22. Che, T., Wu, Z., Wang, Y., Yang, R.: Impacts of knowledge sourcing on employee innovation: the moderating effect of information transparency. J. Knowl. Manag. **23**(2), 221–239 (2019)

23. Chin, W.W.: Issues and opinion on structural equation modeling. MIS Q. **22**(1), vii–xv (1998)

24. Churchill, G.A., Jr.: A paradigm for developing better measures of marketing constructs. J. Mark. Res. **16**(1), 64–73 (1979)

25. Cropanzano, R., Mitchell, M.S.: Social exchange theory: an interdisciplinary review. J. Manag. **31**(6), 874–900 (2005)

26. Cummings, J.N.: Work groups, structural diversity, and knowledge sharing in a global organization. Manag. Sci. **50**(3), 352–364 (2004)

27. De Jong, J., Den Hartog, D.: Measuring innovative work behaviour. Creat. Innov. Manag. **19**(1), 23–36 (2010)

28. Dodgson, M.: Innovation in firms. Oxf. Rev. Econ. Policy **33**(1), 85–100 (2017)

29. Engestrom, Y., Engestrom, R., Karkkainen, M.: Polycontextuality and boundary crossing in expert cognition: learning and problem solving in complex work activities. Learn. Instr. **5**(4), 319–336 (1995)

30. Faems, D., Subramanian, A.M.: R&D manpower and technological performance: the impact of demographic and task-related diversity. Res. Policy **42**(9), 1624–1633 (2013)

31. Fagerberg, J., Mowery, D.C., Nelson, R.R.: The Oxford Handbook of Innovation. Oxford University Press, Oxford (2005)

32. Fonseca, T., de Faria, P., Lima, F.: Human capital and innovation: the importance of the optimal organizational task structure. Res. Policy **48**(3), 616–627 (2019)

33. Fores, B., Camison, C.: Does incremental and radical innovation performance depend on different types of knowledge accumulation capabilities and organizational size? J. Bus. Res. **69**(2), 831–848 (2016)

34. Fornell, C., Larker, D.: Structural equation modeling and regression: guidelines for research practice. J. Mark. Res. **18**(1), 39–50 (1981)

35. Garicano, L., Wu, Y.: A Task-Based Approach to Organization: Knowledge, Communication and Structure. CEP Discussion Papers dp1013, Centre for Economic Performance, LSE (2010)

36. Garud, R.: On the distinction between know-how, know-what, and know-why. Adv. Strateg. Manag. **14**, 81–102 (1997)

37. Githii, S.: Knowledge management practices and innovation performance: a literature review. J. Bus. Manag. (IOSR-JBM) **16**(2), 89–94 (2014)

38. Greenberg, J., Baron, R.A.: Behavior in Organizations: Understanding and Managing the Human Side of Work, 8th edn. Prentice Hall, New York (2002)

39. Grigoriou, K., Rothaermel, F.T.: Structural microfoundations of innovation: the role of relational stars. J. Manag. **40**(2), 586–615 (2014)

40. Hansen, M.T., Mors, M.L., Lovas, B.: Knowledge sharing in organisations: multiple networks, multiple phases. Acad. Manag. J. **48**(5), 776–793 (2005). https://doi.org/10.5465/AMJ.2005.18803922

41. Hassan, H.A., Asif, J., Waqar, N., Abbas, S.K.: The impact of knowledge sharing on innovative work behaviour. Asian J. Multidiscip. Stud. **6**(5) (2018)

42. Helfat, C.E., Peteraf, M.: The dynamic resource-based view: capability lifecycles. Strateg. Manag. J. **24**, 997–1010 (2003)

43. Howell, J.M., Boies, K.: Champions of technological innovation: the influence of contextual knowledge, role orientation, idea generation, and idea promotion on champion emergence. Leadersh. Q. **15**(1), 123–143 (2004)
44. Hoyrup, S.: Employee-driven innovation: a new phenomenon, concept and mode of innovation. In: Employee-Driven Innovation, pp. 3–33. Palgrave Macmillan, London (2012)
45. Hu, L., Randel, A.E.: Knowledge sharing in teams: social capital, extrinsic incentives, and team innovation. Group Org. Manag. **39**(2), 213–243 (2014)
46. Hu, M.L.M., Horng, J.S., Sun, Y.H.C.: Hospitality teams: knowledge sharing and service innovation performance. J. Tour. Manag. **30**(1), 41–50 (2009). https://doi.org/10.1016/j.tourman.2008.04.009
47. Hulme, P.E.: Bridging the knowing–doing gap: know-who, know-what, know-why, know-how and know-when. J. Appl. Ecol. **51**(5), 1131–1136 (2014)
48. Ipe, M.: Knowledge sharing in organizations: a conceptual framework. Hum. Resour. Dev. Rev. **2**(4), 337–359 (2003)
49. Jada, U.R., Mukhopadhyay, S., Titiyal, R.: Empowering leadership and innovative work behavior: a moderated mediation examination. J. Knowl. Manag. **23**(5), 915–930 (2019)
50. Janssen, O.: Job demands, perceptions of effort-reward fairness and innovative work behaviour. J. Occup. Organ. Psychol. **73**(3), 287–302 (2000)
51. Johnson, P., Johnson, H., Waddington, R., Shouls, A.: Task-related knowledge structures: analysis, modelling and application. In: 4th Conference of the British Computer Society on People and Computers IV, Manchester, pp. 35–62 (1988)
52. Kahn, K.B.: Understanding innovation. Bus. Horiz. **61**(3), 453–460 (2018)
53. Kamaşak, R., Bulutlar, F.: The influence of knowledge sharing on innovation. Eur. Bus. Rev. **22**(3), 306–317 (2010)
54. Kankanhalli, A., Tan, B.C.Y., Wei, K.K.: Contributing knowledge to electronic knowledge repositories: an empirical investigation. MIS Q. **29**(1), 113–143 (2005)
55. Karlsson, J., Skalen, P.: Exploring front-line employee contributions to service innovation. Eur. J. Mark. **49**(9/10), 1346–1365 (2015)
56. Kesting, P., Ulhøi, J.P.: Employee-driven innovation: extending the license to foster innovation. Manag. Decis. **48**(1), 65–84 (2010)
57. Khan, N.A., Khan, A.N.: What followers are saying about transformational leaders fostering employee innovation via organisational learning, knowledge sharing and social media use in public organisations? Gov. Inf. Q. **36**(4), 101391 (2019)
58. Kim, D.H.: A framework and methodology for linking individual and organizational learning: applications in TQM and product development, Massachusetts Institute of Technology, Ph.D. dissertation (1993)
59. Kim, H.H., Choi, J.N.: Do they pay back my knowledge? Generalized reciprocity of knowledge and creativity in work teams. In: Academy of Management Proceedings, vol. 2019, no. 1, p. 10911. Academy of Management, Briarcliff Manor (2019)
60. Kim, W., Park, J.: Examining structural relationships between work engagement, organizational procedural justice, knowledge sharing, and innovative work behavior for sustainable organizations. Sustainability. **9**(2), 205 (2017)
61. Kline, R.B.: Principles and Practice of Structural Equation Modeling, 3rd edn. The Guildford Press, New York (2010)
62. Le, P.B., Lei, H.: Determinants of innovation capability: the roles of transformational leadership, knowledge sharing and perceived organizational support. J. Knowl. Manag. **23**(3), 527–547 (2019)
63. Leonardi, P.M.: Social media, knowledge sharing, and innovation: toward a theory of communication visibility. Inf. Syst. Res. **25**(4), 796–816 (2014)
64. Lin, C.P.: To share or not to share: modeling knowledge sharing using exchange ideology as a moderator. Pers. Rev. **36**(3), 457–475 (2007)

65. Lin, H.F.: Knowledge sharing and firm innovation capability: an empirical study. Int. J. Manpow. **28**(3/4), 315–332 (2007)
66. Maqbool, S., Černe, M., Bortoluzzi, G.: Micro-foundations of innovation. Eur. J. Innov. Manag. **22**(1), 125–145 (2019)
67. Marsh, H.W., Hocevar, D.: Application of confirmatory factor analysis to the study of self-concept: first-and higher order factor models and their invariance across groups. Psychol. Bull. **97**(3), 562 (1985)
68. Marwede, M., Herstatt, C.: No innovation for the elderly? The influence of cognitive distance in corporate innovation. Creativity Innov. Manag. **28**(3), 355–367 (2019)
69. Masih, N., Sriratanaviriyakul, N., El-Den, J., Azam, S.: The role of knowledge sharing on employees' innovation initiatives. In: 2018 8th International Workshop on Computer Science and Engineering (WCSE 2018), pp. 697–704 (2018)
70. Michna, A.: The mediating role of firm innovativeness in the relationship between knowledge sharing and customer satisfaction in SMEs. Eng. Econ. **29**(1), 93–103 (2018)
71. Mirzaee, S., Ghaffari, A.: Investigating the impact of information systems on knowledge sharing. J. Knowl. Manag. **22**(3), 501–520 (2018)
72. Moustaghfir, K., Schiuma, G., Mura, M., Lettieri, E., Radaelli, G., Spiller, N.: Promoting professionals' innovative behaviour through knowledge sharing: the moderating role of social capital. J. Knowl. Manag. **17**(4), 527–544 (2013)
73. Muhammed, S., Doll, W.J., Deng, X.: Impact of knowledge management practices on task knowledge: an individual level study. Int. J. Knowl. Manag. **7**(4), 1–21 (2011). https://doi.org/10.4018/jkm.2011100101
74. Muhammed, S., Doll, W.J., Deng, X.: A model of interrelationship among individual level knowledge management success measures. Int. J. Knowl. Manag. **5**(1), 1–16 (2009). https://doi.org/10.4018/jkm.2009010101
75. Muhammed, S., Osmanaj, V., Kulakli, A., Zaidi, S.: Evaluating task knowledge as a mediator in the relationship between knowledge sharing and innovative work behaviour. In: Proceedings of the 12th International Joint Conference on Knowledge Discovery, Knowledge Engineering and Knowledge Management, vol. 3, pp. 40–50 (2020)
76. Mura, M., Lettieri, E., Radaelli, G., Spiller, N.: Promoting professionals' innovative behaviour through knowledge sharing: the moderating role of social capital. J. Knowl. Manag. **17**(4), 527–544 (2013)
77. Musen, M.A.: Dimensions of knowledge sharing and reuse. Comput. Biomed. Res. **25**(5), 435–467 (1992)
78. Nahapiet, J., Ghoshal, S.: Social capital, intellectual capital, and the organizational advantage. Acad. Manag. Rev. **23**(2), 242–266 (1998)
79. Neta, R., Pritchard, D.: Arguing About Knowledge, 1st edn. Taylor & Francis Ltd., Routledge, London (2009)
80. Netemeyer, R.G., Bearden, W.O., Sharma, S.: Scaling Procedures: Issues and Applications, 1st edn. Sage Publications, California (2003)
81. Nonaka, I.: A dynamic theory of organizational knowledge creation. Organ. Sci. **5**(1), 14–37 (1994)
82. Normann, R.: Organizational innovativeness: product variation and reorientation. Adm. Sci. Q. **16**(2), 203–215 (1971)
83. Nurulin, Y., Skvortsova, I., Tukkel, I., Torkkeli, M.: Role of knowledge in management of innovation. Resources **8**(2), 87 (2019)
84. Odetunde, O.J.: Employee innovation process: an integrative model. J. Innov. Manag. **7**(3), 15–40 (2019)
85. Oldham, G.R., Cummings, A.: Employee creativity: personal and contextual factors at work. Acad. Manag. J. **39**(3), 607–634 (1996)

86. Ologbo, A.C., Nor, K.M., Okyere-Kwakye, E.: The Influence of knowledge sharing on employee innovation capabilities. Int. J. Hum. Resour. Stud. **5**(3), 102–110 (2015)
87. Phung, V.D., Hawryszkiewycz, I., Chandran, D.: How knowledge sharing leads to innovative work behaviour: a moderating role of transformational leadership. J. Syst. Inf. Technol. **21**(3), 277–303 (2019)
88. Ping, R.A., Jr.: On assuring valid measures for theoretical models using survey data. J. Bus. Res. **57**(2), 125–141 (2004)
89. Pittino, D., Martínez, A.B., Chirico, F., Galván, R.S.: Psychological ownership, knowledge sharing and entrepreneurial orientation in family firms: the moderating role of governance heterogeneity. J. Bus. Res. **84**, 312–326 (2018)
90. Preacher, K.J., Hayes, A.F.: SPSS and SAS procedures for estimating indirect effects in simple mediation models. Behav. Res. Methods Instrum. Comput. **36**(4), 717–731 (2004)
91. Pulakos, E.D., Dorsey, D.W., Borman, W.: Hiring for knowledge-based competition. In: Jackson, S.E., DeNisi, A., Hitt, M.A. (eds.) Managing Knowledge for Sustained Competitive Advantage: Designing Strategies for Effective Human Resource Management, Pfeiffer, pp. 155–177 (2003). https://digitalcommons.usf.edu/psy_facpub/1067
92. Radaelli, G., Lettieri, E., Mura, M., Spiller, N.: Knowledge sharing and innovative work behaviour in healthcare: a micro-level investigation of direct and indirect effects. Creativity Innov. Manag. **23**(4), 400–414 (2014)
93. Ritala, P., Olander, H., Michailova, S., Husted, K.: Knowledge sharing, knowledge leaking and relative innovation performance: an empirical study. Technovation **35**, 22–31 (2015)
94. Rothaermel, F.T., Hess, A.M.: Building dynamic capabilities: innovation driven by individual-, firm-, and network-level effects. Organ. Sci. **18**(6), 898–921 (2007)
95. Russell, B.: Human Knowledge: Its Scope and Limits, 1st edn. Routledge, London (2009)
96. Schultze, U., Leidner, D.E.: Studying knowledge management in information systems research: discourses and theoretical assumptions. MIS Q. **26**(3), 213–242 (2002)
97. Schulz, M.: The uncertain relevance of newness: organizational learning and knowledge flows. Acad. Manag. J. **44**(4), 661–681 (2001)
98. Scott, S.G., Bruce, R.A.: Determinants of innovative behavior: a path model of individual innovation in the workplace. Acad. Manag. J. **37**(3), 580–607 (1994)
99. Smith, M., Busi, M., Ball, P., Van der Meer, R.: Factors influencing an organisation's ability to manage innovation: a structured literature review and conceptual model. Int. J. Innov. Manag. **12**(04), 655–676 (2019)
100. Stalk, G., Evans, P., Shulman, L.E.: Competing on capabilities: the new rules of corporate strategy. Harv. Bus. Rev. **70**(2), 57–69 (1992)
101. Stoffers, J., van der Heijden, B., Schrijver, I.: Towards a sustainable model of innovative work behaviors' enhancement: the mediating role of employability. Sustainability **12**(1), 159 (2020)
102. Storey, C., Kahn, K.B.: The role of knowledge management strategies and task knowledge in stimulating service innovation. J. Serv. Res. **13**(4), 397–410 (2010)
103. Subramaniam, M., Youndt, M.A.: The influence of intellectual capital on the types of innovative capabilities. Acad. Manag. J. **48**(3), 450–463 (2005)
104. Thomas, S.P., Thomas, R.W., Manrodt, K.B., Rutner, S.M.: An experimental test of negotiation strategy effects on knowledge sharing intentions in buyer–supplier relationships. J. Supply Chain Manag. **49**(2), 96–113 (2013)
105. Tsai, J.C.A., Kang, T.C.: Reciprocal intention in knowledge seeking: examining social exchange theory in an online professional community. Int. J. Inf. Manag. **48**, 161–174 (2019)
106. Van den Hooff, B., de Ridder, J.A.: Knowledge sharing in context: the influence of organizational commitment, communication climate and CMC use on knowledge sharing. J. Knowl. Manag. **8**(6), 117–130 (2004)

107. Von Hippel, E.: Sticky information and the locus of problem solving: implications for innovation. Manag. Sci. **40**(4), 429–439 (1994)
108. Wang, S., Noe, R.A.: Knowledge sharing: a review and directions for future research. Hum. Resour. Manag. Rev. **20**(2), 115–131 (2010)
109. Wang, Z., Wang, N.: Knowledge sharing, innovation and firm performance. Expert Syst. Appl. **39**(10), 8899–8908 (2012)
110. West, M.A., Farr, J.L.: Innovation at work: psychological perspectives. Soc. Behav. **4**(1), 15–30 (1989)
111. Widén-Wulff, G., Ginman, M.: Explaining knowledge sharing in organizations through the dimensions of social capital. J. Inf. Sci. **30**(5), 448–458 (2004)
112. Wong, S.Y., Chin, K.S.: Organizational innovation management: an organization-wide perspective. Ind. Manag. Data Syst. **107**(9), 1290–1315 (2007). https://doi.org/10.1108/026355 70710833974
113. Yang, J.T.: The impact of knowledge sharing on organizational learning and effectiveness. J. Knowl. Manag. **11**(2), 83–90 (2007)
114. Zack, M.H.: Managing codified knowledge. Sloan Manag. Rev. **40**(4), 45–58 (1999)
115. Zaim, H., Muhammed, S., Tarim, M.: Relationship between knowledge management processes and performance: critical role of knowledge utilization in organizations. Knowl. Manag. Res. Pract. **17**(1), 24–38 (2019)

2.0 KMIS and Knowledge Dynamics

Alizee Lacosta(✉) and Catherine Thomas

GREDEG, Université Cote d'Azur CNRS, 250 rue Albert Einstein, Valbonne Sophia-Antipolis, France
{alizee.lacosta,catherine.thomas}@univ-cotedazur.fr

Abstract. Web 2.0 technologies such as enterprise social networking (ESN) tools have a profound impact on knowledge management (KM) within companies towards greater simplicity, fluidity, and dynamism. According to the latest research, the KM information systems (KMIS) from Web 2.0, mobilizing more collaborative technologies, call for a better knowledge sharing and creation, based on their intuitive functionalities and "the wisdom of the crowd". Based on a Design research methodology carried out within an international company, our research provides three main results: (1) implementation guidelines, based on 9 design rules, are provided for an efficient 2.0 KMIS; (2) out of step with the literature, these technologies are efficient for knowledge sharing, but have not proved their efficiency on supporting knowledge creation; (3) the capacity of these tools to motivate users through visibility and centrality creates a tension with the need for a common identity to manage knowledge on this type of information systems.

Keywords: Knowledge management · Enterprise social networking tool · ESN · JIVE

1 Introduction

Interactions between individuals is at the heart of the two knowledge management (KM) processes. The first one, knowledge sharing, requires people to ex-change/interact [1–3]. The second process, knowledge creation, is allowed by people interacting to combine knowledge [3, 4]. Since almost two decades, KM is facilitated by digital technologies, and nowadays, most of the literature around KM is talking about information systems (IS) that support KM [5–9].

These technologies, supporting knowledge management have evolved, from a primary purpose of storing knowledge (traditional KMIS) to exchange and collaborative objectives. Then, KMIS today do not only serve knowledge capitalization, but also collaboration and so, knowledge combination [10–13]. Indeed, KMIS from Web 2.0 (2.0 KMIS) including enterprise social networking (ESN) tools, aim to simplify their usage and streamline interactions [14–16]. ESN-type tools focus on developing virtual social network [17]. Then, by enhancing dimensions of social capital [4], these tools aim to favor knowledge combination [10, 11]. Thus, a question comes around their ability to create ties and more specifically: How to implement these ESN for them to create the social interactions supporting efficient knowledge sharing and creation?

© Springer Nature Switzerland AG 2022
A. Fred et al. (Eds.): IC3K 2020, CCIS 1608, pp. 137–156, 2022.
https://doi.org/10.1007/978-3-031-14602-2_7

To reply to this question, we conducted a design methodology within an international company, as part of a PhD research completed in three years. Starting by put-ting in perspective the KM and the IS literature around knowledge exchange, the methodology will be explained as well as the context in order to present the results through the design of rules in CIMO-logic. This article allows to have a clear vision on the construction of an ESN-type KMIS (JIVE) and provide results on these tools' capacity to support knowledge dynamics. More specifically, (1) we provide implementation guidelines, based on 9 design rules, for an efficient 2.0 KMIS; (2) out of step with the literature, our results show that these technologies are efficient for knowledge sharing, but have not proved their efficiency on supporting knowledge creation; (3) the capacity of these tools to motivate users through visibility and centrality has revealed a tension with the need for a common identity to manage knowledge on information systems.

2   Knowledge Dynamics

2.1   Knowledge Sharing

The key to understand the way knowledge is created is the interaction between tacit and explicit knowledge, but it also explains how it is diffused within a group of people [2]. Tacit knowledge is embodied in individuals and is more experienced than shared, therefore tacit knowledge is difficult to share [3]. Explicit knowledge, also called codified knowledge, can take several aspects, with different degrees of abstraction, about the "how" and the "why" [18]. Knowledge never stays in a fixed status, it moves from tacit to explicit and evolves through social exchange (SECI model - [1–3]). Authors then speak about tacit/explicit knowledge interaction and this interaction is source of dynamics.

However, tacit/explicit interaction is not the only component of knowledge dynamics, there is also the social dimension of the exchange. Even if the focus, in the SECI model [2], is on the tacit/explicit interactions [3], we can see that social exchange is important to favor the virtuous circle between the two types of knowledge. They complement and enrich each other [1, 3].

Moreover, reusing codified knowledge in other contexts requires its combination with different elements to favor new knowledge creation [3]. Nevertheless, the appropriation of codified knowledge can be questioned here, as this knowledge transfer raises the question of the individuals' capacity to use in their practices a knowledge codified in other contexts [19]. The codification process can lead to several forms of codification, more or less abstract, depending on the primary objectives. The question of the abstraction is key to ease knowledge dissemination and communication [20] but can also generate a loss of accuracy in the representation of phenomena, the actors would need, then, to expend major effort on re-contextualization [18].

2.2   Knowledge Creation

According to Kogut and Zander [21] and Nahapiet and Ghoshal [4], sharing and creating organizational knowledge is a social process which contain knowledge exchange, absorption and combination. These latter reflect the entanglement of knowledge forms in an organization as a complex social process. The organization should be capable to coordinate, structure, share and create knowledge to build its intellectual capital, which takes its source in the social capital [4]. From Nahapiet and Ghoshal's study [4], three dimensions compound the social capital: first, the structural dimension that refers to the configuration and the density of the ties which connect individuals; the relational dimension which shapes the social system; and the last dimension, cognitive, that promotes a cognitive alignment of individuals which will facilitate the sharing and combination of knowledge. The second dimension, relational, feeds the sense of belonging in a group and lays the foundations of communication and exchanges between members [8].

Communities of Practice (CoP) represent a good example of organizations capable of coordinating, structuring, sharing, and creating knowledge. They are defined by the sharing of work conditions [22], when this condition is met individuals form a community. This common practice generates a support for collective memory [22], CoP are therefore original social structures.

Yet, knowledge management is nowadays considered with information technologies as they support KM processes [23, 24]. In the last decades, KM tools have evolved a lot, from codified knowledge storage tools to collaborative ones [25], especially these last 5 years to ESN-type tools [26].

3 2.0 KMIS

Enterprise social networking (ESN) tools are part of the wave 2.0 defined as applications facilitating interactive information sharing, interoperability, and collaboration on the Internet [27]. This definition is focused on the participation of actors in the system, rather than on the technology, promoting social exchanges. The link between KM and Web 2.0 can therefore be seen as the path from autonomous process systems to networks and collaboration [25]. Web 2.0 is characterized by the social web, which represents the activities of systems, due to the socialization of the Web, that generate new data, which in turn are processed and reused in other areas [28]. ESN tools have special features, enabling to develop social dimension of knowledge exchange.

Research around knowledge sharing and KMIS have, during the last decade, focused on incentives to motivate people to share knowledge within the organization [6, 23, 29, 30]. As Web 2.0 technologies give prominence to participants, and social aspects of their relationship, it reshapes the incentives and knowledge approach [31].

3.1 ESN Specific Features

Web 2.0 is intended to "simplify" use in order to improve interactivity on the web. Interactivity is enhanced by the ability to comment, like [32, 33] and "tag" documents. This helps to give visibility to the content and/or the person behind the content [33]. McAfee [14] suggests the acronym "SLATES" (Search, Links, Authoring, Tags, Extensions, Signals) to differentiate the key features of Web 2.0 technologies. On this kind of platform, with "SLATES" functionalities, authoring allows content to be created, links and tags link them; and search, extensions, tags, and signals shape structures and patterns of visible content, allowing users to "stay on top" [14]. In addition to the "SLATES" functionalities defined by McAfee [14], there are also social bookmarks, "discussions" and "evaluations", visible to all, without needing to participate on the platform [14, 15, 34, 35]. Social bookmarks, along with tags, allow employees and colleagues to search and locate the contents and their associated experts, in order to "look at" what they have found useful or to discover answers or solutions without interrupting them [34]. Discussions are mainly carried out through "questions/answers" and through comments which contain a lot of useful and valuable information for the "requester" but also available to third parties [33]. These tools also provide the ability to create (written) "discussions" allowing individuals to interact with a large number of people without having to email all participants [34]. Finally, content evaluations and the gain of participation points linked to gamification give visibility to contributors. These assessments provide social recognition of a person's contributions and place a value on the individual's knowledge as well as on their ability to create knowledge [34], evaluations and gamification, thus, impact individual's reputation.

3.2   2.0 KMIS' Influence on Knowledge Dynamics.

As explained in the first section, knowledge dynamics is compounded of the two main KM processes: knowledge sharing and knowledge creation. The previous paragraph has showed all the features that Web 2.0 technologies bring to IS and so to KMIS. Yet, we need to explore what the literature says on the impact of these new technologies on knowledge dynamics.

2.0 KMIS and Knowledge Sharing. ESN-type tools are part of the Web 2.0 and designed as a "social network" application. They are defined as applications that support the development of existing personal relationships, the discovery of potential relationships and should help convert these potential ties into weak or strong ones [34]. These enterprise social networking technologies support emerging communications, collaboration between individuals, and the continuous improvement of a contact directory; they are based on self-organized participation and promote dynamic communication [35, 36]. In addition, the ability to see links between individuals, allows users to identify mutual relationships that can be exploited to match, introduce, or recommend contacts: the important element "It's not who you know, it's what who you know knows" [34]. The visibility of communications and knowledge exchange therefore improves levels of knowledge sharing [35].

These ESN-type tools can assist organizations in creating an online resource containing the accumulated wisdom of the organization by allowing knowledge to be codified, sought out and shared [34]. These characteristics allow these technologies to surpass the limits of traditional KMIS [35–37], by allowing to increase the sharing of unstructured knowledge in organizations [10, 32, 33, 35, 38].

2.0 KMIS and knowledge creation. Web 2.0 technologies are a powerful lever for the sustainable creation of relationships in dispersed social communities [15]. Indeed, the rule "the friends of my friends are my friends" has never been truer than in the context of Web 2.0, and the theory of the strength of weak ties of Granovetter [39] extends with the tools of the social network type, in particular for the personal advancement of the individual in the organization [15]. These Web 2.0 tools - promoting participation through different forms of communication, and in greater number - allow exchanges around common interests and thus create "communities" [12, 40]. It is this multitude of exchanges that leads the literature to consider these tools in a logic of collaboration and less in that of storing and sharing knowledge.

Through the collaborative prism, the literature has studied the influence of these tools on the social capital of the organization, a key element in the creation of knowledge [4]. It is because these technologies have a positive influence on the three dimensions, structural, cognitive, and relational of social capital, that they are supposed to influence the knowledge creation [11–13]. However, the impact of Web 2.0 tools on the relational dimension remains debated: some authors note that trust and identification emerge and grow on these tools [10, 13, 26, 30, 41, 42]; and others consider that the relational dimension is only indirectly affected via the structural and cognitive dimensions [11].

The literature thus assumes the effectiveness of Web 2.0 tools in creating knowledge through their ability to enrich social capital. The effectiveness of these tools on knowledge creation itself is not directly studied.

3.3   2.0 KMIS and Motivation

On traditional KMIS, two main challenges have been raised with regards on knowledge sharing: codification costs [8, 43] and loss of power [8, 30, 44].

First, questions and comments on Web 2.0 tools, are more contextual and require less time to "reply". In addition to this, the different level of "tacitness" provide opportunities to share more tacit knowledge on Web 2.0 tools [10, 13]. We can therefore assume that the cost of codification is reduced by the functionalities of these technologies which make it possible to take advantage of the different levels of "tacitness" of knowledge.

Second, the visibility (popularity, social image, or reputation) provided by Web 2.0 tools can help reduce the feeling of power loss for the contributor [34]. The centrality of the individual within his "online" network, and the social rewards linked to this centrality, give individuals power (social influence) and a reputation, in particular thanks to visibility on the tool [32, 33, 35, 45, 46]. Thus, on ESN tools, it is the perspective of this centrality in his/her network that prevails in motivating contributors to share their knowledge, because this centrality gives them the power of influence [17, 46].

In addition to these traditional KMIS motivation components, ESN-type tools have their own. The way these technologies have been built (intuitive, with ease of use to favor participation) bring a "by default" ease of use and so, a better IS appropriation (see Technology Acceptance Model – TAM - [47–49]). Furthermore, there's a "native" motivator on ESN tools: the gamification [16, 38, 46, 50] defined as the use of game elements in contexts that do not usually use them - non-game contexts - [46, 51]. This "game" introduces additional complexities and poses a challenge in the IS design [46]. By quantifying employee contributions, gamification helps identify "who knows what" and "who contributes to what" (knowing who knows); it thus strengthens the updating of knowledge links and exchanges (ESN characteristics) in order to improve the levels of knowledge sharing [51]. The gamification plays a hedonic role but needs also to bring meaningfulness to users [46]. From the start, it is made to increase the involvement of users on the platform [46], but is also linked to rewardability, visibility and competition [51].

Finally, according to KM literature, norms, climate, and culture positively impact knowledge sharing for contributors. Web 2.0 tools, and more specifically ESN-type tools, are supposed to reproduce the company's social capital on the tool, that is to say, to reproduce the networks of relationships which form a valuable resource for the organization [4]. As a result, ESN-type tools affect both the contributors 'motivation, through the emphasis on social image, and knowledge consumers 'motivation, through collective trust/wisdom of the crowd [50].

On traditional KMIS, ensuring the motivation of users and contributors is the role of the governance, especially to avoid vicious circles [52]. On Web 2.0 tools, the technology's functionalities seem to do the job by themselves.

4 Methodology

4.1 Context

This research is carried out within the framework of a CIFRE (an industrial agreement for training through research in France) PhD thesis within a leader company in the travel industry. The company, we will name Travel-α for confidentiality reasons, is an international company with different management offices in America, Europe and Asia. During 2016, Travel-α initiated a change in its strategy based on a digital transformation. The company's KM strategy is to support the company strategy of Travel-α while assisting its employees in digital knowledge sharing and creation via an ESN-type tool, JIVE (commercial software). Travel-α used several content management platforms, mainly an intranet and SharePoint. The current KM project is to gather most of this SharePoint content on JIVE. The goal is to allow employees to share, exchange, communicate and collaborate as freely as possible.

The objective of implementing this new tool is threefold: (1) share information relating to human resources and HR processes, i.e., the intranet, (2) manage knowledge relevant to customer relations and (3) organize and encourage interactions via the emergence of collaborative groups between Travel-α employees. The last two objectives are managed by the KM function; the study therefore focuses on these two.

4.2 Integrative Design Methodology

In order to carry out this research, we have adopted a design methodology well suited to intervention research where the researcher-actor aims to design and then implement a tool or an organizational device. We applied an integrative design methodology [53] which combines two methodologies: "science-based design" and "human centered – design". The first one corresponds to the development of design rules by mobilizing existing knowledge in the scientific literature; the second one - "human centered – design" approach - focuses on the practitioners' knowledge, on the assumption that successful solutions emerge from design processes involving users and future users and analysis of their needs [54].

The integrative approach thus combines knowledge from the literature and from practitioners; the design rules from the literature are supplemented by the construction of "usage scenarios". These consist of capturing the knowledge of practitioners through the analysis of their practices and the potential expected uses of the tool. The development of design rules will make it possible to design and then implement the organizational mechanism that will accompany the establishment of JIVE to develop a KM strategy of exchange, sharing and creation of knowledge. These rules, written by adopting the CIMO logic model [55] describe the Context, the Intervention performed, the Generating Mechanism activated to obtain the desired result "Outcome".

The design rules from the literature, once implemented, can be tested and a new design loop can be developed. Thus, this methodology is carried out in several loops, each consisting of six stages: understanding the problem, developing design rules, creating usage scenarios, building the artefact, evaluation, and transformation [54].

4.3 Methodology Implementation

The implementation of this methodology was done in three design loops between 2018 and 2020; the last loop could not be completed due to the Covid-19 pandemic. This implementation was done through the implementation of design rules to create and manage KM groups on JIVE. The groups created are identified by their initials. Data collection and analysis are used to understand the problem and create usage scenarios, which are the preliminary steps to developing design rules and then evaluating these rules. The evaluation is both the last step of the current loop and the first of the next loop.

Loop 1. Loop 1 data was collected through two surveys, conducted one year apart. The objective was to fully understand the problems and issues associated with the implementation of JIVE and to develop scenarios of usage. The surveys, with multiple-choice and open questions, were sent (via the Internet) to all departments of the organization: the first survey (more than 400 responses collected), carried out in 2017 just after the launch of JIVE, sought to identify the uses of the different KM tools in Travel-α; the second, carried out in 2018, aimed to identify the changes in use introduced by the new platform. The first survey was followed by semi-structured interviews with a selection of users of the "Customer" function, the first audience of the KM team: 54 interviews of 30 min each, were conducted over 5 weeks in order to identify the most sought-after documents, the processes for retrieving these documents on the different platforms and the new uses developed on JIVE, compared to the uses on SharePoint. The analysis of this data in interaction with the literature enabled the development of the first design rules, tested on three official KM groups, called "pilot groups".

Loop 2. For the second design loop, a third survey was launched (500 responses collected) and was followed by 25 semi-structured interviews of 30 min each. The main purpose of these interviews was to identify 1) the reasons why collaborators were going to JIVE, 2) the type of content sought, 3) the recovery process initiated and 4) the difficulties encountered. In addition, during this second loop, more than 180 meetings with group leaders, contributors and key KM stakeholders were conducted and coded. The analysis of this new data has enriched the design rules of the first loop.

Loop 3. The third design loop could not be completed due to the Covid-19 pandemic. This is why the annual survey was not launched. Only meetings with group leaders, contributors and stakeholders were conducted: 30 meetings in total for the construction of new official KM groups, and 8 meetings to develop governance adapted to the KM system deployed on JIVE.

5   Results

The results of this research correspond to the knowledge created thanks to the de-sign rules conceived and tested in practice, enriched over the three design loops. Intermediate results have been presented in Lacosta and Thomas' article [54] after implementing the first loop and half of loop 2. The current article presents an enrichment of the results with the finalization of the loop 2 and the implementation of loop 3 and provides design rules for the construction of an ESN-type KMIS.

These results are presented following the integrative methodology steps (problem awareness, design rules, artefact construction and evaluation). Each design rule is presented in CIMO-logic format. We will not repeat the context, a multinational firm of American culture, which remains unchanged for the duration of the study.

5.1   Problem Awareness

The first analysis of meetings and interviews allowed us to define problems at two levels: strategic and operational. At the strategic level, expectations were (1) to organize knowledge in alignment with the new strategy and (2) to use JIVE to create a KM system. The second loop added a third strategic issue: a KM governance seems needed but adapted to these web 2.0 technologies. At the operational level, get one platform to store knowledge and content, was the most requested element. But the change from a very centralized platform to a decentralized one was one of the main operational challenges KM team had to solve. The second operational challenge was to manage the transition from SharePoint to JIVE in order to get more collaboration for a richer sharing. In using an ESN-type tool, specific features, like gamification, have been used to motivate users to participate on the platform, however some issues have been raised during the second loop with regards on using gamification on a KM system. Finally, communication around the KM system has and still require improvements.

5.2   Design Rules

The literature in interaction with surveys and interviews has allowed us to gather design rules according to their objectives, into three principles: design rules (1) for the architecture of the system, (2) for knowledge sharing and (3) for the users 'motivation. These principles in interaction with the groups' members were then broken down into 9 design rules. This step therefore mixes steps 2 (design rules) and 3 (usage scenarios).

Design Rules for the KM System's Architecture. The dual purpose of the knowledge management system led us to build the KM solution by combining two types of JIVE groups: first, official KM groups that aim to support the capitalization of knowledge through the exchange and sharing of knowledge deemed relevant, validated and updated; second, collaborative KM groups which aim to strengthen exchanges and the combination of knowledge in order to promote knowledge creation.

Rule 1. Create official KM groups (I) in charge of guaranteeing the quality of the knowledge in the groups (M) in order to increase the perceived usefulness of the KMIS (O). These essential processes to guarantee confidence in the published knowledge (perceived usefulness) and the ability to retrieve the right document (ease of use) requires the implementation of minimal governance.

Rule 2. Encourage the emergence of collaborative KM groups (I) to promote the autonomy and cooperation of actors (M) in order to create new knowledge (O). Their objective is to increase the exchanges and combinations of knowledge not yet stabilized in order to allow the emergence of new knowledge.

Rule 3. Organize interaction modes between official and collaborative KM groups (I) to increase the quantity and quality of knowledge (M) in order to improve the perceived usefulness of the KMIS (O).

These three rules have been created in the first loop of design.

Design Rules for Knowledge Sharing. The move from the previous platform (based on SharePoint) as a single site, to a multitude of groups on JIVE reflects a major change in the KM system. The recognition of official groups, depositaries of validated knowledge, then becomes essential. There are 4 design rules for knowledge sharing and two of them (rule 4 and 5) aim to facilitate the knowledge retrieval in order to increase KMIS' perceived ease of use and therefore its appropriation. The objective of the two other rules (rules 6 and 7) is to strengthen the application of the two first.

Rule 4. Adopt a naming and tagging convention (I) that facilitates document retrieval (M) to improve KMIS' appropriation (O). Rule 4 is based on the adaptation of the naming convention principle found on traditional KMIS and extend it to tags, specific elements of Web 2.0 tools. The naming convention contains mandatory elements in order to allow consistency in indexing the documents between official KM groups and a search mental schema shared by users, which improves keyword search results. Tags make it possible to refine indexing by synonyms, in particular by type of content (e.g. "presentation" versus "deck").

Rule 5. Organize knowledge within each official group (I) to facilitate documents' retrieval (M) to improve the KMIS' ease of use (O).

The intervention was carried out in two ways. The first is based on the creation of "folders" (called "categories" in JIVE), developed from the naming convention. Browsing through these folders provides different access to the sought documents. The second consisted of creating a "content overview" document mapping the types of documents and the hyperlink to documents published by the group. This content overview aims to make the navigation through content easier as well as the retrieval.

The rules 4 and 5 have been created and applied from the very first design loop.

Rule 6. Train official group owners and contributors (I) to ensure the knowledge quality and organization in the group (M) to enable autonomy for KM groups (O) while maintaining the perceived usefulness of the KMIS (O).

Rule 6 proposes to provide training to official KM groups' owners and contributors to enable them to better understand the tool and better understand the rules for publishing content (rules 4) in order to facilitate their appropriation. Through this rule, the appropriation of rules 4 and 5 ensures the KMIS' perceived usefulness.

Rule 7. Communicate on the KM system (I) in order to strengthen the sharing of meaning around the KM system (M) and thus, promote its appropriation (O).

This communication modality aims to share/post on JIVE the launch of KM official groups and to document the 2.0 KMIS (search functionalities, naming convention, etc.) to facilitate its use by users and contributors. This documentation was supplemented by webinars which aimed to convince users to apply the rules in order to facilitate the use and increase the KMIS' perceived usefulness.

These two rules (6 and 7) emerged from the 1st loop's results and has been applied from the beginning of the second loop.

Design Rules for Users' Motivation. As seen in the literature, the motivation to use a Web 2.0 tools comes "naturally" thanks to their intuitive functionalities and ease of use. However, in order to strengthen the sense of belonging and meaningfulness to KM groups on JIVE – essential components of knowledge sharing and for online communities (built on virtual social network – [17]), we provide a rule on the common identity, but also a rule to bring meaningfulness to KM groups gamification.

Rule 8. Provide official groups with a common identity (I) in order to develop a sense of belonging (M) and thus promote KM system's appropriation as a whole (O).

This rule aims first to develop a common identity for all official KM groups. Indeed, the sense of belonging to a group (or community), sharing the same social norms, is recognized by the KM literature [4, 22] and the IS literature [8, 10, 43, 50] as a mechanism that facilitates knowledge sharing. This identity also helps to give elements of social recognition to the groups' owners, fostering the sense of belonging to a community of "knowledge workers/contributors".

The common identity is built around the reuse of the company's brand elements (logo, color, etc.) but also around the same home page template. The latter also allows users to find their way around the official pages and find key information in the same places. The common model ensures similarity between the groups but also leaves a lot of freedom on the rest of the page, so that each group can appropriate it.

This rule, with regards on the common identity, has been created on the first loop and then applied during all loops.

Rule 9. Regulate the quests of official KM groups: (1) KM team should be included in the quest discussions, and (2) quest objectives and end date are required.

ESN tools offer new functionalities, notably gamification with quests and earning points by participation on the platform. Martin Cruz, Martín Pérez, & Trevilla Cantero, in 2009 [29], hypothesized that competition between members encourages employees to perform useful and valuable tasks for the organization. The authors specified that this type of motivation can be a good tool to generate a "basic commitment".

Emerging from observations on the loop 1 and confirmed by the first results of loop 2, this rule could not be implemented until loop 3, especially because the KM team was not responsible of the tool, and so needed to convince and then the approval from Internal Comm (in charge of JIVE) to put this rule in place.

In loop 3, a rule around a KM steering committee was planned to be implemented, with the objective to find the type of governance needed on web 2.0 technologies; unfortunately, the covid-19 pandemic has stopped the research.

5.3   Artefact Construction

As explained briefly above, the methodology of Design Science lives by loops. The first loop, rules creation, was applied on three pilot groups (PO, TC and GSS) in the last quarter of 2018. All three pilots have applied the rules. However, the application of the naming rules (rules 5 and 6) revealed points of tension in one group (GSS) as they did not necessarily understand its interest.

The second loop has been applied on 8 products/services and strategy groups (in the primary KM scope) and 6 other groups related to TX, sales or CX team productions, during 2019 (out of the KM primary scope). During this loop, we did not apply any rule 3 because no collaboration groups have been created. We encountered again these naming tension on Rule 4, as naming turned out to be, for some of them, a way to value their KM group through the choice of vocabulary. The naming of documents can indeed make it possible to stand out and thus serve a need for "representation", which was the case with "strategy" groups which did not follow the naming convention. Also, the Rule 7, around communication has been extended in loop 2, bringing some documentation helping the sharing on JIVE, as naming convention, "KM guidelines" and webinars, have been published and communicated to the whole company, insisting to key stakeholders like KM groups' contributors.

With regards on rules for users' motivation, we noticed that the Rule 8, about identity, only started to work in the middle of Loop 2. Indeed, it is necessary that a certain number of people apply the rule for an identity to emerge and for some social influence to be exerted. However, despite an appropriation of this rule, which extends beyond the initial KM perimeter, we have seen that the desire to stand out (need for representation, cf. naming convention) also appears in the implementation of this rule.

Finally, during the first months of loop 3, we had time to apply rules to 7 product groups, which allowed us to achieve the KM project primary scope. Also, we applied the design rules to 2 other TX groups (out of KM scope). The last document helping on the sharing, "how does the search work?", has been published and shared across all departments.

5.4   Evaluation

The three different design loops allowed us to highlight 3 key results relating to the construction of a KM system on an ESN-type tool: the first is linked to knowledge sharing, the second to knowledge creation, the third result comes to gamification and the last one is related to identity.

Knowledge Sharing: Exchanges Enriched. The main advantages of Web 2.0 tools are the features including likes, comments or questions which allows people to interact easily and rapidly. These functionalities enhance the quality of the knowledge shared, but also develop the quality of ties.

First, through comments, and questions features, users can ask for more information to contributors, interact with them and/or other users on the platform. The example below shows us that a response in a comment can help the user to apply an official document rule to a particular case. Contextualization is done by people who face same situations and share it, as explained by a Program Manager - named here PM-1 (based in Europe) - below in 2019.

> "The question was whether we could put the invoices on [a travel-α product] I raised the question in comment, and I had the answer"

On JIVE, whatever content type you publish, your name appears as it is in the HR system; you cannot use a pseudonym. Thus, all users know who posted what, "who knowns what" or "who owns what", as a Commercial Operator (based in Europe) explained:

> "It is very easy to know who the product owner is, […], who can be helpful. So, it is an easy access information and ex-change platform"

These ESN features extend exchanges with many potential partners and not only with the people who own the content. Below, the combined advantage of (1) the commenting feature and (2) the platform's openness to everyone, enables greater responsiveness because everyone can respond (contributors and other users too), as PM-2 (based in North America) said:

> "One thing I really like is that when you post [a question], you don't hear the owner of the product right away, but you hear other PMs or other people who could answer it"

However, sometimes, users' comment does not add value, as a Sales (based in Asia) said:

> "A lot of people commenting, it's irrelevant"

The multiplication of connections in ESN-type tool allows users to gain new and better access to knowledge.

Second, as the primary purpose of an ESN-type tool is to create virtually the characteristic of a social network, but it also allows to connect with individuals you are not connected with, directly or indirectly. It appears that these tools fulfil well this function of "connectivity" as presented by another Sales (based in Europe):

> "Overall, I think it's a very good tool: the possibility of being able to interact with people is an ergonomic tool"

However, while the tools of Web 2.0 advocate self-regulation, these results were made possible thanks to the implementation of the design rules allowing to identify the official page and running ownership on those groups, as another PM (based in North America) tells us, sharing her screen, that she clicks on the name of the group because it says "official" to find the information and knowledge she needs:

- "Yesterday I clicked on "Places" and then I clicked right here ["PO (official)", the first result].
- Why did you choose the first one?
- Because it says "official"!".

The categorization of documents has been formalized considering the needs of practitioners. In 2019, more than 20% of respondents to the survey conducted on the entire JIVE platform and not only on official KM groups, mentioned difficulties in retrieving documents. In contrast, interviews showed that when the naming was respected and "official" appeared in the group name, retrieval was faster. For example, the "content overview" turn out to be a real success in retrieving documents, as many comments under this page specify:

"Thank you for this page!".

These platforms allow the development of specific uses that will enrich the sharing of knowledge; they encourage connections between individuals that could not have existed without these technologies. However, designed rules seem necessary to facilitate knowledge retrieval, also on an ESN-type tool.

Knowledge Creation: Mixed Results. The distinction between official and collaborative KM groups (rules 1 and 2), and how their interaction can favor a dynamic KM system (rule 3) has been put in place by GSS in the loop 1. GSS owners noted that the interactions between the two types of KM groups allowed them to question critical knowledge. As stated by the GSS' Vice-President:

"What the GSS group has set up is exactly where we want to go to manage knowledge"

Unfortunately, the collaborative group has not been animated and was moved out of priorities. So, we cannot confirm or infirm the results. During the second loop, we have tried to implement more collaborative KM groups in order to get more data, but owners were not interested, as one of them said:

"that's ok, we are already collaborating using mails and calls"

A second collaborative KM group, linked to the PO official group (created in the first loop) has been launched during the second design loop. This group has been mainly used to coordinate the main activities of its members and it worked quite well because members saw the benefit of having "everything in one place". However, the objective was not to facilitate collaboration, exchanges, and combinations of knowledge. This means that there can be a real interest for the employees to get a group to ease the collaboration, but this kind of group has no, or very little, impact on knowledge creation.

Then, it appears that if Travel-α employees take ownership of the knowledge sharing on the tool, the knowledge creation process is not yet appropriate even if it is supported by certain hierarchical levels. These examples show two main needs: first, motivation for knowledge creation as much as knowledge sharing; second, which follows from the first, the need of managers' implication in KM project and awareness about knowledge creation to get dynamics in the KM system.

Motivation: A Better Appropriation of the KM System. ESN-type tools aim to recreate social network characteristic online, and so to foster sense of belonging to a virtual community, where activities from your peers are visible. In addition to the gamification (ESN-type native feature), it generates motivation for users to go on the platform.

First, ESN features allow users to create motivational social bonds. These functionalities of virtually recreating social relationships make it possible to recover some social interactions that individuals could have face to face, in particular congratulations, encouragements, as explained by PM-3 (based in North America):

"If somebody need encouragement, I would definitely encourage them"

Users and/or teams can also share the achievements and successes online, the kind of communication generates lots of likes and comments, which help to feel supported, as explained by PM-4 (based in North America):

"It is also a great place for staying connected [...] we have a page where we can share accomplishment, we can put news, you can ask questions"

In some ways, ESN-type features give users the opportunity to recreate, virtually, spaces for social exchange and bring sense of belonging to remote teams and/or communities. The openness of these platforms brings visibility of posts and thus increase the number of users who can like, comment, and post. The visibility and popularity g-features work like a circle around reputation: the more you or your space/posts is followed, liked and commented, the more you have visibility and the more people like, comment etc.

However, this visibility can be double-edged when it comes to KM. On one hand, these features helped to bring visibility to KM official groups, and so identity, as we have seen in the artefact construction: more groups were implemented, less problems of reluctant people appeared. On the other hand, we have seen some groups not respecting or a little the naming and identity rules in order to differentiate themselves and/or to give themselves visibility and/or "protect their territory of knowledge". Hierarchical support may be necessary to convince the most reluctant group owners and to avoid excesses of customization.

Second, gamification on ESN-type tools allow individuals to earn points by participating. Two ways of earning points exist: first, the more you participate the more you earn points; second, following a "quest".

On one hand, whether it is a like, or a comment, or even a document, each activity gives points to the users. This simple fact is a motivator for individuals who are thus encouraged to use the tool, as explained by PM-3 (based in North America):

> "When I have a little time or depending on the page, when I see my profile, I see that I am so close to the next level so I will pick a quest or I'll do something to pump up my points"

Here, we can see that users are encouraged to "participate" on the platform to earn points and this incentive seems to be well working. However, earning points based on the activity users have on the platform can generate perverse effects, even when users are concerned about their activity's usefulness, as PM-3 explained:

> "I try to comment but I like my comment to be a value, I don't comment just for comment I would really comment if my words would be impactful. [...] I don't want to be the girl that comment "great job everyone" every single time"

As written on the quote, the number of people commenting "great job" is significant enough for her to mention it and to wonder about meaningfulness in this.

On the other hand, a "quest" creates a "path" for the users to take in order to earn points. This "path" leads them to "consume" different content, in different ways: depending on the actions requested in the quest, they have to like, comment, "share" or download content. By encouraging people to do so, the quest can have a positive impact on the knowledge dynamics.

(1) The individual is browsing content that he or she might not have seen without the existence of the quest. Insofar, as the quest can be related to the individuals' tasks, it highlights important content for him or her and, thus, favor its consultation as a priority, as PM-4 explained:

> "There are some products that I really do need, and I want to know about, so I would do that quest"

When a quest is targeting the right and key documents, it allows to counter "information overload" which is often cited by users and the literature of Web 2.0 tools. PM-4 continues:

> "And I think this is going to take me to the right places, make me bookmark the right pages"

(2) These "quests" also allow managers to track people who completed quests, if from their initiative or as a required task. The quests are offering a new form of training for employees as explained by PM-5 (based in North America).

> "We had to complete the [JIVE quest]: we have to go through [JIVE], the learning training thing by August 12. That's really good because when we see that there is a deadline, in my opinion, it forces me to bloc my calendar, take the time and go through it. And it is very [...], easy to follow"

Thus, it came as a good practice for the marketing manager of the new strategy to, first, create a quest to encourage individuals to consume the new strategy content and, second, to incorporate this quest into training for newcomers. If you want to complete the quest, you must complete all the actions listed. It "forces" users to consume and share knowledge.

However, quests may lack of sense to users. Content owners can create quests to make users consume the content but, which, at the end, make no sense for them, as PM-4 explained:

> "Some of the quests want you to share a page or a document. I don't really understand that when we all have access to the same quest. I am like "who am I going to share this with? ". People have all the same access that I have. [...] That's not really working, I'm like "why are we doing this?"

It seems here that the hedonic motivation does not activate when there is loss of meaning. As a reminder, ESN should allow the re-creation of social ties, which partly consist of common meanings, particularly within CoP. In the example above, the person sought to share with his/her community to bring value and help others. This example shows that a poorly designed quest can create information overload.

Yet, we have seen during the JIVE's first year that individuals were motivated to use the tool by the perspective of earning points. Then, our observations allow us to conclude that the gamification does generate a "basic commitment" as the literature points out. Many contributors on the platform made the request to create quests to generate views on their content. Thus, putting in place some rules about the gamification should improve motivation to share knowledge on the platform. This gamification rule allows to avoid vicious circles as mentioned by Garud and Kumaraswamy [52] in a context of financial incentive.

6   Discussion and Conclusion

6.1   Knowledge Sharing Enhanced on 2.0 KMIS

ESN-type tools allow the multiplication of interactions and enrich the exchange of knowledge [10, 32–35, 38, 46, 51]. Indeed, comments, questions and discussions enrich the initial content of documents posted, as additional "less formal" knowledge. It initiates a virtuous circle of knowledge dynamics, as the two forms of explicit knowledge (official documentation and comments) enrich the Nonaka's virtuous circle based on tacit/explicit interaction [1].

This less formal knowledge helps users in its appropriation as it provides context, echoing Echajari and Thomas' work [18] on codification, abstraction and appropriation. Thus, knowledge sharing is enhanced.

However, our study specifies that for the sharing to be effective, certain rules must be put in place, more particularly rules for naming and organizing knowledge. From the literature, web 2.0 technologies allow knowledge to be self-regulated thanks to the wisdom of the crowd [12, 50]. It appears, here, that the wisdom of the crowd is not enough to kick off knowledge dynamics on the KMIS; regulation is then necessary.

6.2 Knowledge Creation on 2.0 KMIS at Half-Mast

Most of the literature around 2.0 KMIS, and more specifically ESN-type tools, focuses on their ability to create knowledge; these studies focused on the capacity of these technologies to generate social capital, which in turn should have a positive influence on knowledge creation [10, 11] but did not study their direct influence on knowledge creation. Our study shows the impact of ESN-type tools on the dimensions of social capital. The links of individual social networks extend beyond the geographic circle and the usual social network (structural dimension); rules 4 and 5, as well as the one on gamification, positively influence the cognitive dimension. However, these elements are not sufficient to create new organizational knowledge. Following inputs from the literature, we created non-regulated collaborative group in order to favor collaboration, but we did not get the expected results. It seems then, that a form of KM governance is needed to support knowledge creation on 2.0 KMIS.

6.3 Motivation Favored with a Risk of Developing Vicious Circles

ESN-type features encourage users to actively participate in the KM processes and help to access the right knowledge by bringing new ways to build social ties. Virtual relationship, visibility [34, 35] and gamification [26] helps to share.

However, motivation is a tricky topic and new features on 2.0 tools bring this trickiness to another level. The intuitive features and the wisdom of the crowd are not working that well when it comes to a KM system, as it needs identity and meaningfulness. Users adhere very easily to the "reputation" game thanks to the openness and popularity in the platform, they can use it for individual or group visibility, thus this visibility works against the KM system. This shows a need for management implication and support on KM system. Furthermore, meaningfulness on the "game" was a request from the users, then to answer it, a regulation of the gamification features is needed.

Also, our study confirms and gives another context of vicious circles around incentives to Garud & Kumaraswamy's research [52]. Gamification is even more dangerous as this practice is easy to implement. They therefore need to be regulated by the KM governance system.

6.4 Limits and New Research Avenues

Three major limitations are present in this study. First, our research focuses on the study of a single international company operating in the travel industry, with a predominant American culture. In another context, the results would most certainly be different. An analytical generalization could only be done in this same type of enterprise. Then, this study was abruptly stopped due to the Covid-19 pandemic, so the finalization of the analysis could not be successful on all subjects. Finally, our results have shown the effectiveness of these tools in promoting knowledge sharing, but under a certain number of rules. However, they did not show ESN-type tools' effectiveness in creating knowledge, and so on knowledge dynamics. This calls for new research on the type of KM governance adapted to 2.0 KMIS, capable of promoting both knowledge sharing and creation, as well as managing motivation risks.

References

1. Nonaka, I.: A dynamic theory of organizational knowledge creation. Organ. Sci. 5(1), 14–37 (1994). https://doi.org/10.1287/orsc.5.1.14
2. Nonaka, I., Takeuchi, H.: The Knowledge-Creating Company: How Japanese Companies Create the Dynamics of Innovation. Oxford University Press, New York (1995)
3. Nonaka, I., von Krogh, G.: Perspective—tacit knowledge and knowledge conversion: controversy and advancement in organizational knowledge creation theory. Organ. Sci. 20(3), 635–652 (2009). https://doi.org/10.1287/orsc.1080.0412
4. Nahapiet, J., Ghoshal, S.: Social capital, intellectual capital, and the organizational advantage. AMR 23(2), 242–266 (1998). https://doi.org/10.5465/amr.1998.533225
5. Gray, P.H.: The impact of knowledge repositories on power and control in the workplace. Info Technol. People 14(4), 368–384 (2001). https://doi.org/10.1108/09593840110411167
6. Hwang, Y., Lin, H., Shin, D.: Knowledge system commitment and knowledge sharing intention: the role of personal information management motivation. Int. J. Inf. Manage. 39, 220–227 (2018) https://doi.org/10.1016/j.ijinfomgt.2017.12.009
7. Jasimuddin, S.M., (Justin) Zhang, Z.: transferring stored knowledge and storing transferred knowledge. Inf. Syst. Manage. 28(1), 84–94 (2011). https://doi.org/10.1080/10580530.2011.536117
8. Kankanhalli, A., Tan, B.C., Wei, K.K.: Contributing knowledge to electronic knowledge repositories: an empirical investigation. MIS Q. 29(1), 113 (2005). https://doi.org/10.2307/25148670
9. Kim, S.H., Mukhopadhyay, T., Kraut, R.E.: When does repository KMS use lift performance? The role of alternative knowledge sources and task environments. MISQ 40(1), 133–156 (2016). https://doi.org/10.25300/MISQ/2016/40.1.06
10. Panahi, S., Watson, J., Partridge, H.: Towards tacit knowledge sharing over social web tools. J. Knowl. Manage. 17(3), 379–397 (2013). https://doi.org/10.1108/JKM-11-2012-0364
11. Bharati, P., Zhang, W., Chaudhury, A.: Better knowledge with social media? Exploring the roles of social capital and organizational knowledge management. J. Knowl. Manage. 19(3), 456–475 (2015). https://doi.org/10.1108/JKM-11-2014-0467
12. Park, H., Park, S.J.: Communication behavior and online knowledge collaboration: evidence from Wikipedia. JKM 20(4), 769–792 (2016). https://doi.org/10.1108/JKM-08-2015-0312
13. Archer-Brown, C., Kietzmann, J.: Strategic knowledge management and enterprise social media. JKM 22(6), 1288–1309 (2018). https://doi.org/10.1108/JKM-08-2017-0359
14. McAfee, A.P.: Enterprise 2.0: the dawn of emergent collaboration. IEEE Eng. Manage. Rev. 34(3), 38–38 (2006). https://doi.org/10.1109/EMR.2006.261380
15. Schneckenberg, D.: Web 2.0 and the shift in corporate governance from control to democracy. Knowl. Manage. Res. Pract. 7(3), 234–248 (2009). https://doi.org/10.1057/kmrp.2009.17
16. von Krogh, G.: How does social software change knowledge management? Toward a strategic research agenda. J. Strateg. Inf. Syst. 21(2), 154–164 (2012). https://doi.org/10.1016/j.jsis.2012.04.003
17. Kane, G.C., Alavi, M., (Joe) Labianca, G., Borgatti, S.P.: What's different about social media networks? A framework and research agenda. MIS Q. 38(1), 275–304 (2014)
18. Echajari, L., Thomas, C.: Learning from complex and heterogeneous experiences: the role of knowledge codification. J. Knowl. Manage. 19(5), 968–986 (2015). https://doi.org/10.1108/JKM-02-2015-0048
19. Ancori, B.: The economics of knowledge: the debate about codification and tacit knowledge. Ind. Corp. Change 9(2), 255–287 (2000). https://doi.org/10.1093/icc/9.2.255
20. Boisot, M., Li, Y.: Codification, abstraction, and firm differences: a cognitive information-based perspective. J. Bioecon. 7(3), 309–334 (2005). https://doi.org/10.1007/s10818-005-3940-x

21. Kogut, B., Zander, U.: Knowledge of the firm, combinative capabilities, and the replication of technology. Organ. Sci. **3**(3), 383–397 (1992)
22. Wenger, E.: Communities of practice: learning as a social system. Syst. Think. **9**, 2–3 (1998)
23. Kannabiran, G., Pandyan, C.: Enabling role of governance in strategizing and implementing KM. J. Knowl. Manage. **14**(3), 335–347 (2010). https://doi.org/10.1108/13673271011050085
24. Schroeder, A., Pauleen, D., Huff, S.: KM governance: the mechanisms for guiding and controlling KM programs. J. Knowled. Manage. **16**(1), 3–21 (2012). https://doi.org/10.1108/136 73271211198918
25. Hayes, N.: Information technology and the possibilities for knowledge sharing. In: Easterby-Smith, M., Lyles, M.A. (ed.) Handbook of Organizational Learning and Knowledge Management, pp. 83–104. Wiley, Hoboken (2015). https://doi.org/10.1002/978111920724 5.ch5
26. Aboelmaged, M.G.: Knowledge sharing through enterprise social network (ESN) systems: motivational drivers and their impact on employees' productivity. JKM **22**(2), 362–383 (2018). https://doi.org/10.1108/JKM-05-2017-0188
27. O'Reilly, T.: What is Web 2.0: design patterns and business models for the next generation of software. In: MPRA Paper, vol. 65. University Library of Munich, Germany, January 2007
28. O'Reilly, T., Battelle, J.: Web squared: Web 2.0 five years on. O'Reilly Media, Sebastopol (2009). Consulté le: 12 août 2021. [En ligne]. Disponible sur: http://search.ebscohost.com/ login.aspx?direct=true&scope=site&db=nlebk&db=nlabk&AN=536514
29. Martín Cruz, N., Martín Pérez, V., Trevilla Cantero, C.: The influence of employee motivation on knowledge transfer. J. Knowl. Manage. **13**(6), 478–490 (2009). https://doi.org/10.1108/ 13673270910997132
30. Razmerita, L., Kirchner, K., Nielsen, P.: What factors influence knowledge sharing in organizations? A social dilemma perspective of social media communication. JKM **20**(6), 1225–1246 (2016). https://doi.org/10.1108/JKM-03-2016-0112
31. Dudezert, A., Fayard, P., Oiry, E.: Astérix et la gestion des connaissances 2.0 : une exploration de l'appropriation des SGC 2.0 par le mythe du Village Gaulois. Systèmes d'information Manage. **20**(1), 31 (2015) https://doi.org/10.3917/sim.151.0031
32. Beck, R., Pahlke, I., Seebach, C.: Knowledge exchange and symbolic action in social media-enabled electronic networks of practice: a multilevel perspective on knowledge seekers and contributors. MISQ **38**(4), 245–1270 (2014). https://doi.org/10.25300/MISQ/2014/38.4.14
33. Leonardi, P.M.: Ambient awareness and knowledge acquisition: using social media to learn "who knows what" and "who knows whom". MISQ **39**(4), 747–762 (2015). https://doi.org/ 10.25300/MISQ/2015/39.4.1
34. Sophia van Zyl, A.: The impact of social networking 2.0 on organisations. Electron. Libr. **27**(6), 906–918 (2009). https://doi.org/10.1108/02640470911004020
35. Sedighi, M., Lukosch, S., Brazier, F., Hamedi, M., van Beers, C.: Multi-level knowledge sharing: the role of perceived benefits in different visibility levels of knowledge exchange. JKM **22**(6), 1264–1287 (2018) https://doi.org/10.1108/JKM-09-2016-0398
36. Faraj, S., Wasko, M., Johnson, S.L.: Electronic knowledge networks: processes and structure. In: Knowledge Management: An Evolutionary View of the Field 2014, pp. 161–178 (2014)
37. Štorga, M., Mostashari, A., Stanković, T.: Visualisation of the organisation knowledge structure evolution. J. Knowl. Manage. **17**(5), 724–740 (2013). https://doi.org/10.1108/JKM-02-2013-0058
38. Grant, S.B.: Classifying emerging knowledge sharing practices and some insights into antecedents to social networking: a case in insurance. JKM **20**(5), 898–917 (2016). https:// doi.org/10.1108/JKM-11-2015-0432
39. Granovetter, M.: The strength of weak ties: a network theory revisited. Sociol Theory **1**, 201 (1983). https://doi.org/10.2307/202051

40. Lin, Y., Wang, C.: Wisdom of crowds: the effect of participant composition and contribution behavior on Wikipedia article quality. JKM **24**(2), 324–345 (2020). https://doi.org/10.1108/JKM-08-2019-0416
41. Levy, M.: Stairways to heaven: implementing social media in organizations. J. Knowl. Manage. **17**(5), 741–754 (2013). https://doi.org/10.1108/JKM-02-2013-0051
42. Singh, J.B., Chandwani, R., Kumar, M.: Factors affecting Web 2.0 adoption: exploring the knowledge sharing and knowledge seeking aspects in health care professionals. JKM **22**(1), 21–43 (2018). https://doi.org/10.1108/JKM-08-2016-0320
43. Bock, G.W., Zmud, R.W., Kim, Y.G., Lee, J.N.: Behavioral intention formation in knowledge sharing: examining the roles of extrinsic motivators, social-psychological forces, and organizational climate. MIS Q. **29**(1), 87 (2005). https://doi.org/10.2307/25148669
44. Škerlavaj, M., Connelly, C.E., Cerne, M., Dysvik, A.: Tell me if you can: time pressure, prosocial motivation, perspective taking, and knowledge hiding. JKM **22**(7), 1489–1509 (2018). https://doi.org/10.1108/JKM-05-2017-0179
45. Zhang, X., de Pablos, P.O., Zhou, Z.: Effect of knowledge sharing visibility on incentive-based relationship in electronic knowledge management systems: an empirical investigation. Comput. Hum. Behav. **29**(2), 307–313 (2013). https://doi.org/10.1016/j.chb.2012.01.029
46. Liu, D., Santhanam, R., Webster, J.: Toward meaningful engagement: a framework for design and research of gamified information systems. MISQ **41**(4), 1011–1034 (2017). https://doi.org/10.25300/MISQ/2017/41.4.01
47. Davis, F.D.: Perceived usefulness, perceived ease of use, and user acceptance of information technology. MIS Q. **13**(3), 319 (1989). https://doi.org/10.2307/249008
48. Venkatesh, V., Davis, F.D.: A theoretical extension of the technology acceptance model: four longitudinal field studies. Manage. Sci. **46**(2), 186–204 (2000). https://doi.org/10.1287/mnsc.46.2.186.11926
49. Venkatesh, V., Bala, H.: Technology acceptance model 3 and a research agenda on interventions. Decis. Sci. **39**(2), 273–315 (2008). https://doi.org/10.1111/j.1540-5915.2008.00192.x
50. Levy, M.: WEB 2.0 implications on knowledge management. J. Knowl. Manage. **13**(1), 120–134 (2009). https://doi.org/10.1108/13673270910931215
51. Suh, A., Wagner, C.: How gamification of an enterprise collaboration system increases knowledge contribution: an affordance approach. JKM **21**(2), 416–431 (2017). https://doi.org/10.1108/JKM-10-2016-0429
52. Garud, R., Kumaraswamy, A.: Vicious and virtuous circles in the management of knowledge: the case of Infosys technologies. MIS Q. **29**(1), 9 (2005). https://doi.org/10.2307/25148666
53. Pascal, A., Thomas, C., Romme, A.G.L.: Developing a human-centred and science-based approach to design: the knowledge management platform project: knowledge management platform project. Brit. J. Manage. **24**(2), 264–280 (2013). https://doi.org/10.1111/j.1467-8551.2011.00802.x
54. Lacosta, A., Thomas, C.: The role of an enterprise social networking tool on organisational knowledge dynamics. In: Proceedings of the 12th International Joint Conference on Knowledge Discovery, Knowledge Engineering and Knowledge Management, Budapest, Hungary, pp. 76–87 (2020). https://doi.org/10.5220/0010120200760087
55. Denyer, D., Tranfield, D., van Aken, J.E.: Developing design propositions through research synthesis. Organ. Stud. **29**(3), 393–413 (2008). https://doi.org/10.1177/0170840607088020

Digital Modeling of a Domain Ontology for Hospital Information Systems

Avi Shaked(✉)

Systems Engineering Research Initiative, Tel Aviv University, 69978 Tel Aviv, Israel
avishakedse@gmail.com

Abstract. Hospital information systems need to rely on a well-defined, coordinated ontological infrastructure. We use conceptual metamodeling to capture and communicate an ontology for hospital operations, which is designated for use by an actual information system under development. We base our metamodel on the system requirements specification. We demonstrate how this ontology evolves throughout development iterations, as well as how it can be used for threat modeling in the early stages of the system development. We discuss the practical and theoretical implications and potential of our approach.

Keywords: Ontology · Domain specific modeling · Digital engineering · Metamodeling

1 Introduction

Information systems are an enabler of modern healthcare [1, 2]. They also impact the organizational structure of hospitals [3]. Such systems rely extensively on the data they store and represent to the user. Data needs to be well organized in order for systems users to discuss it effectively and to provide actionable insights. Preferably, data is expected to be of a standardized form should it be used in collaborative scenarios or shared amongst different systems [3–5].

A further challenge in the design of modern information systems is addressing cybersecurity aspects. Information systems in healthcare are subject to cybersecurity threats [6]. Cybersecurity has been identified as a knowledge management problem, and it is suggested that incorporating a knowledge management oriented cybersecurity view can improve systems design with respect to cyber threats [7].

Ontologies promote good knowledge management as well as the establishment of explicit, sharable, reusable and interoperable knowledge representations [5, 8]. They are therefore expected to contribute to the rigorous engineering of the aforementioned healthcare information systems.

Many healthcare related ontologies were defined as artifacts of academic research. Examples of these include an ontology for healthcare technology innovation [3], ontologies describing ubiquitous computing environment for healthcare [9, 10], an ontology for health care networks [11], a breast cancer imaging ontology [12] and an ontology for medical services [13]. While crucial for organizing existing knowledge, such research

© Springer Nature Switzerland AG 2022
A. Fred et al. (Eds.): IC3K 2020, CCIS 1608, pp. 157–166, 2022.
https://doi.org/10.1007/978-3-031-14602-2_8

derived ontologies often remain theoretical and are not validated in operational environments or applications. The latter ontology, for example, has only been theoretically checked for consistency despite being designated for systems usage.

The "Fast Healthcare Interoperability Resources" (FHIR) specification by the not-for-profit organization HL7 is an attempt at healthcare data standardization from a practitioners' perspective which embeds some ontology-related concepts. However, these concepts are manifested purely as a technical implementation, and consequently require a reverse engineering effort in order to be formulated as an implementation agnostic ontology. Such effort can be deemed inappropriate for addressing real-life operational challenges rapidly. As an illustration, in FHIR, there is no direct relation between a physician and patient; and instead, it is represented by a relation between a patient and a practitioner, with the physician being a specific practitioner type. Furthermore, this relation is expressed using a directional relation from the patient to the practitioner; and consequently a stakeholder who wishes to explore the ontological concepts of a physician as a practitioner has to explore the resource model from the patient perspective – and not from the physician perspective – in order to identify the relation. Moreover, the relations are not illustrated graphically, and this hinders the communicability of the embedded ontological concepts.

In this paper we share our experience using conceptual modeling to capture a primal ontology for hospital operations, while developing a prototype for a hospital information system. We utilize a grass roots approach to defining ontologies, which can promote their practical usage. Furthermore, we demonstrate the value of the ontology in designing cybersecurity aspects of the information system. In Sect. 2 we describe our methods. Then, in Sect. 3, we present the resulting ontology, designed to support a specific hospital operations situational awareness information system. Two versions of the ontology are discussed, showing an evolution which coincides with development iterations. Furthermore, we demonstrate another practical aspect of the ontology: serving as a basis for threat modeling. Finally, in Sect. 4, we discuss the advantages and limitations of our approach as well as suggest potential directions for further research.

This paper extends a previously published work [14], with an updated outlook based on prototyping an information system using the suggested ontology [15]. This includes an updated presentation of our metamodel as it evolved throughout two development iterations, a new cybersecurity related threat modeling based on the ontology and an elaborated discussion.

2   Method

Due to urgent hospital need for digital transformation, expedited by the COVID-19 pandemic outburst, and with hospital personnel being rarely available to provide us feedback, we focused on deriving a minimal yet cost-effective ontology. We aimed to provide the infrastructure for a rigorous information model, which would then be used in the aforementioned healthcare information system.

We derived a hospital operations ontology – designated for organizing information in the newly developed information system – by analyzing a set of requirements which was coordinated with relevant stakeholders. This analysis involved the identification of the relevant entities as well as their relations.

The aforementioned set of requirements was a specification for a hospital management information system, in a very early stage of establishing needs and system concept. The requirements specification is considered intellectual property, and thus cannot be shared in this publication. However, we note that it was in Hebrew and comprised three sections: a mission statement, describing the system's objectives and a basic narrative; an illustration referring to the operational scenario; and a list of high level requirements describing both medical and technical needs in natural language.

We reviewed the specification and derived pertinent domain entities and their relations. We found that some ontological entities and relations were mentioned explicitly while additional entities and relations were mentioned implicitly. During our analysis of the specification we identified some gaps that further implied some of the ontological domain knowledge remained tacit (as opposed to being stated in the requirements). Whenever deemed critical, we filled in these gaps by adding entities and relations.

We used the open-source Eclipse ECORE to formally capture the ontology. ECORE is used for describing metamodels based on the standard EMOF specification [16]. Applying this core component of the software integrated development environment Eclipse – as opposed to applying a specialized ontology tool (such as Protégé) – was intended to secure the continuity of using the derived ontology in actual software implementations of the hospital information system.

We used a variation of the STRIDE methodology for threat modeling [17]. This variation uses our derived, implementation-agnostic ontology as the underlying design for threat identification, as opposed to the classic use of system architecture. This emerged from our need to assess cybersecurity threats in the early development stage where system architecture has not been established. Furthermore, this can be justified as our ontology forms a data architecture, which is further supported by the form follows function design principle [18]. We used the TRADES modeling methodology [19] and its supporting open-source TRADES Tool [20] to formalize our threat model.

3   Results

This section presents the results of deriving the ontology in two iterations of developing a prototype as well as using the ontology for system level threat modeling.

3.1   The Ontology for the First Prototype

Figure 1 shows the derived hospital operations ontology. This standardized ECORE metamodel representation depicts the ontological entities as rounded rectangular nodes and the ontological relations between entities as edges between the nodes. Relations may take various representations reflecting their diverse nature. A diamond headed directed arrow signifies a composition relation, i.e., the source node to which the diamond is attached includes the target node as its component; a bi-directional arrow signifies a bi-directional relation between two nodes; and an arrow attached to a target node using a hollow triangle translates into a "type-of" relation, with the source node being a type of the target node. An example of the latter type is used between the "GeneralEntity" node and many of the other nodes; and this is done from a modeling perspective to add generic features (specifically, the "name" attribute, contained within the "GeneralEntity" node). The cardinality of composition and bi-directional relations is stated using a textual tag on the end of the relation edge. For example, the fact that a hospital can comprise zero to unlimited physical locations is represented as a composition relation with "[0..*] location" cardinality. Similarly, a patient can only be at a specific location in the hospital at a specific time, and this is represented as a "[0..1] location" relation between the Patient and the Location conceptual entities. In both cases, a null (zero) location association denotes that a location has not been specified yet.

We identify seven conceptual entities as types of modeling entities: hospital, location, patient, health indicator, temperature, doctor and department. All of the identified entities appear explicitly in the requirements specification. An eight entity "medical record" appeared originally in the specification, but was removed from our model due to initial customer focus with respect to the information system. Some of these entities appear in the specification using redundant terms, and this was identified in our analysis of the specification. Specifically, the redundancies exist in references to the patient (2 different Hebrew terms), location (4 different Hebrew terms) and doctor (2 different Hebrew terms).

The relations between the entities and their cardinalities are not as explicit in the specification as the entities definitions. Consequently, specifying several relations involved interpretation of the specification's textual content. Few exceptions to this are the following: (1) the location concept is explicitly mentioned in relation with the patient and with the doctor (the nature of these relations, however, is not stated); (3) a location is explicitly mentioned as "inside the hospital," which, implicitly leads to a composition relation, as in "the hospital has locations"; (4) doctors are implicitly mentioned in one statement as "belonging to the hospital," which, implicitly leads to a composition relation, as in "the hospital has doctors"; (5) health indictors and the patient are explicitly mentioned as a construct state, implying a composition relation, as in "a patient has health indicators"; (6) temperature is explicitly mentioned as a type of a health indication.

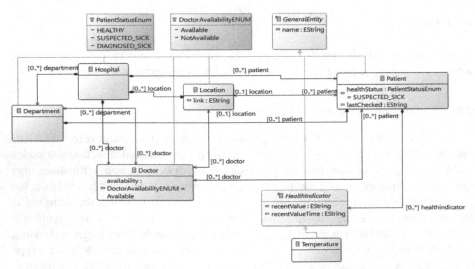

Fig. 1. A conceptual metamodel representing the derived hospital ontology (in ECORE Tools), adopted from [15].

3.2 The Ontology for the Second Prototype

Our prototype implementation uses the "link" attribute of the "location" entity to open a web camera feed. This implied the existence of the additional conceptual entity "web camera" as well as a more generic entity in the form of a "device". These concepts were integrated into our metamodel – and consequently into our ontology – when reflecting on the information system design and improving it for a second prototype. Figure 2 shows this. Our previous metamodel is modified to support the existence of devices and their utilization and management. Specifically, the functionality of opening a web camera feed now uses a web camera device entity, with its address attribute designating the link that should be used to access the device.

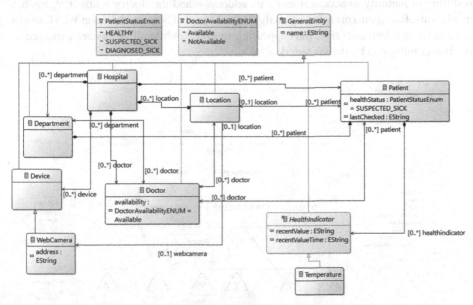

Fig. 2. The metamodel for the second prototype. Newly introduced entities and relations denoted in blue. (Color figure online)

3.3 Threat Modeling Using the Derived Ontology

Figure 3 shows our threat model as captured formally using TRADES Tool. First, the ontology was used to represent the conceptual data architecture of the system: each onto-logical entity was represented as a TRADES component of the system. The hospital entity is considered the top hierarchy, containing the ontological entities connected to it with composition relations. Attributes associated with each ontological entity are included in the information model as data elements contained in their respective components (as can be seen in the "Model Explorer" tab on the left of the figure).

For the threat modeling, we concentrate on entities that included attributes, as these are expected to facilitate threat identification. These are: Patient, Doctor, Health Indicator and Web Camera. We therefore filter the system information model to focus on the ontological entities' attributes (as can be seen on the top of the left panel in the figure, stating "*data" as the filter). Then, conceptual threats based on STRIDE are added to the information model: Spoofing, Tampering, Repudiation, Information Disclosure, Denial of Service and Elevation of Privileges. These conceptual threats are allocated to relevant ontological entities based on the potential risk they introduce to the entity's role and attributes: the Information Disclosure threat allocation to Patient denotes the possibility of disclosing information about the patient (such as his/her health status); Tampering is allocated to both Health Indicator with respect to recent values reported as well as allocated to the Patient with respect to "health status" and the "last checked" timing; Spoofing is allocated to the Web Camera as a hostile device may spoof as the camera using its address; and finally Denial of Service is allocated to both the web camera – resulting in inability to access it using its address – and the doctor – affecting his/her availability. Based on a preliminary analysis, the Denial of Service threat on Web Camera is deemed an acceptable risk, thus appearing in green; while all others are expected to be further mitigated by the system design.

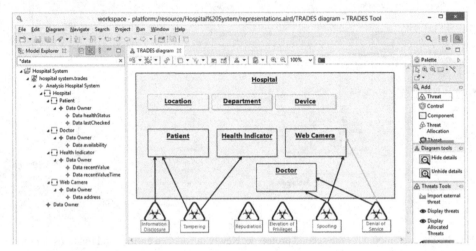

Fig. 3. A TRADES model documenting the ontology based threat modeling. (Color figure online)

4   Discussion

A formal ontology is a key to establishing and coordinating information systems, as it captures and communicates domain knowledge. Here, we articulated a domain-specific ontology for hospital operations, derived from a requirements specification, using a well-defined metamodel.

Using a standardized metamodel as our ontology model was shown to contribute to formalizing pertinent knowledge, designated as the information model infrastructure for information systems realization. Conceptual entities were identified and narrowed down from redundant terms to singular ontological entities. Furthermore, implicit definitions with respect to the relations between entities were translated into explicitly stated relations with their cardinality included.

The concretization of relations definitions reflects design decisions, and it is therefore subjective. Still, it facilitates ontology related discussion with stakeholders. The communication of our design decisions with stakeholders forms a basis not only for delivering an appropriate information system, but also for understanding and possibly even improving domain operations. As an illustration, our conceptual metamodel depicts a centralized approach in which the hospital manages its doctors as a common resource (expressed by compositional relation of the hospital in Fig. 1). Doctors are assigned dynamically to hospital departments (the bi-directional relation between "Department" and "Doctor" in Fig. 1). This approach can be contrasted with an alternative one, in which doctors are considered a dedicated resource of the department.

While being exclusively derived from a practitioner's viewpoint, our initial hospital operations ontology corresponds with the previously conceived, theoretical ontology for medical services [13]. Specifically the "doctor" and "patient" ontological concepts appear in both ontologies. Another common concept is the "health indicator," which is termed "vital sign" in the ontology for medical services, with both ontologies mentioning "temperature" as a specialized type of this concept. Also, both ontologies depict similar relations between the shared concepts: a doctor relates to a patient, and a patient has health indicators. The cardinalities of these relations appear in our ontology exclusively. Also, whereas the ontology for medical services is more comprehensive with respect to the services, our hospital operations ontology includes additional concepts related to hospital organization (e.g., "location", "department", "hospital" and their relations), corresponding with the need to reflect and impact organizational structure design and resource allocations [3]. The lack in some service related concepts in our ontology can be the result of the minimum viable product approach. This is further corroborated as our second prototype's ontology identifies an additional concept which appears in the ontology for medical services – "device." The incorporation of the device concept into our ontology emphasizes the product-service systems nature of the domain: the hospital, which is responsible for providing healthcare services, is also responsible for the acquisition, maintenance and provision of devices that support the effective operation of its departments, and ultimately allow the hospital to provide healthcare services effectively.

Ontologies can be useful in establishing threat models of systems. Here, the ontology translates naturally into a data-oriented composition of the system. This facilitates a systematic approach to establishing a communicable and actionable threat model, in the early stages of design and prior to system implementation.

Our metamodel-based approach to capturing the domain ontology has several limitations. First, the composition-oriented metamodel representation of the ontology only captures direct relations between entities, and is less appropriate for communicating behavioral ontological relations. For example, a particular use case may exist in the form of a doctor examining a patient's temperature, and yet there is no direct relation between the "doctor" and "temperature" elements. We note that systems that implement our metamodel can in fact support such interactions, e.g., by allowing a doctor to query all/some of the patient's relations. Regardless, future research shall consider enhancing metamodel representations with behavioral related relations, to support a more comprehensive representation of ontologies. Addressing this gap may also facilitate the development of systems based on metamodels, reducing the need in some additional behavioral descriptions – such as sequence diagrams – for basic, ontology-derived functions. A possible approach may be in the form of introducing explicit ontological relations into a metamodel. For example, an ontological relation between the "doctor" element and the "temperature" element may be introduced to the metamodel as a new type of relation. This is illustrated in Fig. 4 on top of our original, first prototype metamodel (Fig. 1). The "examines" ontological relation (in dashed blue arrow) is added to the metamodel, depicting the doctor ability to examine the temperature. This ontological relation can then be further specified as a composition of several metamodel relations: the bi-directional relation between "doctor" and "patient," the compositional relation between "patient" and "health indicator," and the type relation between the latter and "temperature." This opens up an opportunity for verifying the completeness of the metamodel with respect to the ontology. For example, orange dashed arrows in Fig. 4 denote the relation route that implements the aforementioned "examines" ontological relation: a doctor relates to a patient, which has a health indicator of type temperature. If, hypothetically, one of the concrete metamodel relations was missing, then the composite relation route from "doctor" to "temperature" could not have been realized, indicating a gap in the design of the metamodel.

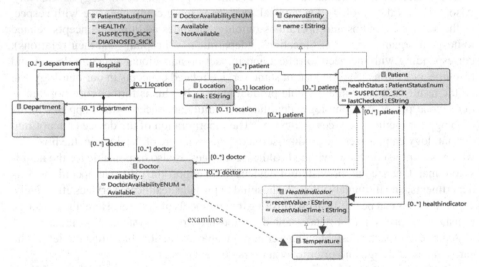

Fig. 4. An illustration of using an ontological layer on top of a formal metamodel. An ontological behavior-related relation is marked in blue, with a metamodel-based route to implement the ontological relation is shown in orange. (Color figure online)

Second, our grass roots derivation of the ontology can lead to an inflation of domain-specific ontologies. While existing ontologies may be used as a stepping stone for creating a domain-specific ontology, the full investigation and/or implementation of existing ontologies can hinder development efforts, and this should not be a barrier for ontology-based engineering [12]. Introducing a grass roots ontology – as we demonstrated – is a legitimate trade-off [21]. In the hospital operations ontology case, for example, the ontological concept of "device" – which exists in the ontology for medical services – was not considered essential for the first prototype, as discussed above. Furthermore, from a technical implementation point of view, model translation tools can be used to harmonize different ontologies (e.g., as a semantic network for integrating different narratives, as recommended by Luokkala and Virrantaus [22]), and specifically to translate a uniquely defined (proprietary) ontology to a standardized ontology. For example, entities of the hospital operations ontology can be translated to a standard definition (e.g., "health indicator" can be translated to the ontology for medical services' "vital sign"). Specifically, our Eclipse-based conceptual model is automatically captured as a standardized XMI technical representation, which facilitates such translation capabilities. This may promote the interoperability of systems and the sharing of valuable information, both identified as recommended long term goals for medical situational awareness [23].

References

1. Meydan, C., Haklai, Z., Gordon, B., Mendlovic, J., Afek, A.: Managing the increasing shortage of acute care hospital beds in Israel. J. Eval. Clin. Pract. **21**(1), 79–84 (2015)
2. Topaz, M., Bar-Bachar, O., Admi, H., Denekamp, Y., Zimlichman, E.: Patient-centered care via health information technology: a qualitative study with experts from Israel and the US. Inform. Health Soc. Care **45**(3), 217–228 (2020)
3. Moreno-Conde, A., et al.: ITEMAS ontology for healthcare technology innovation. Health Res. Policy Syst. **17**(1), 47 (2019). https://doi.org/10.1186/s12961-019-0453-y
4. Schulz, S., Stegwee, R., Chronaki, C.: Standards in healthcare data. In: Kubben, P., Dumontier, M., Dekker, A. (eds.) Fundamentals of Clinical Data Science, pp. 19–36. Springer, Cham (2019). https://doi.org/10.1007/978-3-319-99713-1_3
5. Husáková, M., Bureš, V.: Formal ontologies in information systems development: a systematic review. Information **11**(2), 66 (2020)
6. Willing, M., et al.: Behavioral responses to a cyber attack in a hospital environment. Sci. Rep. **11**(1), 1–15 (2021)
7. Tisdale, S.M., Morris, R.: Cybersecurity: challenges from a systems, complexity, knowledge management and business intelligence perspective. Issues Inf. Syst. **16**(3), 191–198 (2015)
8. Yang, L., Cormican, K., Yu, M.: Ontology-based systems engineering: a state-of-the-art review. Comput. Ind. **111**, 148–171 (2019)
9. Kim, J., Kim, J., Lee, D., Chung, K.-Y.: Ontology driven interactive healthcare with wearable sensors. Multimedia Tools Appl. **71**(2), 827–841 (2012). https://doi.org/10.1007/s11042-012-1195-9
10. Ko, E.J., Lee, H.J., Lee, J.W.: Ontology-based context modeling and reasoning for u-healthcare. IEICE Trans. Inf. Syst. **90**(8), 1262–1270 (2007)
11. Dieng-Kuntz, R., Minier, D., Růžička, M., Corby, F., Corby, O., Alamarguy, L.: Building and using a medical ontology for knowledge management and cooperative work in a health care network. Comput. Biol. Med. **36**(7–8), 871–892 (2006)
12. Hu, B., Dasmahapatra, S., Dupplaw, D., Lewis, P., Shadbolt, N.: Reflections on a medical ontology. Int. J. Hum. Comput. Stud. **65**(7), 569–582 (2007)
13. Zeshan, F., Mohamad, R.: Medical ontology in the dynamic healthcare environment. Procedia Comput. Sci. **10**, 340–348 (2012)
14. Shaked, A.: On the road to hospital digital transformation: using conceptual modeling to express domain ontology. In: Proceedings of KMIS 2020, pp. 265–269 (2020, online)
15. Shaked, A.: Modeling for rapid systems prototyping: hospital situational awareness system design. Systems **9**, 12 (2021)

16. Object Management Group: Meta Object Facility formal specification, version 2.5.1 (2016)
17. Shostack, A: Experiences threat modeling at microsoft. In: Proceeding of MODSEC@ MoDELS 2008 (2008)
18. Ellero, N.P.: Crossing over: health sciences librarians contributing and collaborating on electronic medical record (EMR) implementation. J. Hosp. Librariansh. **9**(1), 89–107 (2009)
19. Shaked, A., Reich, Y.: Model-based threat and risk assessment for systems design. In: Proceedings of ICISSP 2021, pp. 331–338 (2021, online)
20. TRADES Tool. https://github.com/IAI-Cyber/TRADES. Accessed 5 Jan 2022
21. Sandkuhl, K., et al.: From expert discipline to common practice: a vision and research agenda for extending the reach of enterprise modeling. Bus. Inf. Syst. Eng. **60**(1), 69–80 (2018). https://doi.org/10.1007/s12599-017-0516-y
22. Luokkala, P., Virrantaus, K.: Developing information systems to support situational awareness and interaction in time-pressuring crisis situations. Saf. Sci. **63**, 191–203 (2014)
23. Toner, E.S.: Creating situational awareness: a systems approach. In: Medical Surge Capacity Workshop Summary. National Academies Press, Washington (2009)

Author Index

Printed in the United States
by Baker & Taylor Publisher Services